"In this brave, vulnerable book, professor and preacher Matthew Kim reminds us that homiletics also includes diverse humans, both preachers and listeners. He names the elephant in many congregational rooms and aims to prepare preachers to become more culturally intelligent as a means to being more faithful to God and the gospel of Jesus Christ. This is an essential text for anyone who takes seriously the call to love our neighbors through preaching, regardless of denominations, ethnicities, genders, locations, and religions. Readers will step away from these pages with the renewed realization that cultural exegesis not only is important for sermon preparation but is an act of love."

—**Luke A. Powery**, dean, Duke University Chapel

"The art of preaching involves more than simply 'getting the Bible right.' We will not know *what* to preach until we know *to whom* we are preaching. In *Preaching with Cultural Intelligence*, Matthew Kim wisely and adeptly sensitizes preachers to the unexamined cultural and sociological assumptions that inevitably drive their preaching. Throughout the book Kim helps the reader understand the importance of cultural intelligence, showing how self-exegesis, cultural-exegesis, and scriptural-exegesis can all come together in a way that deepens the preacher's capacity to minister the Word of God to the people of God. This is a thoughtful, insightful book that offers more than mere homiletical technique—an important book for pastors."

—**Gerald Hiestand**, executive director, Center for Pastor Theologians; senior associate pastor, Calvary Memorial Church

"As an 'Other' myself—in more ways than one—I found Kim's book to have touched on an issue worth serious consideration by every preacher. This work will start us on the process of becoming more culturally intelligent, whether we are preaching in South Hamilton or South Korea, New York or New Delhi. And, as we engage with this book's concepts, the Word of God will be better served to the community of God from our pulpits, molding a diversity of peoples into the unity of the image of Christ."

—**Abraham Kuruvilla**, Dallas Theological Seminary

"Preachers have been waiting for a smart book on cultural intelligence. Let's face it, we've been behind the ball when it comes to really understanding the cultural diversity of our listeners. Matthew Kim brings us up to speed and gives us practical ways to use cultural intelligence. And he reminds us from the Bible that it is our duty as preachers to work diligently that we might present *everyone* fully mature in Christ."

—**Patricia Batten**, Gordon-Conwell Theological Seminary

Preaching *with* Cultural Intelligence

Understanding the People Who Hear Our Sermons

Matthew D. Kim

2 Tim 4:2

Baker Academic
a division of Baker Publishing Group
Grand Rapids, Michigan

Published by Baker Academic
a division of Baker Publishing Group
PO Box 6287, Grand Rapids, MI 49516-6287
www.bakeracademic.com

Printed in the United States of America

Library of Congress Cataloging-in-Publication Data
Names: Kim, Matthew D., 1977– author.
Title: Preaching with cultural intelligence : understanding the people who hear our sermons / Matthew D. Kim.
Description: Grand Rapids : Baker Academic, 2017. | Includes bibliographical references and index.
Identifiers: LCCN 2017013257 | ISBN 9780801049620 (pbk.)
Subjects: LCSH: Preaching. | Christianity and culture.
Classification: LCC BV4211.3 .K553 2017 | DDC 251—dc23
LC record available at https://lccn.loc.gov/2017013257

In keeping with biblical principles of creation stewardship, Baker Publishing Group advocates the responsible use of our natural resources. As a member of the Green Press Initiative, our company uses recycled paper when possible. The text paper of this book is composed in part of post-consumer waste.

17 18 19 20 21 22 23   7 6 5 4 3 2 1

For my brothers

Timothy David Kim (1979–2015),
the most intelligent, culturally intelligent,
and selfless person I have ever known

and

Dennis Daniel Kim,
who uses his intellect, cultural intelligence,
and relational gifts to change the world one person at a time.

Contents

Acknowledgments   ix
Introduction   xi

Part 1 Cultural Intelligence in Theory

1. Preaching and Cultural Intelligence   3
2. The Homiletical Template   13
3. Hermeneutics and Cultural Intelligence   31
4. Exegeting the Preacher   45

Part 2 Cultural Intelligence in Practice

5. Preaching and Denominations   65
6. Preaching and Ethnicities   95
7. Preaching and Genders   127
8. Preaching and Locations   157
9. Preaching and Religions   185

Conclusion   215
Appendix 1: The Homiletical Template   219
Appendix 2: Worksheet for Understanding Culture   223
Appendix 3: Sample Sermon   231
Notes   239
Index   261

Acknowledgments

I want to acknowledge many individuals who have helped to make this book a reality. First, many thanks to the Trustees, President Dennis Hollinger, Vice President for Academic Affairs Richard Lints, and my colleagues in the Division of Practical Theology at Gordon-Conwell Theological Seminary for generously providing the resources and space during the fall of 2015 to engage in sabbatical research. In particular, thanks to Jeffrey D. Arthurs, Patricia M. Batten, and Scott M. Gibson, my colleagues in the preaching department, for carrying my teaching load and tending to other responsibilities in the Haddon W. Robinson Center for Preaching in my absence. Jeff and Scott, I'm grateful for your constructive input on the Homiletical Template at its early stages. Thank you very much, Scott, for reading the entire manuscript and for fine-tuning it.

President Paul Nyquist, Winfred Neely, John Koessler, and the entire pastoral studies department at Moody Bible Institute in Chicago, thank you so much for the honor of inviting me to give your Homiletical Lectureship on "Preaching with Cultural Intelligence" in October 2015. Your warm hospitality and acknowledgment of my work will not be soon forgotten.

Several Byington scholars, Gordon-Conwell's term for research assistants, developed a bibliography for cultural intelligence: Daniel Walsh, Tiffany Miller, Joshua Cahan, and Kyle Sandison. I cannot thank you enough for your labor and partnership.

Thanks to the MDiv and ThM students who have taken my elective, Cultural Exegesis for Preaching, as well as the Preaching to Culture and Cultures DMin cohort for serving as my guinea pigs to test and challenge the ideas in this book.

Friends and colleagues in ministry, Casey C. Barton and Jared E. Alcántara, graciously read a chapter of the book and offered their instrumental feedback. Thank you, Casey and Jared, for imparting your cultural intelligence to me.

The Kern Family Foundation provided a generous faculty grant during the spring semester of 2015 to explore the intersections of hermeneutics, preaching, faith, location, and work. Many thanks to my surveyed pastors for their honest, insightful, and thorough reflections on preaching in urban, suburban, and rural contexts.

Countless thanks are due to Robert Hosack, Eric Salo, and the entire staff at Baker Academic for seeing the merits of this project and for their tireless attention to details from start to finish in the publication process. Thanks for your patience and grace during my various trials in the course of writing this book.

I am tremendously blessed to have married into the Oh family. Much gratitude is due to my in-laws, Chung Hyun and Jung Sook Oh, whose benevolence and acts of love can never be remunerated. To my wonderful brother-in-law, Yung Oh, and sister-in-law, Suzanne Kim, who show amazing love and support to our family, your overflowing kindnesses remain deeply embedded in my heart.

I cannot thank enough my three precious sons, Ryan, Evan, and Aidan, for their long-suffering in waiting for their dad to finish writing this book. I want you to know that I love you so much, and I am so proud to be your father. I am so sorry for the times that I made you wait to play with you.

Words cannot convey my heartfelt appreciation for my incredible wife, Sarah, who has tirelessly loved me and sacrificed herself for me and our three boys. I will never be able to repay all the love and support you have shown me. Thank you for reading the manuscript and offering your helpful recommendations for improving it. Sarah, I love you very much!

Thanks to my parents, Ki Wang and Taek Hee Kim, who learned cultural intelligence the hard way by immigrating to the United States before our birth to give my brothers and me the opportunities America would offer. Thank you for sacrificing so much for our family and for reminding me daily of God's love, encouragement, and generosity. Your mantra, "You can do it," rings loudly in my mind at all times!

This book is dedicated to my beloved younger brothers, Timothy David Kim (1979–2015) and Dennis Daniel Kim. Both of you enter my mind at some point every single day. Tim, I can't thank you enough for the love, memories, and laughter we will always share. Although I failed to verbalize it, you were an example to me in so many parts of life and taught me so much about how to love and care for others well. Dennis, thank you for your friendship, humor, and encouragement. You two have enriched my life in countless ways. I love you both so much. Tim, I will always carry you and your example of Christ's selflessness in my heart until we see each other again.

To God alone be all of the glory, honor, and praise.

Introduction

A fable exists about two animal friends: a giraffe and an elephant. The giraffe decided to build his family a new residence. Meeting his family's precise dimensions, the abode showcased lofty entryways and majestic ceilings. It was a vibrant expression of the giraffe's creativity and craftsmanship. In fact, it received the accolade of "National Giraffe Home of the Year."

One day, as the giraffe peered out from his woodshop window, he noticed an elephant strolling down his avenue. Having previously served with him on a PTA committee and being cognizant of the elephant's skill in woodworking, the giraffe quickly welcomed him into his home. At that moment there was an obvious dilemma. This house was built for a giraffe and not for an elephant. The elephant could squeeze his head through the doorway, but his corpulent body was quite a different matter. The giraffe proudly proclaimed, "It's a good thing we made this door expandable to accommodate my woodshop equipment. Give me a minute while I take care of our problem." So he took down some adjoining panels to oblige the elephant's girth.

After enjoying a few laughs, the conversation was interrupted by a phone call, which led the giraffe away momentarily. Filling the time, the elephant browsed the room, appreciating the giraffe's workmanship. His curiosity led his eyes to the second floor, but the wooden stairs could not support his weight. The stairs began to fracture with each tentative step. Overhearing the crackling in the next room, the giraffe erupted: "What on earth is happening here?" To this, the elephant responded, "I was trying to make myself at home." The giraffe countered, "Okay, I see the problem. The doorway is too narrow. We'll have to make you smaller. There's an aerobics studio near here. If you'd take some classes there, we could get you down to size."

The elephant was perplexed. "Maybe," he muttered.

The giraffe proceeded with his tirade, "And the stairs are too weak to carry your weight. If you'd go to ballet class at night, I'm sure we could get you light on your feet. I really hope you'll do it. I like having you here."

"Perhaps," the elephant replied. "But to tell you the truth, I'm not sure that a house designed for a giraffe will ever really work for an elephant, not unless there are some major changes."[1]

As an expert in business management, R. Roosevelt Thomas Jr. shares this perceptive fable in response to the mounting challenges of working in a diverse corporate culture. In his book *Building a House for Diversity*, he presents skills that businesspeople require in an increasingly diverse workforce. Thomas observes that giraffes and elephants coexist in every company but he queries whether both are given the permission and the capacity to thrive.

Giraffes represent the majority culture and its leaders, whom Thomas refers to as "the insiders." Giraffes set the tone for the organization's culture, vision, values, and strategies. Elephants, however, represent the minority cultures, "the outsiders" within an organization who must always conform to the ways of the majority culture in order to fit in.

I share this fable because, like the business community, the demographics of our churches have also been diversifying. Most congregations in North America are not as completely homogeneous as they once were with respect to denominational traditions, ethnicity, gender, location, socioeconomics, musical preferences, education, ministry philosophy, theology, ecclesiology, and so on. Manifestations of the homogeneous unit principle as espoused by Donald McGavran, who argued that churches grow most effectively when they are homogeneous, linger in various parts of the country.[2] That is, eleven o'clock on Sunday morning is still regarded as the most segregated hour in the week. Yet in many congregations, widespread demographic shifts are steadily occurring. As preachers, we want to "be prepared in season and out of season," as the apostle Paul encouraged his protégé Timothy not only to preach the Word but also to preach it relevantly to the various types of listeners God sends his way (2 Tim. 4:2).

Elephants or the Others (whomever that term means to us) have already entered the church building. They worship among us, and their diversity may not be revealed only in the hue of their skin. Diversity exists in subtle places concealed from our naked eyes. Elephants sit throughout the sanctuary, hoping to hear a sermon that connects with their lives. We may have noticed them, but have they been permitted and given access to feel truly at home in our congregations? Do we prepare our sermons with them fully in our hermeneutical and homiletical views?

Allegorically speaking, the giraffe's perspective in this fable represents a common attitude among preachers today. We may believe that we are the real architects, contractors, and builders of this organization called the church. That is, we like to call the shots. We determine the blueprint of the congregation through our vision casting and leadership prowess. We pour the church's concrete foundation with core doctrinal beliefs and erect the framework with what we consider essential values for our church. Through ecclesial protocols and policies, we set in place a secure roof that provides welfare for our members. We may even build a hedge around the building through our preaching that communicates either verbally or indirectly what types of people are welcome and those we furtively wish would check out the church down the street.

As an ethnic Korean, born and raised in the United States, the impetus for this book derives from my personal experiences living as an elephant in America. Like the proverbial elephant in the room, I and Others often stand out, and not necessarily for positive reasons. In most contexts, the dominant culture places me in the Other category. In other words, I have never felt completely comfortable in white America, nor am I at ease among Korean nationals and first-generation Korean immigrants. Like sitting awkwardly and uncomfortably between two chairs made of timber, I have always sat in the in-between space, what Gerald Arbuckle calls the state of liminality.[3] In most cases, being in a sanctuary where I am the Other has meant that my background and experiences have been grossly misunderstood or completely ignored.

Being in the position of the elephant is cumbersome and painful. We do not know what it is like until we have actually experienced it. In preaching to diverse listeners, then, we want to be mindful of the Other, especially because we take the second greatest commandment seriously. To love our neighbors means that we will put ourselves in the position of the Other. Like Jesus's example of the good Samaritan, we care for our church members just as we care for our own bodies and souls. We can demonstrate this care even in our preaching.

As preachers, we want to pause and reflect on life and Scripture from the Others' viewpoint. For example, have you ever asked yourself these questions about your listeners during sermon preparation? (1) How would listeners from Life Situation X or from Cultural Background Y read and interpret this Scripture passage? (2) What excites them, and what do they fear? (3) Which illustrations are most relevant and helpful for these listeners? (4) What does life application look like in their specific context? (5) How can we embrace and even celebrate those who are different from us in our preaching ministry and in "doing life" together?

At points in my life, I have also sat in the position of the giraffe, having served as the senior pastor of a church where our congregation's demographic consisted of different ethnic groups and with people from various socioeconomic and cultural backgrounds. Through trial and error, I attempted, albeit imperfectly, to preach God's Word in such a way that the Others would fully recognize and appreciate that I have prepared sermons with them in mind.

Today I serve as a professor of preaching and ministry at an evangelical theological seminary and am seeking to train future preachers from various ethnic and cultural backgrounds. As someone who has wrestled with cultural sensitivity and insensitivity all of my life, I am writing this book to prepare twenty-first-century preachers for the realities of congregational diversity in North America and beyond.

So then, how do we prepare sermons for diverse listeners? Think about it like preparing a meal. In order to create an entrée, we need the proper ingredients. If we frequent many grocery stores, we will have observed that somewhere in the store there is an ethnic or international food aisle. As an ethnic person, I enjoy many types of cuisine—the spicier the better, I say. In this designated aisle various spices adorn the shelves from around the globe. Grocery stores have made the requisite adjustments to diversity. We want our preaching to be well informed and well stocked with the proper ingredients as well.

I once spent part of a summer in Kisii, Kenya, on a short-term mission trip. Wanting to learn more about the local fare, I asked our host missionary what the staple diet is in Kenyan culture. His response was, "We eat *ugali* [thickened cornmeal porridge] at every meal." Likewise, preaching involves three major staples in our sermon preparation: understanding hermeneutics, humans, and homiletics. First, evangelical preachers begin sermon preparation with God's Word. Thus preaching involves hermeneutics, the skill of interpreting the biblical text and its context. Second, we preach to people, so we want to understand humans, which involves preachers building the Homiletical Bridge. Third, we engage in homiletics, the art and science of preaching, which is to take that biblical truth from the text and create and deliver a relevant message for today's variety of hearers.

The elephant is correct when he says that a home "designed for a giraffe will [not] ever really work for an elephant, not unless there are some major changes." The same could be said of our preaching. Perhaps we have been preaching the same way no matter who is listening. In such cases, we have not actually considered the Others in our sermon preparation. Other homileticians value diversity but may not know what questions to ask or what the process involves.

If you are reading this book, you probably, like this giraffe, relish an "I like having you here" feeling toward the Others. If so, we want to reflect on the elephants in the room. We want them to feel noticed, valued, embraced, and celebrated in church life and in our preaching. We want to love elephants in our congregations deeply, just as Christ loved his church. In *Building a House for Diversity*, the author later points out the giraffe's fundamental gaffe: "The house was not built with elephants in mind."[4] Perhaps more often than we would care to admit, our sermons have been written for giraffes and not for elephants. It is never too late, however, to cultivate skills in preaching to both (so-called) insiders and outsiders.

In the chapters to come, we will become equipped with a conceptual framework and practical model to better understand and preach effectively to various types of listeners. The book is divided into two parts. Part 1 serves as an introduction or backdrop to the theory of cultural intelligence. First, in chapter 1, I introduce the concept of cultural intelligence and give us a framework for how our preaching benefits from developing cultural intelligence. In chapter 2, I present the Homiletical Template by which to implement the concept of cultural intelligence in our preaching. Chapter 3 explores the intersection of preaching and hermeneutics and investigates how Others may read and interpret the written Word. In chapter 4, we embark on a journey toward self-exegesis, to consider the preacher's own cultural context and thereby illuminate how one's cultural lenses impact the hermeneutical and homiletical enterprises. This exercise is critical because only after preachers have deeply explored their own contexts will they have the bearings to interpret another culture.

In part 2, we flesh out cultural intelligence as a homiletical practice and explore five cultural contexts and how each type of listener is wired. The five cultural contexts to be surveyed include denominations (chap. 5), ethnicities (chap. 6), genders (chap. 7), locations (chap. 8), and religions (chap. 9). The format for each major chapter is similar, working through the Homiletical Template in three stages. In Stage 1, we commence with the hermeneutics involved in interpreting Scripture as we contemplate cultural variances. In Stage 2, we build the Homiletical Bridge and explore six areas of life for each cultural background. Finally, in Stage 3, we discuss the delivery element of homiletics in communicating more efficaciously to each cultural group.

We preach the Bible to real people—both to ourselves and to our hearers. Preaching effectively to the Other involves what David A. Livermore and others call "cultural intelligence," and that is what we seek to obtain.[5] Moreover, preaching with cultural intelligence requires biblical exegesis *and* cultural exegesis. Sermons deficient in either form of exegesis will be found duly wanting in the ears and hearts of our listeners. Both are indispensable to our calling as preachers. I want to acknowledge up front that *Preaching with*

Cultural Intelligence cannot possibly exegete comprehensively every cultural context being covered or tailor cultural intelligence to a given congregation's precise measurements. Some cultures on the reader's immediate radar will inevitably not be explored. However, I trust that as we embark on this cultural intelligence journey together, even one more listener will exclaim on Sunday morning, "Thanks be to God for this preacher who understands God's Word and understands me." So, thank you for picking up this book and for taking the next step in becoming a culturally intelligent Christian and a culturally sensitive preacher. Our efforts are not in vain, because God is worth it and so are our listeners.

Part 1

Cultural Intelligence *in* Theory

1

Preaching and Cultural Intelligence

Blocks from where I live in Beverly, Massachusetts, lies the Kernwood Bridge, built in 1907 to connect Beverly, known for its scenic public parks and beaches, to the legendary town of Salem, famed for its late 1600s witch trials and modern witchcraft tourism.[1] This bridge not only expedites approximately 7,700 drivers' daily commutes when crossing the Danvers River into the other city; it also serves to bring together these two distinct expressions of New England culture.[2] Just as physical bridges connect landmasses and town cultures separated by bodies of water, bridges are necessary connective instruments in homiletics. Preachers in the twenty-first century require, as John Stott puts it, the dexterities to stand "between two worlds"[3] and engage the world of the Bible and the world of today.[4] This book is an attempt to put additional flesh on Stott's original skeleton for preaching as bridge-building. It is inadequate to study the Scriptures without marrying this biblical exegesis to the pressing cultural issues of our time and valuing the cultural groups embodied in our churches.

Like the sides of an incomplete Rubik's Cube, preachers survey a checkerboard of eclectic people sitting in the pews, trying to make sense of how they can integrate the disparate pieces of their hearers' lives into a clear, contextualized, and unified message. This bridge-building exercise in preaching warrants cultural intelligence. At the same time, the preacher who displays cultural intelligence when preaching is simultaneously and subconsciously building bridges between and among his congregants, who often come from very dissimilar cultural contexts. Congregational cultural intelligence is a trait that is sorely missing in many churches today. That is, people don't have the requisite training to understand each other. In this opening chapter, I want to define culture through the eyes of a homiletician and explore how cultural intelligence conjoins the preaching process. The chapter concludes with a short description of the Homiletical Template that will augment our competence to preach with greater cultural understanding and sensitivity.

Culture and Homiletics

Culture is ubiquitous.[5] Just open your ears to the cacophony of languages in the bustling grocery store aisles or glance at the latest fashion magazines vying for your consumption or absorb cultural sound bites by hearing late night talk-show hosts' monologues on CBS, ABC, and NBC. Culture is life, and life is culture. Yet defining culture succinctly and cogently is quite tricky, is it not? The sheer murkiness of the term has led many in our society to dichotomize or parse out culture. Ask anyone on Main Street or in your church lobby what the term "culture" means today, and you will probably hear particularized aspects of culture named, including language, fashion, social media, trends, worldviews, musical tastes, news, values, politics, race, ethnicity, cuisine, beliefs, gender issues, mores, human sexuality, blue collar, white collar, religious preferences, the arts, sports, hip-hop, church traditions, evangelical, mainline, progressive, liberal, conservative, Baptist, Presbyterian, Anglican, Methodist, R-rated, PG-rated, and so on.

Not only have we compartmentalized culture but also culture is never stagnant. All cultures are fluid and ever evolving. New cultural trends are constantly being instated and reinstated by Hollywood, religious leaders, the media, politicians, marketers, designers, and others. How, then, might preachers define culture with regard to understanding the litany of cultures represented in our congregations? The apostle Paul provides this telos, or end goal, of preaching where he writes to the church of Colossae, "[Jesus Christ] is the one we proclaim, admonishing and teaching everyone with all wisdom, so that we may present *everyone* fully mature in Christ. To this end I strenuously contend with all the energy Christ so powerfully works in me" (Col. 1:28–29, emphasis added). In referring to this text, I am not contending that every single sermon must include Christ, as some propose from the historic-redemptive perspective on preaching.[6] However, I am submitting that it is in the purview of *every* preacher to understand and appreciate *everyone's* cultural nuances, to move them forward in their sanctification process in becoming more Christlike in their maturity.[7]

Take, for example, Philip's encounter with the Ethiopian eunuch in Acts 8:26–40. The Holy Spirit prompts Philip to stop and inquire whether the

Ethiopian understands what he is reading from the book of Isaiah. The Ethiopian eunuch responds in verse 31: "'How can I,' he said, 'unless someone explains it to me?' So he invited Philip to come up and sit with him." At this point, the invitation toward cultural intelligence commences with an exchange of ideas, questions, and dialogue. Then, in verse 35, Philip explains the meaning of Isaiah 53:7–8 and continues to share with him the good news of Jesus Christ. It is not insignificant that Luke records the ethnicity of this Ethiopian eunuch. Here the ethnic moniker of Ethiopian does not refer to modern-day Ethiopia per se, but rather to the Nubian region between southern Egypt and northern Sudan.[8] Through this cultural exchange, we observe that Philip's presentation of the gospel for this Ethiopian government official required cultural intelligence.

As in Philip's divine appointment with the Ethiopian eunuch, to be able to "present everyone fully mature in Christ" requires cultural intelligence. It does not happen without intentionality. It calls for extended labor "with all the energy Christ so powerfully works in me" to preach with cultural intelligence, by getting to know my congregants and their respective cultures. How, then, should preachers interpret the term "culture"? My definition of culture for preachers seeks to be holistic and intentionally broad in nature: *culture is a group's way of living, way of thinking, and way of behaving in the world, for which we need understanding and empathy to guide listeners toward Christian maturity.*[9] In a moment, we will explore what this means in greater detail.

The Genesis of Cultural Intelligence

People working in the business world—what Christians call the marketplace—have acutely felt the pressure to interact effectively with persons who are culturally different from them. A lack of cultural understanding and sensitivity has palpable consequences: a company's loss of revenue. For this reason, business professors P. Christopher Earley and Soon Ang wrote a trendsetting book called *Cultural Intelligence: Individual Interactions across Cultures*, to assist businesspeople in understanding and working with people from different cultures and backgrounds.[10] In this book the authors established a business concept called the cultural quotient theory (CQ), also known as cultural intelligence. They define cultural intelligence as "the capability to deal effectively with other people with whom the person does not share a common cultural background and understanding."[11]

Cultural intelligence (CQ) resembles emotional intelligence (EQ), which measures one's capacity for relational and interpersonal skills.[12] David Livermore

has popularized Earley and Ang's concept and provided a concrete framework
to achieve cultural intelligence in the midst of often complex and varied congregations.[13] Borrowing CQ as a conceptual framework to guide this book, my
goal is to employ cultural intelligence in our significant calling as preachers.
Below is a quick overview of Livermore's four stages of cultural intelligence,
which we will adapt for homiletical purposes.

The Four Stages of Cultural Intelligence

As culturally intelligent preachers, we want to familiarize ourselves with and
develop in all four stages of cultural intelligence.[14] While each of the four
stages is significant to understanding different cultural contexts, the loci of
this book will be centered on CQ knowledge and CQ action. CQ drive will
be the primary subject of chapter 4, and CQ strategy will be considered
more implicitly as we attempt to put cultural intelligence into action via the
Homiletical Template.

CQ Drive

First, Livermore articulates CQ drive as "the motivational dimension of
CQ, [which] is the leader's level of interest, drive, and energy to adapt cross-
culturally."[15] CQ drive reflects an inner longing to better understand similar
and dissimilar congregants. Loving our sheep requires getting to know them
beyond simply their names and professions. Who are they? What cultures and
subcultures do they most identify with? What dreams do they have, and what
are their fears? What beliefs do they hold closely? What causes them pain?

Livermore indicates that CQ drive is the most crucial of the four stages.[16]
Here it gauges the preacher's motivation level in seeking to understand one's
listeners. For example, someone with low CQ may quickly pigeonhole others
without taking any time to consider where such thinking, living, and behaving
derives from and the reasons why. They think to themselves, "That's the way
those people are." Yet those who possess a high degree of CQ drive enjoy
learning about other cultures. They do not consider cultural intelligence as
a burden or a chore. No matter where you find yourselves on the CQ drive
spectrum, my intention is not for you to feel overwhelmed. Rather, the hope
is that cultural intelligence becomes an extension of our everyday lives as we
grow to know our congregants over time.

How can we determine our CQ drive? Imagine this scenario at your church.
A new couple who are recent immigrants from Senegal (ethnicity), transplants
from Grand Rapids (location), or Methodists (denomination) visit your church

for the very first time. Is your natural inclination to greet them and inquire about their cultural backgrounds, or would you dart toward church members with whom you already share a strong camaraderie? (If you are introverted like me, your immediate response may be driven by your introvertedness and may not necessarily be an indication of your level of CQ drive.) Are you willing to pronounce and remember unfamiliar or "foreign" names? Or do you have the patience to watch movies in a different language, reading the English subtitles? My assumption is that you inherently possess at least a moderate desire for cultural intelligence or else you would have avoided this book. Wherever we fall on the CQ drive spectrum, the goal is that God will increase our inquisitiveness and love for Others in our congregations and communities. A more detailed consideration of CQ drive will be taken up in chapter 4.

CQ Knowledge

The second stage toward cultural intelligence is CQ knowledge, which represents "the cognitive dimension of the CQ research, [and] refers to the leader's knowledge about culture and its role in shaping how business [in our case, preaching] is done."[17] The key elements in CQ knowledge are assessing our current knowledge of how cultures are similar and different and "the way culture shapes thinking and behavior."[18] What knowledge do we currently possess about various listeners as we prepare to preach to them? For instance, what beliefs or values influence their daily decisions?[19] Are they individualistic (making decisions based on individual preferences) or collectivistic (making decisions according to what's best for a group)? Would they rather spend time with you (as a being-oriented culture) or accomplish something with you (as a doing-oriented culture)? On what do they spend their time and resources? What types of food do your listeners eat, and what do they decline? What cultural values are most highly esteemed in their culture: honesty, hard work, success, age, education, profession, salary, position, or status? What cultural idols obstruct the gospel from taking root in their lives, and more?

CQ Strategy

Third, "CQ strategy, also known as metacognitive CQ, is the leader's ability to strategize when crossing cultures."[20] Put differently, it is our plan of attack when interacting with those who are culturally different from us. As we strategize, we are engaging in three important tasks. First, we consider our own level of awareness regarding "what's going on in ourselves and others."[21] Second, we plan, thus "taking time to prepare for a cross-cultural encounter—anticipating how to approach the people, topic, and situation."[22] Last, we exercise CQ strategy by "monitoring our interactions to see if our plans and expectations were appropriate."[23] CQ strategy represents the process of creating a viable roadmap to help us become more culturally aware and culturally conversant. Our CQ strategy will be teased out through the Homiletical Template in chapter 2.

CQ Action

Last, in Stage 4, we want to develop CQ action, which is "the behavioral dimension of CQ . . . [and] the leader's ability to *act* appropriately in a range of cross-cultural situations. . . . The subdimensions of CQ action are *verbal actions*, *nonverbal actions*, and *speech acts*—the exact words and phrases we use when we communicate specific types of messages."[24] Put simply, CQ action, for preachers, is the test of how effectively we put into practice our CQ drive, CQ knowledge, and CQ strategy. Once we have implemented our cultural intelligence, we can determine whether our knowledge and strategies have been received well by our listeners and what elements need further calibration.

Becoming Bridgers of Cultures

The demands of pastoral ministry are endless. Growing in cultural intelligence may seem like an unnatural activity, a daunting process, and even an unnecessary inconvenience to an already-crowded schedule. Yet for Christians, cultural intelligence is part and parcel of what it means to be a disciple. By our very vocation, pastors and preachers *are* bridgers of cultures. We are the very transformational agents whom God uses through the act of proclamation to fasten sinners to the Scriptures and meld disparate disciples to one another—especially in such volatile moments of history like today, where our knee-jerk reaction toward Others is one of suspicion, distrust, patronization, dehumanization, fear, hatred, and even violence. We automatically assume the worst in Others and fail to give one another the benefit of the doubt.

In contrast, the apostle Paul prescribes cultural embrace and adoption as ways forward to overcome cultural differences. As an example for all preachers, Paul tells the Corinthian believers, "I have become all things to all people so that by all possible means I might save some" (1 Cor. 9:22). Preaching with cultural intelligence means understanding the various cultures and subcultures (the smaller cultural clusters within a larger cultural context) in our congregations and addressing the various needs and nuances of the people listening to our sermons with a spirit of empathy. Culture-bridgers take unwavering steps toward seeing life from the Other's perspective and experiences and even fighting on their behalf instead of retreating to the solace of the status quo.

Preachers often find themselves in one of two camps. Some acutely feel the burden of this cavity of cultural awareness in their proclamation, while others assume that everyone's needs are being served. For preachers communicating in the twenty-first century, acquiring and utilizing cultural intelligence is really not optional: it is vital to our proclamation lest we accept being dreadfully irrelevant. Michael Quicke reminds us that "myopic preachers are naïve about culture. They fail to give it much thought and prayer."[25] Additionally, Leonora Tubbs Tisdale encourages preachers to engage in cultural exegesis as the way to cultivate "explicit skills and training in 'exegeting congregations' and their subcultures—just as they need skills and training in exegeting the Scriptures."[26] Raymond Bakke comments: "Most of us went to Bible schools or seminaries where we learned to design ministry in our own image, i.e., to sing the songs we appreciate, and to preach sermons we would like to listen to. Unfortunately for us, the challenge now is to retool and design ministry strategies in the image of the unreached who may be very different from us culturally."[27] Much like these thinkers, we may feel the vacuum of specialized cultural knowledge about the diverse range of people in the pews. Cultural exegesis is the process by which we obtain and employ cultural intelligence. It is taking what we know and what we learn about specific cultures and using that to help them apply God's truth in tangible ways and in culturally germane forms.

My hope in writing this book is to offer a practical framework to help us become biblical as well as bridge-building preachers. As biblical preachers, the truth found in the scriptural text dictates and shapes the central idea of the sermon. That is, we preach the main idea of the text. Bridge-building preachers take that main idea of the text into the deeper alcoves of our listeners' hearts and minds, seeking maximum cultural engagement and sermonic relevance. What we are venturing into will not be without resistance. Some of our congregants may find ways to dissent from our seemingly impulsive itch now to cater culturally sensitive meals to the Others on the outskirts. Michael Angrosino warns, "Be prepared to face questions, criticisms, even hostility from those in your community who do not yet see the value of what you are attempting to accomplish."[28] However, through faithfully preaching culturally intelligent sermons, our listeners will in due time see the lasting impact of how cultural intelligence cultivates their appreciation for one another's cultural differences, just as God intended. To facilitate this process in becoming culturally intelligent preachers, we may need new pathways of approaching culture and understanding cultural intelligence.

A New Model of Culture for Cultural Intelligence

To this point, we have been talking about culture by way of definitions, but what might culture look like if it was presented as a diagram? Since some preachers are visual learners, I would like to present the term "culture" as "visually speaking."[29] A common image to display cultural difference is the iceberg: a few aspects of culture are above the surface, and many others (perhaps 90 percent) lie hidden below. For instance, Patty Lane refers to objective and subjective cultural differences. Objective culture represents the visible portions of the iceberg, which include clothing, manner of greeting, food and language; subjective culture "is the internal part of culture that drives or motivates the visible, objective culture"[30] and is less detectable, such as a person's values, feelings, assumptions, and motivations,[31] obscured below the waterline. Earlier in this chapter, I defined "culture" as *a group's way of living, way of thinking, and way of behaving in the world, for which we need understanding and empathy to guide our listeners toward Christian maturity.*[32] What if we create a new visual model of culture for cultural intelligence that includes both visible and invisible components of culture as a triad, seen as a way of living, way of thinking, and way of behaving (see fig. 1.1)?

In many ways Lane's understanding of culture emphasizes culture as ways of living and thinking yet addresses issues of behavior less directly. A more holistic understanding of culture involves all three ways: living, thinking, *and* behaving. The objective here is to incorporate more of each of these cultural dimensions in our sermons. Although the default mode is to start with the most visible cultural element (way of living), we would seek to increasingly utilize newfound cultural knowledge to crystallize our sermon with thinking and behavioral elements as well. Depending on your cultural context, there may be some overlap among these three dimensions to culture. Each aspect of culture below provides six cultural descriptors for further consideration.[33] In your cultural contexts, other germane topics may emerge, while others on this list may seem less pertinent to you.

Culture as a Way of Living

On the surface, we can make cultural connections with people from all cultural backgrounds when we talk about food, clothing, language, music, celebrations, and time. These categories are considered visible or external aspects

Figure 1.1
Model of Cultural Intelligence

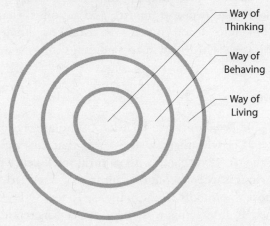

Way of
Thinking

Way of
Behaving

Way of
Living

of culture. Many of these ways of living can be determined by reading books on culture and cultural differences. Of course, the more we spend time with people from other cultural contexts, the more we will be able to experience these ways of living firsthand. Six areas of exploration include food, clothing, language, music, celebrations (national holidays and festivals), and time (as being limited or limitless).[34] Ways of living can become stumbling blocks when Others' ways of life conflict with ours. See appendix 2 for more details.

Culture as a Way of Thinking

In this second section, I am alerting us to some of the important cognitive and experiential thinking that goes on within a particular cultural group. These ways of thinking (beliefs, rituals, idols, dreams, God, and experiences, or BRIDGE) will be integral for employment in the Homiletical Template that will be employed as we build the BRIDGE into our listeners' cultures. More details on these six ways of thinking will be provided in the Homiletical Template in chapter 2 as well as in appendix 2.

Culture as a Way of Behaving

Nearly all behaviors are culturally conditioned.[35] What constitutes acceptable behavior in one culture is not universally prescribed across every culture. Although the Bible clearly identifies types of behavior aberrant from the Christian faith, called sinful practices, here are six ways of behaving to consider with respect to cultural differences: ethics (what is right and what is wrong), decisions (who ultimately makes the decision), mores (what is considered acceptable behavior), love (which expressions of love are culturally appropriate), fairness (what is just or unjust), and actions (behaviors that are often influenced by our cultural context). Assistance on understanding different ways of behaving is provided in appendix 2.

Conclusion

I echo Eugene Peterson when he asks, "Who are these particular people, and how can I be with them in such a way that they can become what God is making them?"[36] Preaching with cultural intelligence prods us to become more voracious learners about the cultures of our particular people and especially those who sit idly on the margins. To love Others means that we will care for them by interacting with them and getting to know them personally, even when it is difficult. As David Livermore observes, "Embodying Jesus cross-culturally is a messy, complicated process."[37] Developing in cultural intelligence does not happen instantly or without intentionality. It ebbs and flows as we preach and minister to different cultural groups. Allow yourself the freedom to make mistakes along the way and show yourself grace in how rapidly or slowly you are tethering cultural intelligence to yourself. In most cases, your listeners will applaud you for acknowledging their presence, and their glowing countenance will become your incentive to learn more. When making unintended errors, seek Others' assistance in learning about their culture and plead ignorance to engender endearment. Preaching with cultural intelligence will require a lucid homiletical strategy. That will be the subject of our next chapter.

2

The Homiletical Template

A vision is only as effective as its strategy. In other words, a conceivable and practical strategy puts legs on a budding vision, enabling it to be achieved. God's vision is to develop culturally intelligent preachers who rigorously study the biblical text and today's cultural context. This vision requires a plan. Here I present the Homiletical Template for preaching with cultural intelligence as a practical CQ strategy. This template will be divided into three stages: Stage 1 explores hermeneutics through the acronym HABIT; Stage 2 helps us build the Homiletical Bridge by using the BRIDGE acronym; and Stage 3 concludes with the delivery aspects of homiletics via the acronym DIALECT (see fig. 2.1). In utilizing this template, five basic provisos are in order.

First, only in Stage 1 is it strongly recommended that all five steps be completed weekly for sermon preparation. Since hermeneutics is indispensable to the task of preaching, rigorously explore the biblical context and the author's cultural context in partnership with studying your church's cultural context.

Second, Stages 2 and 3 can be understood as à la carte practices. Depending on the subject matter or content of the sermon, use discretion to locate cultural connection points by using the acronym BRIDGE. To augment your communication, intentionally consider one or more elements in the acronym DIALECT. The complexity of your cultural context, however, will stipulate which of these seven communication tools requires additional exploration.

Third, for each of the five major cultural contexts considered in this book, I will provide examples for the nuances of exploring the eighteen stages of

Figure 2.1
The Homiletical Template

Stage 1: Hermeneutics	Stage 2: The Homiletical Bridge		Stage 3: Homiletics
HABIT	**BRIDGE**		**DIALECT**
Historical, Grammatical, and Literary Context	**I**dols	**D**reams	**D**elivery
Author's Cultural Context	**R**ituals	**G**od	**I**llustrations
Big Idea of the Text	**B**eliefs	**E**xperiences	**A**pplication
Interpret in Your Context			**L**anguage
Theological Presuppositions			**E**mbrace
			Content
			Trust

the Homiletical Template. Yet each major chapter will incorporate context-specific elements that will be tailored for each particular cultural group. That is, not all chapters will have a cookie-cutter pattern and be approached in exactly the same fashion.

Fourth, I regret that this book cannot be comprehensive due to the volume and diversity of CQ knowledge that is required for such broad cultural contexts. As a corollary, remember that each of the major cultural contexts covered in this book (i.e., denominations, ethnicities, genders, locations, and religions) is not monolithic, and the preacher will invariably find exceptions to the "cultural" rules. People within a given culture do not embody an identical DNA or share replicated life experiences.

Fifth, adapting this book for each congregation will require specialized cultural intelligence. In certain congregations, homogeneity in terms of race, ethnicity, economic class, denominational affiliation, and other characteristics may be normative. That is, people will be very similar on a surface level. When a visitor enters your sanctuary, they instantly think, "This church is [*whatever*]." You will need to determine which cultures are invisible to you and the majority culture. Your growth edges for cultural intelligence will involve learning about those on the margins who differ in both conspicuous and subtle ways from the majority culture. In other congregations, the demographics of the members vary broadly, and you will need to be selective as to which cultures you will explore in a given week. Remember, you cannot address every single culture in every single sermon. Make it a goal to target your sermons for one or two cultural groups of listeners each week, and prepare the sermon with them in mind. Even if the sermon does not address every culture's specific concerns, you are still building the bridge to help them grow in cultural intelligence about the Other.

Let's begin our CQ strategy by starting with God's Word.

Stage 1: Hermeneutics—Follow Your HABIT

This book seeks to approach our calling as preachers with a balanced understanding of exegeting the Bible and contemporary culture. Recent books on the subject of preaching and culture focus principally on understanding modern cultural overtones and say little to nothing about hermeneutics.[1] Remember, we are not modifying the core gospel message or massaging biblical truth to fit the various cultures and subcultures to which we preach. The gospel message and the biblical text are resoundingly clear, presenting the true account of Jesus Christ's life, ministry, death, burial, and resurrection. Preaching with cultural intelligence does not, by any means, extend liberty or license to distort this good news and biblical truth. In preaching with cultural intelligence, we remain steadfast to interpret Scripture faithfully and to preach sermons that accurately reflect the biblical author's intention conveyed in each pericope. Put simply, the substance or content of the sermon is not altered because of our cultural exegesis or cultural intelligence.

However, interpreting Scripture with an eye toward culture recognizes that humans interpret Scripture through their own cultural lens. In *Misreading Scripture with Western Eyes*, E. Randolph Richards and Brandon J. O'Brien argue that Westerners often read and interpret the Bible fundamentally through a Western cultural perspective, which does not always accurately represent cultural nuances in the Bible well or take into consideration how non-Western thinkers would read and interpret the text. Consequently, preaching can be error-prone when we read the text only from *our* limited cultural point of reference.[2] Thus interpretive methods ought to take into consideration our listeners' cultural context, particularly their assumptions, conflicts, and questions about any given text.

In addition, interpreting Scripture with culture in view does not replace the historical-grammatical approach to hermeneutics. To be clear, preaching with cultural intelligence requires biblical exegesis *and* cultural exegesis. This entails proactively exploring the culture of the biblical author as we simultaneously wrestle with the cultural questions that our listeners bring to the worship service. The acronym HABIT (historical, grammatical, and literary context; author's cultural context; big idea of the text; interpret in your context; and theological presuppositions) provides us with a straightforward sequence to engage hermeneutically with our listeners. Below is a brief description of the HABIT, which we will elaborate on further in chapter 3.

Historical, Grammatical, and Literary Context

For many decades, the traditional hermeneutic approach to interpreting Scripture taught in evangelical seminaries has been the historical-grammatical method. As its name implies, preachers have been instructed to determine the biblical author's originally intended meaning by studying the historical setting of the text in its context as well as the grammar and literary genre. In his widely used preaching textbook *Biblical Preaching*, Haddon W. Robinson defines expository preaching as "the communication of a biblical concept, derived from and transmitted through a historical, grammatical, and literary study of a passage in its context, which the Holy Spirit first applies to the personality and experience of the preacher, then through the preacher, applies to the hearers."[3] Not diverging from this hermeneutical process taught at Gordon-Conwell Theological Seminary and in many other seminaries around the world,[4] the initial step of our sermon preparation commences with biblical exegesis and a historical, grammatical, and literary study of our Scripture text.

Author's Cultural Context

What can get shortchanged or hurried in the hermeneutical process, however, is intentional exploration of the biblical author's cultural context.[5] For example, when we preach through Genesis 15:21, how much sermon time do we allot for characterizing the "Amorites, Canaanites, Girgashites and Jebusites"?[6] To effectively communicate Scripture to the range of cultural groups in our congregations, a more keen appreciation for and comprehension of the biblical author's background and cultural context (i.e., issues beyond authorship and date) will serve preachers well. The purpose of this second step is to provide insight into how the cultures in our churches mirror or conflict with the biblical author's world. In doing so, the goal is to present as accurately as possible the cultural dynamics between the biblical world and the modern context—that is, their similarities and incongruities. Specifically, in each major chapter we will consider one or two dominant cultural practices that permeated the biblical author's time and place. Our listeners will find either resonance or dissonance with these ancient cultural practices.

In most, if not all, cases our initial exploration and interpretation of the author's cultural context will be colored by our own cultural biases and blind spots. Gary Burge cautions: "We must be careful lest we presuppose that our cultural instincts are the same as those represented in the Bible. We must be culturally aware of our own place in time—and we must work to comprehend the cultural context of the Scriptures that we wish to understand."[7] Burge gives some common examples of the kinds of cultural considerations that we may forget to ask or simply be ignorant about:

> In what sense, for instance, did the physical geography of Israel shape its people's sense of spirituality? How did the story-telling of Jesus presuppose cultural themes now lost to us? What celebrations did Jesus know intimately (such as a child's birth, a wedding, or a burial)? What agricultural or religious festivals did he attend? How did he use common images of labor or village life or social hierarchy when he taught? Did he use humor or allude to politics?[8]

The more we familiarize ourselves with the author's cultural context, the more effectively we can raise the cultural consciousness of our listeners, who will either find commonalities or discontinuities with the cultures of the biblical world.

Big Idea of the Text

As we explore the biblical world, pursue a solid understanding of the biblical text in front of us. Specifically, we want to be able to answer this question: What is the central truth or main idea being communicated by the author in our Scripture passage? One way to locate the main idea is by asking two basic questions of the text: (1) What is the author talking about, which Haddon Robinson labels the subject question? (2) What is the author saying about what he's talking about, which is the complement or complete answer to the subject question?[9] Combining the subject and the complement to form a complete sentence or thought is what Robinson calls the exegetical idea, or *the big idea.* An example of how to determine the big idea of the text will be provided in chapter 3.

Interpret in Your Context

Consider the range of questions your listeners are asking about the text based on their cultural vantage points. Anticipate the specific assumptions, conflicts, and questions your listeners have regarding this passage and the biblical truth it communicates. John Koessler observes, "It is true that the biblical author and the life situation of the original audience dominate the exegetical and hermeneutical phases of the sermon. Yet even in the early stages, those who will be listening to us are never far from view."[10] What we are dealing with here may not always be a difference of interpretation but rather of application since "many diversities of interpretation are differences over the way a story applies to different people or in different contexts rather than differences about its inherent meaning."[11] Yet as we study the passage, some natural interpretive rifts will emerge for preachers to acknowledge and probe further on behalf of their hearers.

Theological Presuppositions

Finally, theological presuppositions are any "primary foundational commitments"[12] that we make about the Triune God—Father, Son, and Holy Spirit—and other Christian doctrines, or about ministry philosophies and practices. Theological presuppositions are the topics of contention where Christians exclaim, "Of course, that's the way it is or the only way to do it!" Theological presuppositions often derive from what one has been taught by parents, family members, pastors, teachers, and friends, gatherings from personal study, and one's experiences in the world. Theological presuppositions are powerful and yet limiting because they constitute binding assumptions, which frequently limit a person from seeing the Other's perspective. For example, many have internalized theological presuppositions about the Trinity, election, salvation, atonement, baptism, spiritual gifts, women's and men's roles in ministry, Christ-centered preaching, historic-redemptive or dispensational preaching, and many others. The purpose of this final segment on hermeneutics is to be intentional about the theological presuppositions we and our listeners hold that influence the preacher's hermeneutics and the resulting proclamation.

Stage 2: Build the BRIDGE

In this second stage of the Homiletical Template, we will learn about six concrete ways to build the bridge with our listeners by using the acronym BRIDGE. Again, becoming bridgers of cultures between the biblical world and ours, as well as between diverse cultures represented in the church, is our twofold objective. Rather than being paralyzed by the enormity of our task, building the bridge vis-à-vis accumulating cultural intelligence is not as complex as we might think. Exegeting listeners, particularly those who are different from us, will propel us to forge organic opportunities to learn about the Beliefs, Rituals, Idols, Dreams, (view of) God, and Experiences of our hearers. Cultural intelligence or cultural exegesis can take several forms:

(1) reading books that include the literature and historical experiences of a different culture; (2) engaging in participant-observation by attending events and activities of a particular culture, participating as much as possible, and jotting down notes of what you have learned; (3) conducting focus-group interviews to ask questions about a select group of individuals and their cultures; and (4) spending time with congregants from various contexts, especially in their natural environments such as in their homes and in other cultural settings (e.g., ethnic restaurants, birthday parties, and events to commemorate cultural holidays and celebrations).

To ease the pressure that is probably rising in your bloodstream, the expectation is not that we investigate all six spheres of life every week and include our findings in every single sermon. Rather, developing in cultural intelligence is a nimble process of gradually opening ourselves to learning more about others, their cultures, and their experiences. The image of the BRIDGE reminds us of six areas of life that, if explored, will facilitate our ability to preach culturally intelligent messages. In some weeks we may be able to include only what we learn about congregants' idols. During other weeks we might learn about multiple topics and find strategic points in the sermon to incorporate our newfound cultural intelligence. In practical terms, our schedule in one week may allow having coffee with a parishioner or attending a birthday party of a child from another cultural group. The BRIDGE acronym may be limiting for certain cultures, so you may want to find other topics to investigate as well. Here is a brief synopsis of what we are trying to learn about each culture as we build the BRIDGE.

Beliefs

Begin with learning about your listeners' beliefs. What is a belief?[13] In simple terms, a belief is "an acceptance that a statement is true or that something exists."[14] In general, beliefs can be sorted into three categories. First, some are *confessional* beliefs, which function as cognitive ideas, focusing on the intellect.[15] For instance, I may embrace the confessional belief that advanced forms of technology do not innately advance the human race. Second, *convictional* beliefs resemble values and impact one's behaviors and actions.[16] A young person who believes that education matters will find a way to finish college or graduate school. A person who believes that there is a God will take proactive steps to find out who this God is (e.g., attending a religious service or reading books on religion). Beliefs are "different from feelings or opinions because they make a 'cognitive claim'—that is, a claim to some kind of knowledge."[17] Third, *cultural* beliefs are culturally determined. For instance, Americans may believe that the United States of America is the greatest nation on earth. Others may believe that their own native country is the greatest. As preachers, we are constantly shaping the beliefs of our listeners through the truth of Scripture. Familiarizing ourselves with our listeners' beliefs is paramount to effective communication within and across cultures.

Rituals

The second section of the BRIDGE regards rituals.[18] Simply put, a ritual is a "series of actions or type of behavior regularly and invariably followed by someone"[19] or by some collective group. Every person and every congregation exhibits various rituals, whether spoken or tacit. The significance of rituals is not simply the routine, habit, or practice, but also the meaning behind them. "Rituals, then, are powerful tools by which a society sets boundaries, confers status, and marks changes in some state of affairs."[20] Churches follow rituals, including how Communion is celebrated, musical preferences, liturgy, the order of worship, baptism, celebration of holidays, serving meals or donuts or nothing during the fellowship time, and so on. Such rituals express the local church's heartbeat and put on display the church's specialized beliefs and values. Rituals are accepted practices that are often culturally conditioned, such as wearing one's shoes in the home (Western cultures) or removing one's shoes on entering the home (Eastern cultures). Some rituals are idiosyncratic to a particular culture and will not warrant biblical correction, such as our shoe example. Other rituals, like consistently missing Sunday worship in order to watch NFL football games, show the need for scriptural teaching to challenge the validity of certain rituals or traditions, even if they are passed down from one generation to the next.

Idols

Third, locate the idols in your cultural context.[21] Idolatry is "imagining and trusting anything to deliver the control, security, significance, satisfaction, and beauty that only the real God can give. It means turning a good thing into an ultimate thing."[22] Anything in life can become an idol. These idols do not necessarily manifest themselves in physical form, like the golden calf erected by the Israelites in Exodus 32. Idols can be sharply wedged into the spiritual heart, blocking the necessary flow that brings life to the Christian. An idol can be finding hyper-significance in our race, ethnicity, gender, family upbringing, birth order, profession, financial security, marital status, children, sexual preference, religious affiliation, church membership, denomination, theological convictions, neighborhood, social media image, hobbies, having a green lawn, and all other ontological classifications that can saturate one's thoughts and behaviors. Sometimes particularly cultural idols can be so steeply embedded in the culture that they become normative and completely acceptable, as in Korean immigrant culture, where young adults are sometimes encouraged to find an ethnically Korean marriage partner, even if not a Christian. The cultural idol here is maintaining an alleged ethnically pure bloodline.

However, Gregory K. Beale stresses the prevailing consequences of idolatry: "*What people revere, they resemble, either for ruin or restoration.*"[23] Like a thick fog that settles, idols creep in and cloud our vision from what really matters to God, causing many Christians to "wander through life merely existing instead of living the reality of who God has called them to be."[24] In the task of preaching, Timothy Keller endorses a process of discerning, exposing, and destroying the various idols in our churches.[25] Similarly, we want to uncover these idols in the consciousness of our hearers and help them wrestle with them biblically so that their process of maturity does not become stymied.

Dreams

A fourth strategy to find connection points is to unveil listeners' dreams. Years ago, in my doctoral studies, I came across the work of social psychologists Hazel Markus and Paula Nurius, who taught at the University of Michigan. They developed a conceptual model called the possible selves theory. In it, they tried to understand people's self-perceptions based on what they hoped for, what they expected of themselves, and what they feared.[26] Markus and Nurius's theory of possible selves revealed the power that internalized possible selves, or hopes and dreams, have in people's lives. Dreams are powerful. To varying degrees, every day our listeners have dreams or possible selves for their lives. They may dream about becoming popular in high school, going to a certain university, getting married, starting a family, establishing themselves in a lucrative career, making professional advances, owning their own home, driving a particular type of car, having successful children, not getting cancer, and the list continues. They have fears of the unknown, the symbiotic fears of failure and rejection, fears of terminal illness, the fear of dying, the fear of suffering, and more. Understanding the dreams or

possible selves of our listeners is an all-important first step toward cultural
intelligence, because a person's dreams and possible selves are a reflection of
the way culture has shaped their lives and how their past experiences shape
their future aspirations.

Translating the possible selves theory into a Christian context, preachers can
present listeners with sermonic challenges to channel greater energy toward
their spiritual possible selves, letting hopes and dreams facilitate their progress
toward Christian maturity.[27] What spiritual possible selves are provided in
the biblical text? For instance, in 1 Peter 2:1–5 the apostle states the existing
compromised condition of his readers:

> Therefore, rid yourselves of all malice and all deceit, hypocrisy, envy, and slan-
> der of every kind. Like newborn babies, crave pure spiritual milk, so that by it
> you may grow up in your salvation, now that you have tasted that the Lord is
> good. As you come to him, the living Stone—rejected by humans but chosen
> by God and precious to him—you also, like living stones, are being built into a
> spiritual house to be a holy priesthood, offering spiritual sacrifices acceptable
> to God through Jesus Christ.

We skip down to verses 9–10: "But you are a chosen people, a royal priesthood, a holy nation, God's special possession, that you may declare the praises
of him who called you out of darkness into his wonderful light. Once you were
not a people, but now you are the people of God; once you had not received
mercy, but now you have received mercy." Peter reminds his people of their
earlier condition, stuck in the mire of their depravity, and provides new, godly
dreams or possible selves for their lives. He calls them to cease living as babies
and to grow up by becoming like the images of "living stones," "a spiritual
house," "a chosen people," "a royal priesthood," "a holy nation," "God's
special possession," "the people of God," and to demonstrate for the world
the benefits of the mercy they have already received from God.

The preacher can similarly help listeners see how they can practice their
spiritual possible selves or dreams in their daily lives. The weekly sermon becomes the preacher's platform to remind listeners of God's dreams for them,
which combat the world's dreams for them as widely disseminated through
television, radio, music, podcasts, blogs, movies, and the internet. In many
passages of Scripture, God provides his people with a dream that differs from
their former or current reality. Preachers can employ the sermon to imprint
on the listener God's dreams for their lives, dreams infinitely more gratifying
than anything that this world has to offer. Help your listeners dream godly
dreams without even sleeping during the sermon.

God

Next, how do our listeners view God? For most Christians, their perspective on who God is depends on numerous factors that are often shaped by their lived experiences. Depending on their cultural context, they may tend to emphasize certain characteristics of God as opposed to others: God's eternality, jealousy, love, wrath, mercy, patience, justice, holiness, power, goodness, sovereignty, faithfulness, and so much more. For some, God bears resemblance to a hovering, impossible-to-please mom, or a doting, pushover grandfather who capitulates to the child's incessant pleas. Widely read books like atheist Christopher Hitchens's *God Is Not Great*, atheist Philip Pullman's *His Dark Materials* series, or William Paul Young's *The Shack* are examples of authors who are daring society to reassess God's omnipotence, omnipresence, and omniscience. Paul Froese and Christopher Bader, in their book *America's Four Gods*, present data that reveals Americans' perception of God as fitting into four classifications: authoritative, benevolent, critical, and disengaged.[28] According to Froese and Bader, many Americans' perception of God is less than favorable. Even in the church, our listeners' perceptions of God may reflect the culture more than we think. On the opposite spectrum, Christians hyperemphasize God's unconditional love and grace to the exclusion of his holiness, or glamorize God's lavish generosity, giving him the countenance of a cosmic genie. Even further, certain Christians syncretize the Christian God with the deity of their particular religious expressions. Our exegetical work as preachers is to determine what view of God our listeners possess and build the BRIDGE into their lives to paint a more holistic, balanced, and affirming portrait of who God truly is.

Experiences

Last, our life experiences invariably color the way we view life. Listen to people's narratives. Provide space for them to share the highest and lowest points of life, which invariably alter their perception of the world over a lifetime. For example, if a traumatic event happens to a child at a young age and revises her childhood, such as the death of a parent or experiencing some type of verbal or physical abuse, the child may be stuck in childhood and never grow out of a childlike state even as an adult. As we work with people in ministry, we often wonder why people act the way they do. Once we understand their past, we are able to show them more grace because their idiosyncrasies are often the result of disturbing events, moments, or hardships in their recent and distant pasts. Knowledge of others' past experiences is crucial to the task of preaching. The past experiences of the preacher and listener, especially traumatic moments, indwell the person for decades. Every preacher comes to the task of preaching, as well expressed by Henri Nouwen, as "wounded healers," who then preach to heal other "wounded healers."[29] Moving listeners toward Christian maturity requires culturally specific discipleship in the full-orbed sense of the word. This requires ample understanding of our listeners' beliefs, rituals, idols, dreams, (view of) God, and experiences.

Stage 3: Speak Their DIALECT

Last, in Stage 3 the climax of each chapter offers homiletical devices by exploring seven mechanics of preaching as they pertain to each distinct cultural group. As Kenneth Burke points out, "You persuade [people] only insofar as you can talk [their] language by speech, gesture, tonality, order, image, attitude, [and] idea, identifying your ways with [theirs]."[30] Here communication issues will be considered by using the acronym DIALECT: delivery, illustrations, application, language, embrace, content, and trust are to be appropriately customized for each cultural context. David Hesselgrave explains, "The word *communication* comes from the Latin word *communis* (common). *We must establish a 'commonness' with someone to have communication.*"[31] To communicate with cultural intelligence is not something that occurs haphazardly on an ad hoc basis, but rather is a process that requires a preacher's thoughtfulness and sensitivity.

I intentionally selected the acronym DIALECT to shape our strategy for homiletics because in every culture people speak the native language with a particular dialect. A dialect is a "particular form of a language which is peculiar to a specific region or social group."[32] Put another way, Clive Upton says: "Most of us who have roots in one particular area have special words, or use well-known words in a special way, that we only discover are 'strange' to others when we travel away from home."[33] The North American context alone harbors eight English dialects.[34] At least ten dialects of Spanish are spoken around the globe today.[35] What this means is that speaking the same language (English or Spanish or another) does not automatically denote that one person will understand the other. When we speak the same dialect as another person, common ground can be established where misunderstandings are reduced and buoyantly eliminated. Using the same analogy, to preach using someone's DIALECT means being intentional in our homiletics so as not to preach generic sermons that we hope will address everyone. We will begin with delivery.

Delivery

Every cultural context requires a custom-made or culturalized sermon delivery. When preaching is at its best form, the delivery adapts to the various listeners sitting in the worship service. I am not arguing for a put-on, disingenuous, hypocritical mode of communication. Rather, preaching with cultural intelligence invites opportunities for preachers to adjust communication styles and thereby relate to as many cultural groups that worship together as possible. Calvin Miller observes, "Ours is a relational day and age. We are not heard very well beyond the borders of our relationships. In spite of this most preachers continue to work on content and give very little attention to congregational rapport. Indeed, few preachers really train themselves for relational delivery."[36] "Relational"—or in our terms, culturally intelligent delivery—will emphasize delivery aspects such as sermon structure, tone, pathos, voice, gestures, rate of speech, and so forth, depending on the cultural context of the listeners.

Illustrations

As its etymology suggests, preachers use examples to illustrate or clarify something for the listeners in a sermon. Oftentimes a preacher who stays in ministry in a particular context for a long time will rely on hobbyhorse illustrations retrieved from the same few barrels. What we take for granted in one culture as an effective illustration may completely miss others from a different cultural situation. For example, Wayne Harvey encourages preachers to ask themselves, "*Will this illustration be sensitive to people in the congregation?*"[37] He continues: "Do most of your listeners read *Vogue* or *People*? Do they watch professional wrestling or public television? Do they prefer jazz or country? Every church is different, so some illustrations will work better than others."[38] Becoming familiar enough with cultural contexts to illustrate appropriately will take time, and inevitably we will make mistakes. However, as Matthew Soerens and Jenny Hwang observe in their book *Welcoming the Stranger*, we may even be surprised at how many commonalities we share with the Others, beginning with "a taste for good food, a concern for your families and very often a common Christian faith."[39] Culturally intelligent illustrations will be one of the delivery aims in chapters 5–9.

Application

Applying the sermon for listeners is one of the ultimate goals of biblical preaching. However, offering tailor-made applications for a specific cultural context may prove challenging for many preachers. The vacuum of relevant and textually faithful application has persisted for too long. Abraham Kuruvilla laments, "A robust hermeneutic for making this move from text to audience, which places preaching and application within the larger scheme of spiritual formation and discipleship of God's people, has been sorely wanting."[40] Haddon Robinson agrees: "More heresy is preached in application than in Bible exegesis. . . . Sometimes we apply the text in ways that might make the biblical writer say, 'Wait a minute, that's the wrong use of what I said.' This is the heresy of a good truth applied in the wrong way."[41] Furthermore, as John Koessler maintains, "We may draw conclusions from the text that its human author never envisioned, but we cannot make applications that are incompatible with the author's intent."[42] The added complexity of an unfamiliar cultural context exacerbates our applicational blunders.

Typically, preachers thinking about applications logically gravitate toward action steps with respect to what listeners must do immediately after the worship service to fulfill God's instructions in the text. While there is nothing wrong with this perspective per se, it presents an incomplete understanding of what application is. In light of this, Timothy Keller suggests that application requires equilibrium and "includes, at least, (a) warning and admonishing, (b) encouraging and renewing, (c) comforting and soothing, (d) urging, pleading, and 'stirring up.'"[43] Yet Keller's fourfold strategy for application deals more with the preacher's tone in application than with concrete tips on how to apply the Bible faithfully.

While no universal best practice exists for application, here are three items for consideration when preaching to various culturally different listeners. First, we want to find a greater balance between individual and corporate applications. The American church context is hyperindividualistic. We read the Bible passage and instantly ask ourselves, "So, what does this mean to *me*, and what should *I* do about it?" Although personal application is significant and even necessary for the believer, many non-Western cultures (including ancient biblical cultures) are collectivistic rather than individualistic. Whereas Western Christians drift toward personalized application, many ethnic or non-Western congregants also expect some biblical application that influences the entire church, neighborhood, and especially the family. In general, regardless of congregational demographics, a heightened awareness of communal application will benefit churches in the long run. How we apply the Word individually *and* corporately is a question we want to raise in every sermon, to create a sense of balance, especially with culturally diverse listeners.

Second, try to provide a balance of *being* versus *doing* applications. Many preachers in the United States apply the text with respect to doing more frequently than being. We hear applications such as "Serve food to the hungry, tithe 10 percent of your income, call your mother on Mother's Day, share the gospel with your coworker on Monday morning, visit prisoners and shut-ins," and so on. We forget that the Bible also commands us "to be" in relationship with God as Father, Son, and Spirit, and with other people. In John 15:5 Jesus tells his disciples, "I am the vine; you are the branches. If you remain in me and I in you, you will bear much fruit; apart from me you can do nothing." Thus Jesus places priority on our being with him, which then expresses itself in doing good works for him. When God says in Psalm 46:10, "Be still, and know that I am God; I will be exalted among the nations, I will be exalted in the earth," God reminds the Jewish people of his sovereignty over all creation, nations, and kingdoms. The Lord simply wants their complete trust in him. Many cultures are *being* cultures rather than *doing* cultures. Both sides of application are necessary for all of Jesus's disciples.

Third, certain preachers like to offer applications by naming various implications of a biblical truth. The implication spectrum suggests the following: "Implications may be necessary, probable, possible, improbable, or impossible."[44] Remember that many applications and their implications are culturally conditioned. That is, we should not presume a one-to-one correlation of application and implications across all cultures. As an example, the necessary implication of "You shall not commit adultery" (Exod. 20:14; Matt. 5:27) means one must avoid any sexual relations with someone who is not one's spouse.[45] Robinson states, "An improbable conclusion is [that] you should not at any time have lunch with someone who is not your spouse."[46] However, what is an improbable implication for Western Christians would more likely reflect a necessary, probable, or possible implication in Muslim cultures since unrelated men and women do not eat together unless they are sitting next to their spouse.[47] Therefore, applications and implications require further investigation in the cultures represented in our congregations. Do not assume that an application or implication can be universally employed.

Language

Find a common language with your listeners. Whichever language is spoken in our preaching, the goal is to use vocabulary, images, cultural references, idioms, cognates in other languages, and definitions of terms that our diverse listeners will comprehend. In his book *Rewiring Your Preaching: How the Brain Processes Sermons*, Richard Cox contends, "The vocabulary of the listener determines whether the sermon will be accepted or rejected. An immediate response is required and always given. However, since many times the language of the sermon is foreign to the listener, it is like a package being refused because the recipient can't understand the delivery person. Language determines if the message is simply *delivered* by the speaker or *heard* by the listener."[48] A helpful way to assess whether your language is understood by your listeners is to write out a complete manuscript of the sermon. As you read it over, consider the various cultural groups represented in your church and fill in any question marks by locating words, phrases, idioms, and images that will not make sense to them.

Embrace

Referring to the opening story about the giraffe and the elephant, our preference is to minister and preach to people who are just like ourselves. Like attracts like. However, in our diversifying world we can no longer afford to preach nontargeted sermons. Those on the margins will feel our embrace or lack thereof more acutely than those in the majority.[49] What we are called to do in preaching with cultural intelligence is to acknowledge our prejudices and find Christlike ways to embrace Others who do not fit the "we" category. As Mark Labberton explains starkly, "Crosscultural experiences may be ones we seek or avoid in part because of the comfort or discomfort *we* may have with that 'other.' . . . If we accept the invitation, we can learn with some measure of openness and hope. But *we* typically don't give them such opportunity or entrée. Instead, they are just placed in a box labeled 'they.' We place *them* where *we* think they belong. And *we* move on."[50]

Preaching with cultural intelligence creates opportunities for the preacher to embrace people from all cultures and backgrounds and to remove "we versus them" distinctions. Our initial awkwardness can be overcome with Christian love when we truly embrace the Others in our congregations. The Gospels show Jesus embracing his followers in culturally intelligent ways. He did not embrace or demonstrate love to his followers in exactly the same way in each setting. For instance, Jesus exhibited directness coupled with gentleness toward the Samaritan woman. For the ten lepers, Jesus modeled extraordinary compassion to travel to a place where others were unwilling to go. For the sinful woman, Jesus accepted her extravagant gift of perfume and her anointing of tears. Likewise, how we embrace our listeners will look different depending on our cultural context. As we do so, we are reminded of the well-known principle: "People don't care how much you know until they know how much you care." This same principle rings true especially in cross-cultural preaching. Put differently, "People don't care what we preach about until they know how much we care." Whenever possible, we can find opportunities to embrace our listeners. In each major chapter, some suggestions will be offered on how to do so.

Content

Pastors are notorious for preaching on their preoccupations and other important yet esoteric doctrines. We assume that everything that interests us will enliven our listeners and nourish their souls. Pastors spend an exorbitant amount of the church's calendar in preaching through their favorite books of the Bible, yet without consultation or consideration of their listeners. Scott M. Gibson laments, "Too many preachers have their needs, their concerns, their pet theological positions, and their darling texts to promote or emphasize when they choose texts for preaching."[51] Going forward, the content of our sermons as culturally intelligent preachers may require some revamping. I am referring not solely to the content or "the meat" catered in the message such as dispensing golden nuggets from our biblical exegesis. Here content also refers to themes or topics on which listeners from a particular cultural context would appreciate hearing from the preacher's perspective. In what ways can we demonstrate greater cultural intelligence by preaching on topics that are most germane to our listeners' lives?

Trust

Last, preaching with cultural intelligence necessitates trust. Perhaps in no other profession is trust a more valued commodity than in pastoral ministry. On different occasions the apostle Paul exhorted his protégé Timothy (and fellow elders) about the gravity of ethos and character to earn congregational trust. For instance, Paul reminds Timothy of the expectations placed on overseers (pastors) in 1 Timothy 3:2, with the first qualification being most notably that they are "to be above reproach"; he warns Timothy (and us), "Watch your life and doctrine closely. Persevere in them, because if you do, you will save both yourself and your hearers" (1 Tim. 4:16). Trust is indispensable in preaching. But it does not come without displaying integrity in and out of the pulpit. Jeffrey D. Arthurs declares that "our words and actions outside the pulpit greatly determine the efficacy of our words inside the pulpit."[52]

Earning the trust of the people in our congregations will vary depending on our listeners' cultural contexts and their experiences. For some, earning trust means preaching a faithful, biblical sermon each week that they can apply to their lives. For others, it means spending time with them. For certain pockets of listeners, trust is given only when the preacher remains in the church at least five to seven years. For some ethnic cultures, the preacher must partake of the ethnic cuisine, even if it may be unsavory or undesirable to the palate. Trust is foundational for pulpit ministry, especially when navigating among the various listeners and what calls for trust in their minds. A culturally intelligent preacher will figure out how to earn and maintain that trust.

Conclusion

In this second chapter, I have laid out the overarching framework for our CQ strategy to preach culturally intelligent sermons. The task before us now is to discern which steps of the Homiletical Bridge and delivery are most pressing for our varied listeners today. In the next chapter, we will explore a new hermeneutical model to facilitate a deeper understanding of the biblical author's culture and our own cultures.

3

Hermeneutics and Cultural Intelligence

As North American congregations become increasingly diverse, individualistic, and pluralistic, the cultural diversity beckons preachers to assume that someone in the pews is objecting, "Pastor, I disagree with your interpretation!" The hermeneutical process cannot be completely separated from our cultural backgrounds, theological presuppositions, and life experiences, because our interpretation will be colored by the lenses we wear.[1] As evangelicals, the ultimate aim, hermeneutically speaking, is to derive the same interpretive conclusion while recognizing that the applications we provide will reflect the congregation's various hues. Yet we are not naive enough to think that interpretive variances do not exist; instead, they are often forthrightly defended with great zeal. The history of Christianity, in light of both subtle and overt nuances, shows how varied biblical interpretations can be.

Consequently, this chapter seeks to provide a new hermeneutical model for preachers that will guide us as we consider the cultural diversity of our listeners. This hermeneutical model will be employed in each cultural context that we explore in the rest of the book. How do we faithfully interpret Scripture while keeping in close view the listeners who may read and interpret Scripture differently? How can we more effectively engage interpretively with their cultures, experiences, questions, and concerns, and still remain faithful to the original authorial intention of the text? These questions will be the focus in what lies ahead.

Hermeneutics for Homiletics

Definitions for hermeneutics abound. One of the trailblazers in hermeneutics, Anthony Thiselton, defines it in this manner: "Hermeneutics explores how we read, understand, and handle texts, especially those written in another time or in a context of life different from our own. Biblical hermeneutics investigates more specifically how we read, understand, apply, and respond to biblical texts."[2] Hermeneutics, put simply, is the art and science of interpreting the Bible. Preachers employ hermeneutics to understand the meaning of the text and then apply this meaning to their listeners' lives. John Goldingay notices the tight-knit relationship between hermeneutics and homiletics: "Arguably any true biblical interpretation must eventually take the form of preaching, and vice versa, because 'the Bible itself is preaching.'"[3] While theoretically a straightforward task, myriad factors influence how we read and interpret the Bible. It is worthwhile to consider these challenges to a faithful interpretation of the text.

Preunderstanding

Every student of Scripture approaches the text with his or her own preunderstanding. In their helpful resource *Grasping God's Word*, J. Scott Duvall and J. Daniel Hays define preunderstanding as "all of our preconceived notions and understandings that we bring to the text, which have been formulated, both consciously and subconsciously, *before* we actually study the text in detail. . . . The danger here is for those who assume that their preunderstanding is always correct."[4] Taking a somewhat different slant, Walter C. Kaiser Jr. writes, "The interpreter must bridge the gulf of explaining the cultural elements that are present in the text of Scripture, acknowledge [one's] own cultural baggage as an interpreter, and then transcend both in order to communicate the original message of Scripture into the culture of the contemporary audience."[5]

In other words, our preunderstanding is textured with numerous elements that influence our interpretation of the text: our sinful nature, family, friends, cultural backgrounds, life experiences, worldviews, theological presuppositions, what pastors and influential others have instructed us, opinions (whether acknowledged or unacknowledged), and other factors. In the same vein, our listeners similarly approach the text with their own preunderstanding of what a given text means, which complicates the entire hermeneutical process. The fundamental responsibility of evangelical preachers, then, is to determine first the authors' (i.e., divine and human) meaning of the biblical passage or pericope—"a segment of Scripture, irrespective of genre or length, that forms the textual basis for an individual sermon"[6]—as we acknowledge and make sense of the preunderstanding of the preacher and of the listeners.

Authorial Intention versus Reader-Response

A growing movement in hermeneutics concerns whether modern readers of Scripture can actually ascertain a single authorial meaning. Authorial intention places meaning in the hands of the author and is determined by the author.[7] On the flip side, others have argued for reader-response, which places the onus of meaning on the reader irrespective of what the author intended to communicate to the readers. In our increasingly individualistic culture, Christians are gravitating precariously toward reader-response in bypassing the original meaning and going straight for "relevance," cultural engagement, and individualized application of the Word. Especially in biblical interpretation where we still hold delicately various cultures in view, evangelical preachers must squeeze tightly to authorial intent lest we fall into a scriptural free-for-all where the Word of God can mean anything we (or any cultural context) want it to mean.

Although the number of denominations and ecclesial factions seem to contradict my position, we commit ourselves to the belief that preachers can still discover the authors' intended meaning (a *single* meaning).[8] Andreas Köstenberger and Richard Patterson exhort interpreters: "We should engage in interpretation responsibly, displaying respect for the text and its author. There is no excuse for interpretive arrogance that elevates the reader above text and author."[9] As we submit to the Scriptures and receive the Holy Spirit's guidance, we trust that it is possible today to determine the authorial intention of the text. How can this be accomplished while still acknowledging the cultures and experiences of our varied listeners?

The Relationship between the Bible and Cultural Context

When we think about tailoring the message for a particular cultural group, some preachers start with people and then try to adapt or modify God's Word to fit the values and perspectives of that cultural context (see fig. 3.1). The danger is that following this model forces the preacher to dart too quickly to application. We are trying to apply the meaning of a passage that we do not understand. In contrast to this view, the starting place in sermon preparation should always be God's Word. We suspend application

Figure 3.1
Commonly Understood Relationship between the Bible and Culture

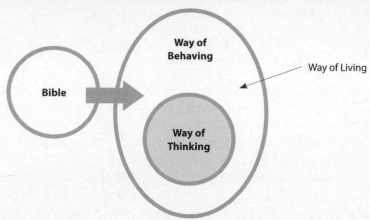

by first determining the meaning of the text in its context. Once we properly understand what Scripture means, we can then apply it to our varied listeners (see fig. 3.2).

Thus preaching with cultural intelligence begins with hermeneutics and not with the values of a particular cultural context. In every text we first determine the unchanging truth found in God's Word, and only then do we try to figure out how best to "explain, prove, and apply" this text to a particular group of people. The difference in perspective between these two views is subtle but profound. If we start with understanding humans today, our preaching and teaching are susceptible to *eisegesis*—reading into the text what is not there, based on our specific cultural lens. The more appropriate perspective, beginning with God's Word, enables us to keep our preaching grounded in the truth of Scripture, and only then do we apply it to a specific context. Even in topical preaching, the preacher will need to determine which Scripture passage best addresses the topical issue for a given sermon.

Find the Single Meaning

I am writing this book from an evangelical perspective, endorsing the position of biblical inerrancy: Holy Scripture in the original languages, both Old and New Testaments, is free from any trace of error. By holding to this position, I advocate the ability to discern a single meaning in any given Scripture passage. Those who have jettisoned biblical inerrancy as a central value distrust the accuracy and reliability of Scripture. Therefore, keeping a tight grip on

Figure 3.2
Necessary Relationship between the Bible and Culture

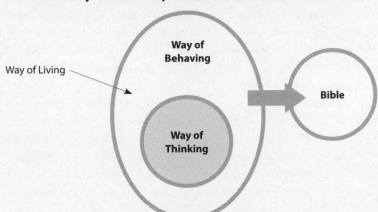

inerrancy enables us to remain faithful to the meaning of the text and not be swayed by reader-response and more sociocultural and experience-centered interpretations.

The single meaning of the text, or "real meaning," as John Broadus put it, seeks to understand the original meaning as intended by the author.[10] The single-meaning view came out of the school of Antioch, where "the Antiochians claimed that an event in Scripture had only one meaning . . . [and that] the spiritual truth was not a double sense or meaning but a single sense as originally intended by the writers of Scripture."[11] In modern Western evangelical circles, the primary vehicle to determine meaning in the text has been the historical-grammatical method. In 1890, Milton Terry understood the historical-grammatical approach to hermeneutics in this way: "In distinction from all the above-mentioned methods of interpretation, we may name the Grammatico-Historical as the method which most fully commends itself to the judgment and conscience of Christian scholars. Its fundamental principle is to gather from the Scriptures themselves the precise meaning which the writers intended to convey."[12]

How do we determine the single meaning today? There is no reason for us to reinvent the wheel here. In *Biblical Preaching*, Haddon Robinson writes, "We try to pull up our chairs to where the biblical authors sat. We attempt to work our way back into the world of the Scriptures to understand the original message. . . . As much as possible, expositors seek a firsthand acquaintance with the biblical writers and their ideas in context."[13] Robinson then provides a helpful interpretive tool to discern the authorial meaning of a passage. The method of interpreting the single meaning is what he calls finding "the big idea" of the text. "When reduced to its basic structure, an idea consists of only two essential elements: a *subject* and a *complement*. . . . While other questions emerge in the struggle to understand the meaning of a biblical writer, these two ('What precisely is the author talking about?' and 'What is the author saying about what he is talking about?') are fundamental."[14]

In Robinson's movement from hermeneutics to homiletics, the exegetical idea from the text is then put into a modern phrase when communicating this truth to the listeners (called the homiletical idea). Once we figure out the exegetical idea of a passage, only then should we consider the cultural context(s) to which we are preaching. Due to limited space here, I commend Robinson's textbook *Biblical Preaching* to you for your additional assistance. Once we have discerned a clear exegetical idea, the task before us is to consider the cultural context of the people to whom we are preaching.

Toward an Authorial-Cultural Model of Interpretation

What is expository preaching? Definitions for expository preaching or biblical preaching are copious. As a short list, here are three recent examples from noted evangelical homileticians. First, Bryan Chapell declares, "Expository preaching endeavors to discover and convey the precise meaning of the Word. Scripture rules over what expositors preach because they unfold what it says. The meaning of the passage is the message of the sermon."[15] Another worthy definition comes from Ramesh Richard: "Expository preaching is the contemporization of the central proposition of a biblical text that is derived from proper methods of interpretation and declared through effective means of communication to inform minds, instruct hearts, and influence behavior toward godliness."[16] Third, Haddon Robinson posits, "Expository preaching is the communication of a biblical concept, derived from and transmitted through a historical, grammatical, and literary study of a passage in its context, which the Holy Spirit first applies to the personality and experience of the preacher, then through the preacher, applies to the hearers."[17]

Absent from these traditional evangelical definitions is the interpretive lens offered by culture. While culture is often implied or assumed in the study of the ancient world's historical context, I would insert "cultural" study as an intentional fourth dimension to the task of sermon preparation. Perhaps more than any other area, preachers today lack a meticulous exhuming of the biblical cultures represented in Scripture as well as concomitantly exploring the various cultures represented in today's world. Preachers have a tendency to deliver sermons that are monolithic and thereby monocultural. We conveniently skip over the names, places, geographical locations, and cultural issues and practices in Scripture that in some shape or form delay the application for the message today. What I am proposing is a new hermeneutical paradigm, which I call the *authorial-cultural* model of biblical interpretation. As preachers, we want to be highly familiar with the authorial intention, which presumes historical, grammatical, and literary study, yet also highlight the author's cultural context—the biblical culture(s) in which the writer lived.[18] Coupling this knowledge base with modern cultures will give preachers the requisite cultural background they need to interpret Scripture effectively.

How often have we read Scripture with our modern lenses only, without apt consideration of the biblical cultural context? As Walter C. Kaiser Jr. observes, "The Bible was written within the confines of certain cultures and times. No interpreter has the right to make that text say whatever he or she wants it to say. The text must be allowed to say what it wants to say but with due respect for the particular setting and culture in which it was based."[19] While many preachers nod their heads to the Bible's cultural contexts, such as Babylon or Nazareth, preaching in an increasingly diverse twenty-first century will necessitate greater intentional engagement with both the biblical and the contemporary cultures.

The hermeneutic model that I provide here underscores the importance of the biblical author's culture and then progresses toward understanding contemporary cultures in the pews. First, we begin with the author's cultural context. For instance, all preachers will have presumably studied and preached sermons from the four Gospel accounts. How does a clear description of the biblical author's cultural context in Mark's Gospel strengthen the sermon and enable listeners to relate the Bible more effectively to their own cultural context? What are the cultural practices embedded in Matthew's or Luke's perspective? How does Matthew's previous occupation as a tax collector or Luke's profession as a physician inform or give color to their writing? How is Matthew's heart for the Jewish people reflected in his Gospel, and Luke's emphasis on physical, cultural, and social outcasts reflected in his? The writings of Matthew, Luke, and the other biblical authors are inseparable from each of them as embodied, culture-specific individuals. How does their particular humanly authorial-cultural context inform our cultural practices in the here and now?

As stated, the *authorial-cultural* model of interpretation does not forego or replace the great tradition of understanding the historical, grammatical, and literary context but simply inserts into the exegetical process the biblical cultural context, which often gets overlooked in sermon preparation. Understanding the cultural context of the author enables modern listeners to see their cultural and personal story within the continuum of the larger biblical narrative. Only when listeners become familiar with biblical cultures can they make sense of how God's Word has an impact on their cultural context. It is naive to think that we can bypass the important step of understanding the cultures in the biblical world. Although the Bible's story is our story, we recognize that cultural similarities and differences in the ancient world cannot be left unmentioned.[20] Our listeners can envisage how to compare and contrast the ways that biblical and modern cultures are similar and divergent. At the same time, understanding the authorial-cultural context will help listeners bridge the gap between the Bible and their modern culture as well as build a bridge between themselves and culturally different listeners seated next to them in the pews.

The Authorial-Cultural Model in Practice

In the second half of this chapter, my goal is to introduce and apply how we can interpret Scripture and consider the ancient and contemporary cultural contexts of our listeners by using the acronym HABIT, as mentioned in chapter 1 and described in chapter 2. This hermeneutical sequence (historical, grammatical, and literary context; author's cultural context; big idea of the text; interpret in your context; and theological presuppositions) is meant to be flexible for interpreting every Scripture passage. Thus in this chapter on preaching and hermeneutics, my goal is to demonstrate how this *authorial-cultural* hermeneutical model works. Interpreting the Bible for all the varied listeners in our churches in any comprehensive fashion is not feasible. For this reason, using this hermeneutical sequence will provide a user-friendly template for learning about the cultures of the biblical world and relating them to the current cultural contexts and concerns that our listeners bring with them to the worship service each week. I am not trying to alter the normal routine in sermon preparation. Much of what I present here are hermeneutical steps that already come naturally in your preparation. Rather, wherever and whenever possible, we can pursue a more vigorous exploration of the cultural context of the biblical author. Since this book is written primarily for preachers, let's work through a Bible passage together first by getting the exegetical idea of the text and then employing this hermeneutical sequence to guide us in augmenting our cultural intelligence for preaching.

Stage 1: Follow Your HABIT

Scripture Text
Psalm 133

Let's become acclimated to the *authorial-cultural* model by way of Psalm 133. This particular psalm may not be widely used for sermons, which may enable the preacher to employ our new hermeneutic approach with a fresher perspective. Even in this brief song of David, we receive interpretive angles to help us understand the Jewish cultural context. What can we learn from this psalm, and how can we understand our cultural context in light of King David's historical and cultural background?

Historical, Grammatical, and Literary Context

Historical Context

As many translations note in the heading, Psalm 133 served as one of the Psalms of Ascent for pilgrims traveling to Jerusalem for religious festivals.[21] Scholars agree on the simplicity and complexity of the psalm, or song, but disagree on its historical context with respect to verse 1 and whom the psalmist is referring to when using the term "brothers" (RSV).[22] For instance, "In a local context, it could encourage the members of a household to stay together or live in harmony, maybe especially after the death of the head of the household."[23] Another interpretation is that it "was used as a greeting from a guest on entering a home where brothers lived together as an extended family."[24] A quite different interpretation is presented by the Reformer John Calvin in his commentary: "I have no doubt that David in this Psalm renders thanks to God for the peace and harmony which had succeeded a long and melancholy state of confusion and division in the kingdom, and that he would exhort all individually to study the maintenance of peace."[25] For Calvin, King David, the author, praises God for his goodness in bringing unity and peaceful relations between the divided monarchy of Israel and Judah.[26]

While interpretations will vary, the preacher's initial interpretive decision regarding the historical nature of the psalm will be to ascertain whether this is a general song of ascent about the importance of peace in community, about harmony in family relations, or particularly about unity between Israel and Judah. Your interpretation of the historical context will be paramount because it will shape how you present the background of the psalm to your listeners. Once you determine your interpretation of the historical context, set the scene for your listeners early in the sermon to give them a panoramic view of the biblical setting.

Grammatical Issues

In terms of grammar, the preacher may be drawn to the poetic structure of the psalm or conduct word studies on the meaning of "good" or "siblings/brothers/kinship." In addition, the reference to Aaron, the high priest, in verse 2 and the two landmarks named in verse 3, Mount Hermon and Mount Zion, may deserve the preacher's special attention. The interpreter's question is to determine why the psalmist refers to Aaron, Mount Hermon, and Mount Zion, and what their significances are in helping to clarify the main point in verse 1. For instance, that Zion is mentioned in this context may directly correlate to the fact that "Yhwh ordered that Zion would be a place where harvests flourished because (among other things) plentiful dew would fall there at the time it was needed. . . . But by speaking of Zion in these terms, the psalm more directly suggests that Zion would be the source of such blessing, no doubt not just for its immediate environs but [also] for the land as a whole."[27]

Grammatically speaking, two dominant images, in this case similes of oil and dew, serve to illustrate the celebration of unity as expressed in the first verse. First, the psalmist compares unity to the anointing of priests with oil. In this case, he specifically likens it to Aaron's consecration as a high priest.[28] The second image is that of dew, which the Israelites living in a desert climate received from the Lord as a gift of grace.[29] While the image of dew does not elicit a second glance from many modern readers, dew possessed much gravitas in the ancient Middle East.[30] The Hebrew participle for "coming down," *yored*, is used three times, which calls attention how oil and dew have heavenly or divine origins.[31] Since unity is compared to blessings from heaven, we readers must appreciate how valuable to God is harmony and peace among his people. Try to learn as much as you can about oil, dew, Aaron's beard, the priestly garments, Mount Hermon, and Mount Zion in the Jewish context. As we study the grammatical issues in Psalm 133, we will acquire a wider cultural lens to grasp the meaningful symbols (similes) in the ancient Jewish world and the emphases placed on these symbols by the biblical author. What might be the equivalents to the similes of oil and dew in your local church context?

Literary Study

There is scholarly debate about whether this psalm is one of the Songs of Ascents, a Song of Zion,[32] or a wisdom psalm.[33] During your study, you will eventually land on one side of this debate. This will inform your teaching on the literary nature of the psalm. Taking it to be a song of ascent, from my perspective the goal is to learn about the Jewish culture's use of the Songs of Ascents, as found in Psalms 120–34. A readily accepted understanding of the Songs of Ascents is that they were used as worship songs during pilgrimages to Jerusalem.[34] In this particular example, Psalm 133 is often listed under the category of didactic psalms, because it teaches the Jewish community a lesson about the importance of unity.[35] As you read over this psalm, consider its tone. The Songs of Ascents engender joy and celebration. They are completely disparate from the psalms of lament. In preaching this psalm, our pastoral tone should be one of encouragement and hope as we remind our listeners to pursue unity in Christian community.

Author's Cultural Context

A helpful approach to learn more about the author's cultural context (that we will employ throughout this book) without duplicating the information from the historical context is to gain an appreciation of the cultural practices in the biblical author's day. In the time of King David, the gathering of God's pilgrims to Jerusalem (Zion) for times of festival worship were high points of the year. According to Charles Briggs, these pilgrim feasts brought "a blessing not only to the permanent inhabitants of the city, but [also] to all those who come up to the pilgrim feasts to share with the inhabitants in the common national worship, which brings upon them the divine blessing and fresh life and vigour with which to return to their homes."[36] The Jewish people went on pilgrimages three times per year to Jerusalem for the annual feasts.[37] Kevin Green explains, "The feasts, or sacred festivals, held an important place in Jewish religion. They were religious services accompanied by demonstrations of joy and gladness."[38] Festival worship is a foreign concept to modern readers of this psalm. As we consider the author's cultural context and the importance of these feasts to the Jews, the preacher may see the benefit of finding modern parallels to the Jewish feasts. In the sermon we can explain further the priestly tradition of pouring oil and the significance of dew. "The ritual that set apart Aaron and his sons for priestly service involved pouring oil on their heads and garments."[39] The dew was a Hebrew symbol of condensation or rain, providing the Israelites with "conditions of refreshment."[40] What cultural references today in your context would resemble the pilgrimage to Jerusalem? To which destination might our listeners travel in order to worship God with others in community? How do we partake in the cultural practice of singing songs of ascent in our cultural context? Or is this a completely foreign concept that would require extra time for explanation?

Big Idea of the Text

Subject: Why does King David exhort the Israelites to live in unity?

Complement: Because through unity they will receive the blessings of God.

Exegetical Idea: King David exhorts the Israelites to live in unity because through unity they will receive the blessings of God.

Homiletical Idea: Unity in the body leads to God's blessings.

Interpret in Your Context

Assumptions

Once we have a working knowledge of the author's cultural context, we move into the realm of considering our listeners and their interpretive concerns. To interpret in our context involves three target points of connection: assumptions, conflicts, and questions. First, what assumptions might our listeners have as they read or hear this passage? One of the central assumptions that our listeners can make regards to whom King David is referring in his use of the Hebrew noun *'akhim* for "brothers." A listener who interprets the Bible literally might assume that David is applauding the unity of brothers, siblings, and one's family, especially if there is disharmony in the home. Others might make the assumption that the term "brothers" signifies the wider Israelite community. The assumptions that the listeners make about our text may be addressed particularly by providing a range of different applications for our hearers, but we must assume that assumptions are being made.

Conflicts

A second approach to interpret the Scripture in our context is to address the conflicts that listeners have with the text. While in many ways King David delivers a glowing exhortation to live in harmony with one another, the reality is that many, if not all, churches today struggle to have unity. Disagreements permeate the church regarding theological differences and ministry practices, such as how best to steward the church's budget, which programs are worthy of our financial support and which ones should be discarded, what type of material should be used for Sunday school curriculum, whether the church should remain in a particular denomination, who is selected for leadership positions, gender roles in ministry, racial and ethnic conflicts in the church, class conflicts between the haves and have-nots, and many other issues that disrupt a church's harmony. Listeners who are cognizant of specific congregational tensions will naturally think of existing conflict between church leaders or a dissenting cluster in the church who are causing problems. For listeners experiencing disunity, the message of King David will be jarring as they are confronted by their current spiritual condition. Being aware of our listeners' conflicts with the text and even raising their objections will help us to communicate God's truth in more culturally tangible ways.

Questions

Third, we want to consider what questions this passage raises for our listeners. A large number of our listeners will want to know the meaning behind verses 2 and 3 and the cultural significance of unity being compared to oil and dew. Our Bible-conscious listeners may have exegetical questions about the last line of the psalm and its reference to blessing and "life forevermore." Is the blessing limited to the geographic location of Mount Zion, or is it speaking of the overall blessing that comes to God's people who live in peace with one another? Skeptical or more cynical listeners will expect the preacher to comment on why God still seems to bless those who are the agents of disunity in the community. What if two pockets of listeners are in conflict over a particular ministry issue? How does one group pursue unity with their adversaries when they believe they are in the right? Globally minded listeners will question how this verse applies to the world where conflict is both ubiquitous and constant. Increasing our ability to interpret our context with their assumptions, conflicts, and questions about the Scripture text will lengthen our sermon's reach as we address our listeners with their cultural questions and concerns.

Theological Presuppositions

The fifth and final component of the hermeneutical process is to identify the theological presuppositions that the listeners embrace regarding our text. Theological presuppositions represent what people believe to be true of God, or they are the ways our listeners articulate, "This is the way God is." Here this psalm infers that God is displeased with divisions among his people. The psalm compels believers to identify and own up to the frictions and fractions within the family of God. Stated positively, God blesses unity in the community of faith. Unity brings about a life abundant in blessings for all. In short, God is the God of unity. One of the dangers that the preacher must handle gingerly is not to shame congregants who already feel condemned by their disobedience to the Lord's command to live in unity. The Holy Spirit will convict our listeners' hearts so that they will confess sin and find restoration. Regardless of one's cultural context, listeners who struggle with a particular sin, in this example disunity, feel condemned by God and condemned by those with whom they share a conflict. However, in church ministry the preacher's word choice and tone can make all the difference as to whether church members in conflict with others will leave as a result of their shame or remain invested in the church. This particular sermon can communicate hope and encouragement as the preacher balances the delicate subjects of sin and grace to manifest to the listeners that God blesses the unity of believers in Christian community. And yet God simultaneously embraces those living in disharmony and calls for repentance and spiritual renewal. What other theological presuppositions might your listeners hold as they read Psalm 133?

Conclusion

In this chapter I have constructed a road map to guide the hermeneutical sequence for preaching with cultural intelligence. The premise behind the *authorial-cultural* model is to determine the author's main idea and intentionally highlight the biblical author's cultural context so that listeners will receive a faithful interpretation of the text and enlarge their understanding of the biblical world and its various cultures. When listeners become familiar with the ancient cultures of the Bible, they will be in a better position to situate their cultures in relation to the cultures found in the biblical text. Before we explore five different cultural groups, we would be well served to understand ourselves better as people and as preachers. This will be the subject of our next chapter.

4

Exegeting the Preacher

Preaching books·rarely discuss the need for preachers to understand themselves except for perhaps the occasional reminder not to neglect one's prayer life.[1] In preaching we can be so listener-focused that we forget to consider how the sermon is informed by and impacts the self. In this chapter we seize the rare opportunity to pause, take a step back, and engage in self-exploration. In his book *Toughest People to Love*, Chuck DeGroat observes that "self-awareness . . . leads to greater transparency—a cornerstone of effective leadership."[2] The transparency that we seek is not full self-disclosure from the pulpit per se, but rather the ability to see ourselves for who we really are. It is not about who we project ourselves to be at church, but an honest inventory of who we are and how our culture(s) and past experiences shape our communication today. As DeGroat indicates, by its very essence transparency is required of leaders, and that includes preachers as well. To have a proper and healthy view of self can be one of the most empowering and encouraging tools one can possess in the pulpit. But, with the busyness of life and being swayed by "the tyranny of the urgent,"[3] seldom do we think about who we are, where we have been, and who we are becoming as persons and as preachers.

The renowned painter Rembrandt was known for his self-portraits. Not the most attractive of men, he painted numerous accurate representations of himself and did not seek to embellish his looks. When asked about why he painted himself so frequently, he responded, "Unless I can really paint myself the way I am, I can't paint others the way they are."[4] We too view ourselves, the world, and others through the lens of our life experiences and culture(s). Like Rembrandt, before we can begin to explore Others and their

45

cultural contexts, we want to know and understand ourselves. The concept of cultural intelligence, as Jared E. Alcántara states in his book *Crossover Preaching*, lacks self-exploration: "In many ways, Earley, Ang, and Tan [the early architects of cultural intelligence] do not go far enough in their discussion of culturally strategic thinking. They leave out an all-important step: *critical reflexive thinking about one's own cultural framework*. Being a student of other cultures is insufficient. One must also scrutinize and interrogate one's own culture."[5] Similarly, Michael Angrosino agrees with the salience of church leaders knowing themselves:

> Be prepared to acknowledge and confront our own discomfort and anxieties regarding differences. . . . Know your own culture first. Do not assume that your own way of thinking or doing things is somehow "normal," "universal," or "natural." You have culture just like everyone else—culture that was learned, and which can therefore be modified. Engage yourself in an honest appraisal of your own culture.[6]

To facilitate this self-exploration process, we will divide this chapter into three parts. Part 1 will identify our levels of CQ drive and our attitudes toward other cultures with the goal of moving toward cultural empathy and celebration. Part 2 will serve as an opportunity for preachers to explore their personal and family histories by way of a preacher's timeline and journal project, which will unearth various repressed areas of life and cultivate greater empathy for Others. In part 3, I will briefly encourage preachers to work through the various cultural markers in the Homiletical Template for themselves before they try to undertake it for their listeners.

Part 1: Develop Your CQ Drive

The preacher's inclination is to travel immediately to the world of the listener. We are predisposed to first consider what God's Word has to say to them, the listener, the Other. In doing so, we remove the preacher from an all-too-important facet of the homiletical equation. In *Preaching to Every Pew: Cross-Cultural Strategies*, James Nieman and Thomas Rogers observe that many pastors and preachers do not take requisite time to consider their own background and culture: "Many of our interviewees said that one of their biggest mistakes came in ignoring their own culture. They were intimately familiar with the cultures in which they were raised and still lived, but rarely did they consciously consider the assumptions on which their daily activities and interactions rested."[7] Consequently "preachers seldom ask questions like,

'Why am I doing this as a white, North American, middle-aged preacher?'"[8] Equally crucial is the ability to ask ourselves where our beliefs and attitudes originated from and how we respond to Others who come from very different cultural contexts. Cultural intelligence is a spectrum where each preacher possesses varying levels of CQ drive. This chapter will provide a three-part road map on how to engage in self-exploration to facilitate our calling to be culturally intelligent preachers. In this first part, the goal is to transition from low to high CQ drive in three increments. We want to move from xenophobe to xenophile, from relying on cultural stereotypes to fostering cultural empathy, and from cultural assimilation into cultural celebration.

From Xenophobe to Xenophile

Preaching with cultural intelligence pertains to building bridges. What is our attitude toward members of different cultures? If we take an honest inventory of our feelings and attitudes, many, if not all, would confess some type of fear or perhaps concealed prejudice against those who are different from us. Prejudices form as a result of *xenophobia*, which is the Latin way of saying, literally, "the fear [*phobia*] of Others [*xeno-*]." More precisely, a common definition of xenophobia is the "fear and hatred of strangers or foreigners or of anything that is strange or foreign."[9] However, we can employ it here more loosely to include all types of cultural differences. We usually form prejudices based on our experience or inexperience with those we consider the Other. For instance, if a person from a particular race, social class, gender, denomination, religion, or any other demographic harms or offends us, we will consequently view all Others from that same classification with suspicion and even fear. Anything or anyone falling outside the realm of normalcy for us becomes unwanted or unnecessary. This rejection of the Other is our way of simultaneously protecting ourselves and maintaining distance and thereby comfort.

Instead of holding pejorative feelings toward Others who look and act differently from us, we can learn to appreciate and embrace them on even the most basic of human levels. That is, we trust Scripture when it says in Genesis 1:27 that God created men and women "in his own image." Every human being possesses innate value and positive qualities that are God-given. The person sitting next to us who has different beliefs, skin tone, style of clothing, taste in music, citizenship, and family upbringing still has the same basic human needs that we do, such as love, food, water, shelter, education, work, money, and so forth. The people sitting next to us in the worship service also want their children to be safe and want their family to have equal rights, as do all families living in America. In short, all people are important and valuable in God's eyes.

Most important, on a pastoral and spiritual level, all humans share a common need (whether they realize this or not) for the forgiveness of their sins and the salvation that is found only in the person and work of Jesus Christ. The writer of Ecclesiastes said it memorably when he declared that God "has also set eternity in the human heart" (Eccles. 3:11). But sadly, our disinterest or disdain for the Other can become, as the apostle Paul said in 1 Corinthians 1:23, a "stumbling block" that interferes with Others' ability to hear the Word preached. Even young children are cognizant when adults brush them off as nuisances. How much more the adults in our midst, regardless of their cultural differences? Matthew 9:36 provides the perfect picture of Jesus who possessed empathy for everyone: "When he saw the crowds, he had compassion on them, because they were harassed and helpless, like sheep without a shepherd." Jesus is our ultimate exemplar of a culturally intelligent person and preacher! Similarly, as we consider how to preach effectively in the twenty-first century, we want to move toward loving our neighbors by growing in cultural intelligence, by becoming xenophiles, "lovers of Others," and practicing CQ consistently in our ministry practice in general, and in our preaching in particular.

From Cultural Stereotypes to Cultural Empathy

Second, we want to examine our overall CQ drive. Do we care to learn about people from other cultures? Our default position is to stereotype those who are different from us. That is, we often make assumptions about people because they, from our estimation, fall into a certain category of people. When we meet someone for the first time, David Smith explains that we usually put them into mental categories "(young men, middle-aged women, blondes, sporty types, immigrants, academics, rednecks, foreigners, and so on) to help us keep our world straight without mental overload—and to protect our comfortable ways of organizing our world."[10] A stereotype is a generalization where all people from a particular cultural group are placed into a neatly defined box who (according to the stereotype) live, think, and behave in certain ways as members of that culture. Take, for example, the most recent visitors to your church or those you met at a recent social gathering. Did you size them up? That is, did you stereotype them based on their height, weight, appearance, race, ethnicity, accent, occupation, marital status, educational background, and so on?

Since my physical characteristics place me by default in the Asian category, it is assumed by others that I was born in Korea and that I speak Korean or should be able to speak the language even though I am a US-born citizen. Rarely, if ever, am I considered by white Americans to be "fully" American. Years ago when I was studying for my doctorate in Scotland, a fellow American (Caucasian) student asked me how I learned to speak English so well. I responded, "I was born and raised in Chicago. I'm American." To this, he replied, "You speak English well enough, so I guess that makes you *somewhat* American." I was outraged, but this exclusivist attitude that only whites are American was nothing new to my Asian American experience. It was just another life moment that reinforced racial discrimination. But this pervasive attitude toward Asians and other ethnic minorities should not be condoned, especially in the church. As human beings, we are constantly making judgments about others based on their race, appearance, accent, or other categories. To grow in cultural intelligence, we must in many ways unlearn our natural inclination to stereotype others and suspend judgment so that we can accurately understand each person and their unique backgrounds and cultures.

The task before us feels herculean. We can never completely understand or appreciate a person from another culture. However, we can grow in cultural intelligence and cultural *empathy*, which is "the ability to understand and share the feelings of another"[11] and is distinct from sympathy, which amounts to "feelings of pity and sorrow for someone else's misfortune."[12] Nieman and Rogers affirm the preacher's need for cultural empathy:

> The church has always been understood as a community whose members are fundamentally different from each other. The apostle Paul describes the church using the image of the human body composed of parts as different as hands, feet, and eyes (1 Cor. 12:12–26). In so doing, he argues for the necessity of such differences. . . . It is necessary for members of the church to be different in order for the church to be the body of Christ in and for the world.[13]

Therefore our goal in cultural intelligence is to grow in empathy and begin to embrace cultural differences so that we can fully function as the body of Christ.

Cultural or contextual empathy invites us to ask questions typically omitted from our consciousness: What does their life look like on a daily basis? What sensitivities are heightened for this individual who comes from a particular marginalized ethnicity or culture? What pain has this woman in my congregation experienced as a result of her gender? Why do people from a Buddhist or Muslim culture think and act in the ways that they do? If I were an immigrant and didn't speak the local language or know the local culture, how would my level of empathy for immigrants increase? Is this new transplant from Los Angeles having a difficult time adjusting to our small town in the

Midwest? My assignment for you is to introduce yourself to those who are different from you. Instead of making quick judgments in your mind about who these people are, what they should be like, what they can or can't do, get to know them for who they are and learn about their cultural differences.

From Cultural Assimilation to Cultural Celebration

Finally, we want to transition from the expectation of cultural assimilation to cultural celebration. By this I am referring to whether we celebrate other cultures or whether we simply expect the Others to assimilate or become just like the dominant majority group (whoever that may be). Jennifer Durham writes: "By definition, a bounded set view is one in which belief and behavior determines who is in the club, and who is excluded. It draws boundary markers by which one is considered 'in-group' or 'out-group.'"[14] Durham continues: "The 'bounded set' mentality is perpetuated by simple behavior modification. Those who embrace the 'in-group' norms are rewarded with acceptance. Those who reject these norms are punished by varying degrees of rejection, thus becoming the 'outgroup.'"[15] Who is on the inside, and who is the out-group in your church? Do members of the out-group have to assimilate and become like insiders, or are they celebrated for who they are?

In the biblical world, Judaizers could be described as cultural assimilationists. They required Gentile converts to behave and conform to Jewish customs and traditions as depicted in Acts 15.[16] In most cases, members of the dominant group seldom consider what life in community feels like for the Others. When we are in the majority, we are blinded to how those on the outskirts regularly experience feelings of being ignored or being unwelcomed. Majority groups often unconsciously perpetuate an atmosphere where Others are simply required to think and act like them if they are to continue worshiping among them.

For some years I served as the senior pastor of a predominantly Korean American church in Denver. We had a number of Caucasians and some other Asian ethnic groups represented. However, rarely did the Korean American congregants stop to think about whether non-Koreans felt accepted or celebrated. The critical mass was tolerant if non-Koreans wanted to come to the church but they were not going to alter the predominantly Korean American ethos to accommodate and welcome non-Koreans into the fold. This attitude is true of most contexts where there is a visible majority culture. Since Korean Americans represented the majority culture, assimilation to "Korean American" became the norm. In some cases, non-Korean parishioners pretended to be Korean, even though they were members of a different ethnic group.

The culturally intelligent preacher creates a vision for a church culture that not only welcomes the Others but even accepts and celebrates their culture. They will integrate the best of all cultures to display to the world that "God created us as cultural beings and [that God] values diversity in all of creation."[17] Through our preaching and teaching, we can create an environment of cultural celebration where all people, no matter what their background or culture is, can offer the church a richer experience as each person employs their gifts to build up the body of Christ. Where are you on the spectrum of CQ drive? My hope in writing this book is that incrementally we will move from xenophobe to xenophile, from cultural stereotypes to cultural empathy, and from assimilationists to celebrators.

Part 2: The Preacher's Timeline and Journal

The literary genre known as autobiography is fascinating because readers gain entrance into the thought world of influential people both past and present. Of course, autobiographies cannot nor should they expose every confidential detail about the author's life. Nevertheless, some of the defining moments in one's life are brought to the level of consciousness through autobiography, as for instance, in Corrie ten Boom's *The Hiding Place* or *Just As I Am* by Billy Graham. Similarly, as preachers we want to engage in self-exploration through the unnatural activity of opening ourselves to our own story, our own autobiography. In this section, we will work on a two-step project that will be called the Preacher's Timeline and Journal.[18] What we will discover in doing this exercise is for our personal enrichment and not necessarily information to be shared publically in Christian community. Yet the reality will sink in that our past and present follow us into the study and into the pulpit each week. My desire is that you will take the opportunity to confront pain in your life so that you will grow in greater understanding and empathy for Others, which is one of the foundational premises of the book. Our experiences and identities influence who we are and how we communicate scriptural truth. Put simply, who we are and what we've experienced in life influence who we are today and even how we preach.

Try to set aside a couple of hours on your day of rest to create a timeline of your life. In this timeline, we want to explore two general areas (events and relationships)[19] to help us process where we have been, who we are now, and how we interact with Others. See figure 4.1 for an example of a timeline. While Terry Walling encourages using Post-it Notes, using pen and paper will work just fine.[20]

Figure 4.1
The Preacher's Timeline

At the approximate age, write above the horizontal line each event and relationship that has impacted your life in both positive and negative ways.

```
0    5   10   15   20   25   30   35   40   45   50   55   60
```

The temptation may be to shortcut the process and just get it done. However, reflect deeply and ask the Lord to reveal the critical events and relationships in your life that perhaps you do not even realize have had a profound influence on your life. We will write journal entries on four specific topics (family, ethnicity, cultural attitudes, and pain) to help us grow in cultural intelligence and contextual empathy. While these journal entries will not necessarily fall under the rubric of culture, writing about our attitudes and pain will nurture our love and empathy for the Others in our churches. To omit thoughtful consideration of this part of the homiletical journey would prove detrimental to our preaching ministry in the long run, like skipping several steps in an instruction manual when assembling a bicycle or a lawnmower. Take your time with this exercise and allow God to speak into your life to encourage and heal you. By remembering key moments, people, and interactions in our lives, we will be able to understand ourselves so that we can identify with the lives of Others.

Step 1: Create a Timeline

What are the significant or defining moments in your life? In this timeline, the goal is to raise important things to the level of consciousness: (1) *events* in your life that have shaped who you have become, and (2) *relationships* with others that have aided your development and maturity.[21]

Begin by taking out a sheet of paper. Draw a horizontal line (representing your life) and delineate it into individual years, five-year increments, or decades. Try to recall important landmarks and events in your personal journey. What would you say are the defining moments in your life, whether negative or positive? For some, a pivotal, life-altering event may be the heartbreaking news that your parents were dissolving their marriage or experiencing abuse from a trusted authority figure. A positive life experience may be a celebratory event, such as finishing your college degree, getting married, adopting a child, or successfully completing your denomination's ordination process.

As you work through this timeline, God may help you recall a time when your view of self or view of culture was transformed. Oftentimes, through this process of self-discovery, God will reveal moments from our lives that we have forgotten but have played an important part in shaping us. For instance, in compiling my personal timeline I remembered an experience in elementary school that forever shattered the self-perception of my ethnicity. Growing up as the only Asian Americans in our Chicago suburb, my two younger brothers and I grew up thinking that we were white. One day my teacher asked me to stay after class to discuss the possibility of befriending two recent Korean adoptees who began attending our school. In many ways, I was coerced or perhaps more accurately shamed into meeting these two brothers. The basic gist of the conversation went like this: "You're Korean, so I want you to help these boys fit in." The friendly Caucasian mother of these adoptees brought my brothers and me to her home after school every day for a few weeks to help her new children acclimate to American society and to their new surroundings. Reality stung when they did not speak any English or understand my very limited Korean. Up until that time, I had always viewed myself only as American and even as white. Seeing these Korean adoptees became a painful reminder of my Other ethnicity, which at the time I was ashamed of. I resented that my teacher had placed me in the Other category. This life event altered my existence, forcing me to understand that American society would never see me as white. The dominant culture expected me to befriend these two Korean brothers and speak to them in my "native" language. While much progress has been made internally in coming to terms with my Korean and American identity, I still experience the shame of being seen as different from the majority culture. I would surmise that your nonmajority ethnic listeners feel kinship with this narrative.

Take a moment to write down some positive and destructive life-defining moments. These life experiences are part of your personal history and influence who you are today. Sometimes people suppress painful memories to escape the pain. Others embrace the hurtful experiences of their lives and live comfortably with this extension of their identity even if they are not willing to explore or confront such events. They believe it's just part of who they are. Stretch yourself to bring up one or two recurring positive and negative experiences that continue to manifest themselves in your life and ministry today. We cannot undo the past, but we can evaluate how these moments have helped or crippled us in our life, ministry, and preaching. Some of the most jarring life experiences may cause us to react poorly in real-life church situations where dormant feelings and attitudes are triggered by members of the congregation.

A second area to explore in this timeline concerns your relationships with others. Perhaps you have influential people or mentors in your life who have guided your journey. What people have mentored you over the years? Write down their names and the ways that these individuals have influenced you. What did you learn from them? How did God use these people in your life? Going a step further, ask yourself some culturally related questions: In what ways did this person influence your view of different cultural groups, as explored in this book, such as people from other denominations, ethnicities, genders, locations, and religions? The people in our lives shape who we are even from a very young age: parents, grandparents, siblings, friends, extended family members, coaches, teachers, pastors, neighbors, coworkers, and so forth.

After you complete your timeline, ask God if there are any moments or people you have missed. What has God taught you through this exercise? What painful moments were recalled that have been buried in your soul? Who has shaped your view of different cultures, and what did these mentors say about them? How do your past experiences inform the way you preach today, especially to those who do not share your same cultural background? Allow God to heal you of any wounds that reopened, and celebrate God's faithfulness in your more affirming moments. Finally, ask the Lord to help you identify areas of connection with others in your congregation who have undergone similar struggles in their journeys.

Step 2: Write Journal Entries on Your Experiences

A second approach to gain a deeper understanding of ourselves is to write journal entries about our experiences. In particular, we want to concentrate on four topics that mysteriously nudge their way into our preaching ministry and pastoral work: family dysfunctions, ethnicity, cultural attitudes, and pain. After completing this second phase, the hope is that God will open our hearts for greater sensitivity toward people's experiences and their pain.

JOURNAL ENTRY 1: WRITE ABOUT YOUR FAMILY'S DYSFUNCTIONS

It might seem strange to launch our first journal entry with family dysfunctionality, but there is a method to the madness. Iterations exist for the saying: "You can take the boy out of Texas, but you can't take Texas out of the boy." Likewise, "You can take the child out of the family, but you can't take the family out of the child." Think about your family upbringing. DeGroat writes, "Families are often a source of our later dysfunction, and lots of good clinical work revolves around systemic family issues. But in the effort to find a cause or a culprit for our difficulties, it's easy to miss the opportunity to trace the dark shadow through our pasts and into our present."[22] Wouldn't it relieve much stress or even be a life-giving step to admit that we come from dysfunctional families? Even the most loving and affirming of families have their share of dark moments. We are the products of generational sin, as evidenced in Scripture such as Exodus 34:7, which says that God "punishes the children and their children for the sin of the parents to the third and fourth generation." The hard and necessary truth that we need to hear is that to varying degrees we all do sin, including your parishioners. All families have a mix of cultural distinctives that are both healthy and caustic. These familial cultures can be heavily steeped in ethnic rituals or even bound by generational sins. Each Sunday, whether we like it or not, we bring the beliefs, voices, mantras, and philosophies of our family members into the pulpit.

Here are some questions that we can ask of ourselves concerning our family: In what type of familial environment were you raised? Are your parents divorced or happily married? Were your parents hospitable? Were your parents giving of their time and resources? Did your parents make decisions biblically or culturally? What were your parents' strongest beliefs and values? Who made the decisions in the home: mom, dad, or both? What sins did your parents struggle with, and what addictions held them captive? What did your mother or father say about people who were from other cultures? How was anger expressed in the home? Were you the victim of abuse: verbal, physical, or sexual? Where are you in the birth order? Are you the firstborn, lastborn, or a middle child? Are you an only child? Do you need to be the center of attention, or do you prefer to go unnoticed? In your estimation, were you the favored child in your family, or do you feel like you were ignored? Were your family members encouraging or disparaging in their speech? How we communicate with others in the context of the local church often and in surprising ways stems from our family upbringing. Take some time to reflect on and write about your family upbringing. Lingering wounds may emerge that need healing. Present these wounds to God and ask for the power to receive healing and to forgive your family members. As God leads you, talk with family members and take necessary steps to seek reconciliation with the family members from whom ties have been severed. Praise God for the ways your family has positively constructed a healthy sense of self.

Journal Entry 2: Understand Your Ethnic Background

A person's race and/or ethnicity innately places them in either a position of hegemony or marginality in the wider society. In their thought-provoking book *Being White: Finding Our Place in a Multiethnic World*, Paula Harris and Doug Schaupp candidly observe, "Two dynamics are operating to maintain a racially stratified system. As a white person I am very privileged. . . . The other dynamic operating is that people of color are victims of racist discrimination."[23] As preachers, a profound aspect of our lives that we cannot escape is our race and ethnicity, which are the first things people see other than our gender. My ethnicity and race will, in many ways, influence whether my listeners will hear what I have to say and the judgments they will make about who I am as the preacher. An immediate question listeners ask is apparent: Does this preacher understand me?

However, issues of race and ethnicity are not daily considerations for members of any dominant culture. In a preaching elective that I teach at Gordon-Conwell Theological Seminary, Cultural Exegesis for Preaching, one of the course topics regards race and ethnicity. During one class, a Caucasian male student expressed how he never wakes up in the morning and says to himself: "I am a white male, and I'm going to see life through this lens of white male privilege." For any majority-culture person, race and ethnicity do not naturally register in the mind until one becomes a minority when choosing to enter a minority's world and culture. My Caucasian friends who have traveled outside the United States to a non-Western culture have sampled what life is like for a minority person, but only during their travels. They have tasted the local spices, interacted with the locals, seen the sights, smelled the streets, and gained some valuable cultural experience. However, they come right back to their normal, privileged life as members of the dominant culture. Being a member of the majority culture does not preclude one from thinking about how this advantaged position in society or in the church influences the totality of one's existence as well as the task of preaching. For minorities, however, one's race and ethnicity are front and center in one's thinking. On a daily basis, the minority confronts the reality of their skin color and other noticeable differences. Stated frankly, ethnic minorities are forced to deal with differences because of the pejorative way they are treated in American culture and the way these differences receive ongoing attention from the dominant culture.

I remind us that each person possesses an ethnic culture. If you are Caucasian, your ancestors originally emigrated from another country, such as Poland, Scotland, or Germany, to the United States. You may be second-, third-, fourth-, or fifth-generation American, but you remain a product of your ethnic heritage. In other words, you are ethnic. My parents are first-generation immigrants from South Korea. I, however, am a second-generation Korean American who was born and raised in Chicago, in the United States. Therefore, while I am ethnically Korean (the background of my family ancestry), I am both American and Korean culturally, which causes tension depending on my circumstances and the people in my immediate context. A modern example may be the American and Greek cultural dichotomy that we observe in the movie *My Big Fat Greek Wedding*. Tula, the main character in this movie, wants to go to college. She feels that it is her American right to become an educated person and to advance in her career trajectory rather than working at her parents' Greek restaurant. However, her family/ethnic culture does not believe that women need a college degree. In her Greek family, a woman's purpose in life is to get married to a Greek man and to have Greek babies. So Tula wrestles with her American identity/rights and her familial/ethnic identity/rights, among other cultural topics.

An oft-unexplored area of life for members of the dominant culture concerns ethnicity, which impacts our relationships and communication with those of different ethnic groups. Here are questions we can ask about our ethnicity: When was the last time I considered my ethnicity? In what context did my ethnicity enter the conversation or situation? How is my particular ethnicity perceived by others in society? Is my ethnicity privileged or seen as a problem? What misunderstandings do I have about other ethnicities? Is ethnicity taken into consideration during my sermon preparation process? Why or why not? Do I possess a single ethnicity? Am I bicultural or multicultural? In which situations does ethnicity inform my thoughts, decisions, and actions?

Identify and write down some reflections on your ethnic culture or cultures. What do you already know about your ethnic background, what knowledge are you lacking, and how has your ethnicity impacted your preaching? What cultural assumptions do we hold that listeners from other ethnic groups may not have? Begin asking your family members questions to learn more about your ethnic heritage. Read cultural histories about the immigration experiences of your ancestors. Sit down and ask your parents, grandparents, and other relatives what their experiences were like in coming to America. What challenges did your parents, grandparents, or great-grandparents face as immigrants to this country? In what ways did they tangibly suffer in a new land? The more we learn about our own ethnic heritage, the greater we will be able to understand and empathize with others from various ethnicities. For further discussions on race and ethnicity, refer to chapter 6.

Journal Entry 3: Identify Your Cultural Attitudes

In this third entry, identify your attitudes toward other cultural groups. If we can be vulnerable for a moment, my assumption here is that every person struggles *at times* with sinful thoughts and derogatory attitudes toward members of different cultural contexts. For instance, we may harbor ill feelings toward others based on their spoken languages, dress, gender, race, ethnicity, class, occupation, musical tastes, theological presuppositions, doctrines and beliefs, ministry philosophies, or simply because they don't do things just like we do. But where did these cultural attitudes come from? Write a journal entry and name the sinful, destructive cultural attitudes that we internalize about others. Get as specific as possible by writing down names, particular cultural contexts, life moments, what it is about their culture that is distasteful to you, and why you struggle to love them. Write down moments when you secretly mocked the Other in your heart or when you condemned them under your breath. While God already knows our dispositions, it is critical for preachers to identify our prejudices and bring them to Christ.

Many preachers operate out of a sense of obligation, and we are taught to put on a smile. We feign love when our insides are churning. In this journal entry, be real with God. As DeGroat writes, "All of us wrestle with the false self, the parts of us that live out of deceit and pretense."[24] We are not exempt from the sin of prejudice. What we write down in this section may alarm us or even be shameful, but until we clearly identify our cultural attitudes, our preaching to "those cultures" will fester falsity and lack candor. In this journal entry I was forced to write down reprehensible moments of displaying my repulsive attitude toward Others such as the time when I was stopped at a red light and immediately locked my doors when a person of a particular color walked near my car. He heard the locks click, and his reaction of utter disappointment will never be erased from my mind. The book of James uncomfortably prompts us all, especially preachers, to look straight at our face in the mirror regularly so that we do not forget what we *really* look like (1:23–24).

Journal Entry 4: Connect with Your Pain

People live with all types of pain: an assortment of physical, psychological, emotional, relational, economical, or spiritual inflammations and ailments. Oftentimes pain comes in the form of realizing our unhealthy cultural differences. Those who are different from the majority stick out, and these so-called unlovable qualities become painful blemishes that leave scars. Sadly, the evangelical church tends to promote doxology and celebration while failing to acknowledge people's identification with theodicy and lament.[25] Soong-Chan Rah says this about the nature of lament: "Lament in the Bible is a liturgical response to the reality of suffering and engages God in the context of pain and trouble. The hope of lament is that God would respond to human suffering that is wholeheartedly communicated through lament. Unfortunately, lament is often missing from the narrative of the American church."[26] DeGroat writes, "In many ways, we've been complicit in our culture in training people to be incapable of dealing with loss, with pain, with failure, with despair."[27]

Cultural intelligence trains us to become agents of healing because we will first confront our suffering and pain and thereby assist others with theirs. My wife took counseling classes at Denver Seminary while I served as a pastor in Colorado. In one of those classes, she learned a simple but profound truth: "People's pain is people's pain." That is, everyone experiences pain differently, whether we consider their pain an actual pain or merely self-pity. The point is profound: it is not in our jurisdiction to dismiss another's pain simply because it fails to meet our criteria for what denotes *real* pain. Remember the time in elementary school where during recess nobody chose you to play kickball on their team, or in high school where you couldn't find a date for the school dance? Now, decades removed from the incidents, you would say these examples weren't a big deal. But go back to those moments. They were quite painful, weren't they?

Which pains lie dormant in your soul? We bridle a kaleidoscope of silent pain from an absentee parent, loss of a parent, relational distress, barrenness, wayward children, losing a child or a loved one, financial instability, job loss, addictions, recurrent sins, being recipients of hate crimes, racism and prejudice, cancer and other incurable sicknesses, distrust in a marriage relationship, adultery, involuntary singleness, stunted language and cultural acquisition, gender discrimination, educational struggles, and innumerable other forms of pain. In other words, our lives transport wounds daily from place to place, and Band-Aids slapped over them serve as poor substitutes for genuine healing and restoration. Parker Palmer explains, "The divided life is a wounded life, and the soul keeps calling us to heal the wound. Ignore that call, and we find ourselves trying to numb our pain with an anesthetic of choice, be it substance abuse, overwork, consumerism, or mindless media noise. Such anesthetics are easy to come by in a society that wants to keep us divided and unaware of our pain."[28]

As preachers, it does not help that we tend to keep our own wounds hidden from others. Yet it is only a matter of time before the wound implodes or exposes itself. Our inability to care for ourselves or confront our pain will inevitably manifest itself in the pulpit, whether verbally or via the incapacity to care for our listeners. Stated more strongly by DeGroat: "If we ignore the darkness in ourselves, others, and our world, we do not know ourselves, and we cannot possibly relate to or care for others or our world. We become impotent, unable to lead with a substantive vision. We become phonies, leading by technique rather than by character."[29] Reflect on enduring areas of pain in your life. How might this pain influence your preaching ministry? How might pain impact your listeners in direct and indirect ways? In what ways can your identification with pain enable you to show empathy with Others?

Particularly for extroverts, share your timeline with trusted friends and mentors. Oftentimes extroverts process better externally. Processing your timeline aloud with others will enrich your self-exploration. Also, take opportunities to guide your church leaders and perhaps the entire congregation through the same process toward self-discovery.

Part 3: Explore the Homiletical Template

The third part of this self-inventory simply serves as a reminder for preachers to participate as much as possible in exploring the components of the Homiletical Template for ourselves as we do likewise on behalf of our listeners. In particular, in consultation with Stage 2: The Homiletical Bridge, we want to verify where our beliefs, rituals, idols, dreams, (view of) God, and experiences intersect with and diverge from our congregants. While it is commonplace that preachers partake in a form of self-exploration every time they preach, working through the BRIDGE sequence will make us aware of the ways we find continuity and dissonance with those who are culturally different from us. By doing so, our preaching will not only be communicated from our limited cultural perspective, but also locate moments of convergence to speak into the cultural contexts of our hearers.

Conclusion

Preachers have the extraordinary opportunity to shepherd God's people by preaching sermons that address the experiential knowledge of various cultural groups who worship among us. When cultural differences are unwelcome or vilified, the preacher will be handcuffed in leading the people toward spiritual maturity. What we want to do as preachers is to equip and enable our listeners to glorify Christ in their bodies just as God created them. As Paul Tokunaga writes, "Our lives in Christ, coupled with our heritage as Asian American Christians, are not without purpose. It is certainly no mistake on his part that we were born into our families and cultures, that we live in America and that we are redeemed. Rather than live in denial of any of these three facts, we should be asking, 'OK, God, you did this for a reason. How can I best bring you honor and glory?'"[30] God has permitted each person to embody an ethnicity, experience particular cultures, and have unique life experiences, all to be used in building up his church in the midst of a fallen world. It is, then, our pastoral delight to equip our varied listeners from all cultural backgrounds to develop in their spiritual maturity and to bring glory to God.

In preparation for understanding other cultures, we have allocated indispensable time to learn about ourselves, our experiences, our culture, and our pain. Curt Thompson helps bring our thoughts in this chapter to a close: "It is only when we are known that we are positioned to become conduits of love. And it is love that transforms our minds, makes forgiveness possible, and weaves a community of disparate people into the tapestry of God's family. . . . To be known means that you allow your shame and guilt to be exposed—in order for them to be healed."[31] Self-exploration for preachers is not a stand-alone event. As God continues to prune us and heal us, we can take what we have learned about ourselves and begin to apply this cultural intelligence for the cultural contexts to whom we communicate. That is the next step in the journey.

Part 2

Cultural Intelligence *in* Practice

5

Preaching and Denominations

Who can forget this unforgettable historic scene in John 17? Jesus awaits his impending betrayal, trial, and crucifixion. As spiritual preparation for what is about to come, Jesus stays up late to pray in the garden of Gethsemane. What does Jesus pray for in his final moments of earthly ministry? He offers up prayers for unity. Specifically, Jesus asks the Father in John 17:21 to sanctify all believers in truth and "that all of them may be one." The raison d'être for this unity is so that a nonbelieving world will witness the church's unity and "believe that you [the Father] have sent me [Jesus]."

Fast-forward two thousand years, however, and differences in scriptural interpretation and sinful proclivities toward authority and "spiritual correctness" have wrought the very disharmony that Jesus prayed against. Jesus never intended for such expansive disunity in the body of Christ. The stark reality of the Christian church today is that we are a disunified bunch. A recent study shows that the years 1800–2008 showed an astronomical increase in denominations, from 500 to 39,000. In 2012 there were approximately 43,000 Christian denominations around the globe. By the year 2025, the number of denominations is projected to explode to 55,000.[1] While many believe that we are now entering a postdenominational age, with numerous denominations in decline, denominations still tarry on, and every minister enters a pastorate that is either affiliated with a denomination or is nondenominational, with its own inherent traditions, ministry philosophies, and preaching distinctives.[2] To dismiss or claim ignorance about these denominational nuances could involuntarily place the preacher's foot on a ministry land mine.

The purpose of this chapter is to discuss ways to preach with cultural intelligence across denominational lines, from mainline Protestant traditions to evangelical renewal movements. To avoid elevating or excluding particular denominations, we will limit ourselves to more high-level issues with respect to denominational, hermeneutical, and homiletical concerns, although certain denominational beliefs, traditions, and practices will be referenced as examples. We will focus on homiletical issues but also raise some awareness regarding worship, theological differences, and ecclesiological matters that warrant pastoral attention when preaching within Protestant traditions.[3] This chapter is written with novice preachers in mind, as they enter their first pastorate within a denomination, but a subsequent goal is to facilitate the thinking of more seasoned preachers who may be looking toward a denominational transition. The following two themes related to our common identity as Protestants will initiate our discussion on denominations and remind us of our shared history and mission.

Protestantism: A Shared History

Jesus was resoundingly clear. Christianity was always intended to be a unified movement and not a partitioned organization. However, it did not take long before schisms broke out among his followers. For Protestants in particular, our differences may appear insurmountable, but might I remind us that we share a common history? Timothy George flags the importance of "the Second Diet of Speyer which also gave us the word 'Protestant,' understood not merely in the sense of 'protest against' but also 'witnesses on behalf of' (*pro-testantes*)."[4] This protest in the sixteenth century came as a reaction to some dubious teachings and practices of the Roman Catholic Church. Historically, the trouble for Protestants has been that our theological and ministerial emphases have been more on the protesting rather than on the witnessing. Denominationally speaking, we are known especially for what we stand against rather than what we stand for and put into practice.

I am not saying that doctrinal differences don't matter. Of course they do. Doctrines and beliefs cost many Christians their very lives. Erwin Lutzer explains in his book *The Doctrines That Divide*, "In days gone by, many believers were tortured, eaten by wild beasts, or burned at the stake because of their doctrinal convictions."[5] While such violent reactions to theological and ministerial variances have tempered some over the centuries, the reality within Protestant circles is that we have not been all that charitable toward one another. Doctrinal differences have engendered local church splits, caused entire denominational rifts, and let individual sheep drift away from the faith.

An expectant outcome from this chapter is for all preachers to grow in transdenominationalism. That is, we want to find avenues to work across denominational variances and also to preach in such a way that we do not demonize those who espouse other theological presuppositions and biblical interpretations, but rather develop greater appreciation for them and their views. In short, we build bridges with other denominations by remaining faithful to our own traditions while espousing a posture of learning from others. Increasingly in this world that is hostile to Christianity, pastors and church leaders must find greater alignment with one another.

The Great Commission: A Shared Mission

Not only do we as Protestants share a common history; we also share a common mission as instructed by our Lord Jesus Christ in Matthew 28:18–20. The well-known evangelist Billy Graham writes, "We are not meant to live for ourselves; Christ has commanded us to tell others of his saving and transforming power. Thus evangelicals have always given priority to evangelism. Evangelicals may disagree on some minor points of doctrine or practice, but they unite on their common commitment to evangelism."[6] Steve Wilkens and Don Thorsen concur with Graham and say, "Evangelical Christians are people of the Great Commission. They seek to understand what Jesus meant by his parting words to the disciples (Matt. 28:16–20). Then they seek to embody and live it out through everything that they think, say, and do."[7]

While theological issues and ministerial philosophies perpetuate Christians of different stripes, who mark their territories and grapple over interpretive nuances in the text, we are losing precious time and ground in bringing people to a saving knowledge of Christ. In *The American Church in Crisis*, David Olson grieves over the ongoing decline of church attendance in the United States.[8] Our Christ-given command is to deliver the good news of Jesus Christ to every person on earth and to make disciples of all people. We can so easily become distracted by nonessential matters and lose sight of "keeping the main thing the main thing."

Regardless of our denominational commitments, ministers are tasked to consider sobering questions about how we and our congregations are faring in terms of spiritual development. Craig Groeschel asks, "Do the people we lead really care about the Gospel? Are they really growing closer to Christ? Is the world any better because our churches exist?"[9] May this chapter serve as a clarion call to preach the good news of Jesus Christ and to preach to help our communities and neighborhoods see the far-reaching impact of the good news we proclaim. To put it bluntly, ministry in the twenty-first century demands the same attitude as that of John the Baptist, and it must declare: Jesus Christ must become greater; our denominations must become less! (cf. John 3:30).

We will now work through the three stages of the Homiletical Template as described in chapter 2. The first stage concerns hermeneutics and follows our HABIT (Historical, Grammatical, and Literary Context; Author's Cultural Context; Big Idea of the Text; Interpret in Your Context; and Theological Presuppositions.)

Stage 1: Follow Your HABIT

Scripture Text
Ephesians 4:1–6

Historical, Grammatical, and Literary Context

Historical Context

From a Roman prison cell, Paul writes this letter to the Ephesian believers in approximately 60–61.[10] Known as a circular letter, Paul writes to "Gentile believers in the churches of southwestern Asia Minor."[11] Having ministered and preached to the Ephesian Christians for more than two years, Paul understood the unique challenges they were facing (see Acts 19:10; 20:17–21). Ephesus was an influential trading city located off the Aegean Sea and currently sits "on the west coast of modern-day Turkey."[12] Clinton Arnold observes, "It would be accurate to characterize Ephesus as the leading city of the richest region of the Roman Empire. At this time, only Rome and Alexandria were larger."[13] As per the religious climate, the city of Ephesus, at the time of Paul's writing, was a haven for the worship of the goddess Artemis, who, as Demetrius the silversmith unabashedly confesses, brought him much business from shrine making (Acts 19:24–27). The city's temples also hosted a number of deities, such as Aphrodite, Zeus, and Dionysus, making polytheism the cultural norm of the day.[14] While no explicit "problem" is mentioned in the letter, Paul writes to remind Christians of their identity as God's reconciled people and how they ought to live in light of this new identity as people united to Christ and bonded to one another.[15]

Grammatical Issues

The limitations of space preclude us from addressing the larger pericope of 4:1–16. Therefore, we will concentrate our efforts on 4:1–6. Chapter 4 marks a distinct shift from the previous three chapters of Ephesians. Harold Hoehner explains, "Ephesians, similar to other Pauline letters, is divided into two main parts: doctrine or theology (chaps. 1–3) and duties or ethics (chaps. 4–6)."[16] In the first three chapters, Paul shares a doctrinal treatise on the person and work of Christ. He reports that "in Christ" the Ephesian believers have everything they need to be reconciled to God and to one another. After dictating his doxological prayer at the conclusion of Ephesians 3, Paul employs the word "therefore" in the beginning of chapter 4, in recognition of what Christ has accomplished, "I urge you to live a life worthy of the calling you have received." In essence, Paul "provides the rationale for behavior by grounding the imperative in the indicative."[17] On account of all that Christ has done (chaps. 1–3), "live a life worthy of the calling you have received." This exhortation is the primary message of the entire pericope and perhaps of the rest of the letter. The calling is for fellow members of the body of Christ to live in unity. In verses 2–3 Paul spells out four how-to's, and later in verses 4–6 he lays out seven theological rationales for living out this Christian unity.

In this section on grammatical issues, a primary consideration for preachers with respect to denominational commitments concerns how your denomination's theological commitments show partiality toward one or more of the seven rationales articulated by Paul for unity in Christ (i.e., one body, one Spirit, one hope, one Lord, one faith, one baptism, one God and Father of all). For example, how might your congregation interpret the statement that there is "one baptism"? Would your sermon primarily emphasize the issue of baptism and serve as a keepsake to remind your listeners of your denomination's position on baptism? While there is, of course, nothing wrong with underscoring how we understand any of these seven topics, it can be eye-opening for the preacher to recognize to what extent denominational/theological commitments shape one's preaching and ministry practices. Recently I read a dispute on social media between a pastor and his congregant on a nonessential theological issue. Sadly, the pastor publicly humiliated the church member with hurtful words because the two did not hold the same position. Thus questions need to be faced: Are we shaming our congregants in our preaching ministry without our knowledge? What is gained and what is lost when our theological allegiances sway the content and shape of our message yet do not represent the central thrust of the text for the day?

Literary Study

As is common knowledge, the literary genre of Ephesians is a letter also known as an epistle. However, the contents in Paul's Letter to the Ephesians are markedly different from his situational letters, where Paul writes to address a specific issue in the church or region, such as in 1 Corinthians or Galatians. Francis Foulkes observes, "In many respects Ephesians reads more like a sermon—in some parts more like a prayer or a mighty doxology—than a letter written to meet some special need in a church or group of churches. It is like a sermon on the greatest and widest theme possible for a Christian sermon—the eternal purpose of God which he is fulfilling through his Son Jesus Christ, and working out in and through the church."[18]

What stands out in this Scripture text is Paul's mentioning of his circumstances in writing this letter "as a prisoner for the Lord" (Eph. 4:1). To begin chapter 4 by naming his location in being imprisoned is no small matter. In New Testament times, the epistle served as a "substitute for the personal presence of the author."[19] Unable to speak directly to them in person due to his incarceration, Paul eagerly wishes for the Ephesian Christians to know that the unity of which he speaks is pressing. Foulkes continues to explain Paul's urgent plea for unity in the body on all fronts: "Where differences in essential doctrine and contradictions in ethical teaching make such divisions, he [Paul] would strive to know and uphold the way of Christ in each detail. Where differences are caused merely by superficial things or by the selfish individualism of members, he would toil and fight for the breaking down of barriers and the working out of genuine fellowship."[20] For Paul, disunity is not an option. At all costs, Christians are to work toward and even "fight for" their unity (cf. v. 3). When we preach from the Epistles, oftentimes we can become so myopic about the doctrine and theology that the epistle imparts that we forget to remind ourselves and our listeners that this is a heartfelt letter from the author to his recipients, whom he loves. Consideration of the literary genre matters in preaching, and in this case highlighting the genre—as a personal letter to fellow Christians—will be significant to the overall communication of the sermon.

Author's Cultural Context

With a blend of Jewish and Gentile believers, the Christian community in Ephesus presented noticeable obstacles for Paul concerning the unity in Christ that he prescribes. Clinton Arnold suggests two major cultural dynamics that made it necessary for Paul to write the Letter to the Ephesians. First, he maintains that "the Ephesian church was most likely struggling with a problem of Jew-Gentile disunity. The problem may have been exacerbated by a large influx of Gentile believers into the community in the years since Paul ministered in Ephesus. Not only was there already a natural and cultural tension between Jews and Gentiles, but Gentile converts often lacked an appreciation for the Jewish heritage of their new faith."[21]

It makes sense that disunity represented a foremost cultural concern in Ephesus since Paul refers specifically to his Gentile readers on more than one occasion (see 2:11–22; 3:1–13). He goes out of his way to remind both Jews and Gentiles that their Gentile brothers and sisters have also been adopted into God's family. In other words, Gentiles are legitimate family members in the body of Christ, and therefore unity is expected from both parties. In Paul's day, Gentiles were permitted access to the outer portion of the temple in Jerusalem, but a physical barrier of 4.5 feet was constructed to prevent Gentiles from entering the inner part of the temple, a wall to which Paul refers in 2:14 as the "dividing wall of hostility."[22] In Christ, however, Jews and Gentiles are no longer divided physically or spiritually. In light of Paul's cultural context in Ephesus, what comparisons can be drawn with your denomination and church context? What barriers still exist theologically and culturally that drive a wedge between your congregants?

A second cultural issue for Ephesus regards Christians' participation in culturally perpetuated sinful practices. In Ephesians 5, Paul particularly names the variety of immoral behavior that was practiced by the worshipers of Dionysus, commonly known as "the god of wine." Scholars tell us that "Dionysus worship was notorious for its unrestrained, orgiastic character, involving wine, music, dance and sex."[23] Paul warns the Ephesians in 5:3, "But among you there must not be even a hint of sexual immorality, or of any kind of impurity, or of greed, because these are improper for God's holy people." He continues in verse 5: "For of this you can be sure: No immoral, impure or greedy person—such a person is an idolater—has any inheritance in the kingdom of Christ and of God." The weightiness of Paul's words points to the fact that culturally permissible sins were plaguing God's people in Ephesus, and Paul sought to curb these practices quickly and thoroughly. With respect to our topic of denominations and congregations, are similar types of cultural sins being perpetuated? For instance, does our denominational affiliation and its theological beliefs encourage us to speak negatively of other Christians and their denominations? Have we bought into "foolish talk" in condemning other Christians because of their allegedly "erroneous" beliefs?

Big Idea of the Text

Subject: How does Paul exhort the Ephesian Christians to walk in a way that is worthy of their calling?

Complement: By demonstrating unity through selflessness and remembering their shared identity and faith in the one True and Triune God.

Exegetical Idea: Paul exhorts the Ephesian Christians to walk in a way that is worthy of their calling by demonstrating unity through selflessness and remembering their shared identity and faith in the one True and Triune God.

Homiletical Idea: Walk in unity through humility with all believers in Christ, because we are one in the same Triune God.

Interpret in Your Context

Assumptions

What assumptions might those in your church/denomination hold as they read Ephesians 4:1–6? The major assumption our listeners may consider is whether they are personally living in unity with fellow believers. John Mac-Arthur points out, "Most of us will admit that we tend to be so self-oriented that we see many things first of all—and sometimes only—in relation to ourselves."[24] However, Paul's central point in this text is not simply individual obedience (which is of great significance) but also corporate unity across segmented populations within Christian community (e.g., across denominations). Even if our congregation is currently experiencing a period of harmony, a concomitant question is whether we are united with believers who may disagree with us theologically and philosophically when it comes to ministry praxis. Here the preacher's temptation is to quit while we are ahead and not extend our purview beyond the four walls of the church. This assumption leads to an oversimplification of Paul's message that perpetuates the status quo of disunity within the larger body of Christ.

Conflicts

At the heart of this Scripture passage is Paul's admonition to love one another. Without love, it is impossible for Christian communities to be unified. The troublesome issue is that love does not come naturally to the Christian. Jonathan Swift writes, "We have just enough religion to make us hate but not enough religion to make us love one another."[25] This passage stretches us to confess the ways in which our church or denomination has veered away from this text by avoiding or intentionally slandering fellow believers because of theological disagreements (e.g., baptism, women in ministry, predestination, or spiritual gifts). As we pray for our congregation and denomination, the Holy Spirit will bring to our consciousness the specific topics that stymie peace. What conflicts exist among your congregation's members and among churches in your local area? In this sermon, the preacher's task is to expose and name the conflicts so that listeners will be encouraged to pray for the unity to which we have all been called. Do not let this opportunity pass by with respect to dealing with sinful and detrimental attitudes, which negate Paul's instruction in verse 3, "Make every effort to keep the unity of the Spirit through the bond of peace."

Questions

Many listeners, regardless of their denominational affiliation, will seek practical answers on how the believer or believing community embodies Christian unity amid an endless array of denominations and fractions. Does unity mean that we relinquish our theological distinctives as a denomination and church? What does this mean practically for congregations? Are ethnic and cultural differences getting in the way of biblical unity? Another way to frame these questions is via the subject of ecclesiology, which requires more intentional reflection in churches of all denominations. Jackson Carroll defines ecclesiology as the "branch of theology that deals with the nature, constitution, and functions of the church."[26] What is the church called to be, according to our particular congregation or denomination? How does this ecclesiology work itself out in Ephesians 4:1–6? Daniel Treier states, "For all church contexts, ecclesiology proves to be a crucial issue regarding theological interpretation of Scripture."[27]

Churches vary greatly in their perspectives on maturity and obedience to the Word. Timothy George tells a humorous story about passing by an evangelical congregation in Kentucky that enticed people to enter with this statement: "The Church that asks nothing of you."[28] In response to this signage, George says: "This seems a long way from the church of the apostles and martyrs which asked everything of you!"[29] The oneness that we share in Christ will provoke myriad questions for our hearers, depending on our Protestant tradition. Anticipating what questions our listeners will ask of the text will enable us to present a relevant message that addresses their curiosity.

Theological Presuppositions

Perhaps more than any other subject, our preunderstanding of the text (see chap. 3) is most visible when it comes to theological presuppositions. The sheer volume of different Protestant denominations suggests that Christians have innumerable theological differences. Robert Stephen Reid and Lucy Lind Hogan have this to say about different theologies within Protestant traditions: "Sacramental theology can differ at key points from Reformed theology; Anabaptist theology differs from Pentecostal theology. Conservative theologies differ from progressive ones. There are many resources that can help preachers consider what makes for reliable and faithful ways to interpret and communicate the theological commitments of their traditions."[30] However, Martin Marty contends: "To be sure, there are distinctions, some of them having to do with emphases. . . . Followers of John Calvin ('Reformed' Protestants) begin with witness to the sovereign God and relate God's graciousness to it. Lutherans begin with God's grace and have to work out what this means for God's sovereignty."[31] The two examples above demonstrate a theological presupposition that undergirds the interpretation of the text.

Moreover, theological presuppositions become the overall framework or blueprint for how we interpret the entirety of Scripture. A study was conducted among radiologists concerning chest X-rays and whether the doctors could locate cancer in the lungs. Researchers at Harvard University secretly inserted an image into the X-ray without the radiologists' knowledge: a person in a gorilla costume. To their utter amazement, the researchers found that only 17 percent of radiologists noticed the gorilla in the X-ray. The study concluded that "what we're thinking about—what we're focused on—filters the world around us so aggressively that it literally shapes what we see."[32] Similarly, in every passage of Scripture we are reading into the text a specific theological perspective based on what we want to, hope to, or expect to see in the text. Our interpretive lenses, in many ways, are looking to find a particular meaning based on our presuppositions: thus we may (1) emphasize what is not inherently present and (2) fail to see, at times, the meaning that is right in front of us.

Theological presuppositions express themselves in different forms. Several years ago I attended a preaching conference with local church pastors and seminary homiletics professors. In one of the paper presentations, the topic for mutual consideration was God-centered preaching. Over the next few minutes, the temperature of the room escalated as a group of pastors from a tradition espousing christological preaching voiced their conviction that *every* single sermon from *every* single Scripture text must include the person and work of Jesus Christ. Citing texts like Colossians 1 and Luke 24 (Jesus on the road to Emmaus), this group of Christ-centered preachers relentlessly contended for their theological presupposition on preaching.[33]

No matter which denomination you align yourself with, you will preach with a sentient or subconscious theological presupposition in mind. Are you aware of the specific theological presuppositions that color your interpretation of Scripture and how they impact the thrust of your weekly messages? Sometimes we are blind to the theological leanings expressed in our sermons. For instance, Baptists may preach through the lens of Christology. Pentecostals may preach by focusing on pneumatology and the role of the Holy Spirit. Reformed Presbyterians may preach historic-redemptive messages. Dispensationalists may preach on eschatology and interpret Scripture based on various dispensations. The list of particular leanings goes on and on. While preaching with a theological bent is normative across denominations, by no means do I suggest that this is an "erroneous" homiletical practice. Rather, the culturally intelligent preacher demonstrates theological awareness about doctrinal positions and contextual empathy for listeners who do not share our theological perspectives. In addition, ultimately the hermeneutical goal (i.e., *authorial-cultural* model) is to allow the text to speak for itself rather than prescribing our theological presuppositions. We are bridgers of denominational cultures.

Stage 2: Build the BRIDGE

Beliefs

David Buschart, in his book *Exploring Protestant Traditions*, explains that denominational beliefs or doctrines can be viewed as being either unique or nuanced. That is, certain beliefs are specific to a particular denominational tradition, whereas others are commonly held by many yet have their own varied meanings and nuances. Buschart gives us an example:

> In some cases, the doctrine is unique to the tradition, such as the Pentecostal belief that speaking in tongues is the initial sign of baptism in the Holy Spirit, and that this baptism is normative for the life of all Christians. In other cases, such as the Lutheran doctrine of justification by faith, the doctrine is not unique to the tradition, but it is formulated and emphasized in such a way that one cannot fully understand or appreciate the tradition without understanding its distinctive approach to this doctrine.[34]

The primary beliefs or doctrines that are considered "essential for denominational orthodoxy" include credo-baptism for Baptists; infant baptism for Presbyterians, Anglicans, and Methodists; Arminian theology for Nazarenes and Methodists; unconditional election for Reformed and Presbyterians; charismatic gifts for Pentecostals and Church of God; and eschatology for Christian and Missionary Alliance and dispensationalist churches.[35] I spoke with a younger pastor who recently candidated at a church. To his surprise, most of the interviewers' questions centered on the issue of eschatology. Particular beliefs and doctrines will be at the forefront for specific churches and denominations, even if those issues are not pressing for the preacher.

Secondary beliefs or doctrines, often referred to as nonessential doctrines, include how often we celebrate Communion, women's roles in ministry, social justice issues, divorce and remarriage, worship music preferences, political views, and more. Preaching excessively on primary and secondary beliefs can pit members of a congregation against one another. We often assume that everyone in the congregation subscribes to a certain belief or doctrine on the simple fact that they attend our denominational or nondenominational church. Years ago, when serving as a senior pastor, I preached a topical series of sermons called "What Do I Believe?" The purpose of the sermon series was to educate the congregation on what the church's position was on various doctrines—both primary and secondary—but also to encourage listeners to be thoughtful Christians, like the Berean believers in Acts 17:11, who "received the message with great eagerness and examined the Scriptures every day to see if what Paul said was true." On completing this sermon series, we learned that our congregation was divided on several theological and ministry issues, including predestination, baptism, and women's roles in ministry.

This sermon series was illuminating because it obliged me in future messages to consider the contrasting perspective on various doctrinal beliefs that were presumed to be normative. Commitment to a particular theology is not the most important criterion for institutional allegiances. A *Christianity Today* article discusses a recent trend of seminarians choosing to study at a particular seminary not based on theological alignment but rather based on the convenience of its location. In this article, Ligon Duncan comments, "Many [seminarians] are choosing to attend regional institutions with which they have less theological affinity in order to stay in the same city."[36] What this means for preachers is that the diversity of beliefs held among listeners within a local congregation—including beliefs not endorsed by the denomination—exist and may vary widely. For instance, some congregants may be worshiping at your church simply because of its proximity and not because they share your doctrinal leanings. What beliefs or doctrines do we assume of our listeners that are not necessarily championed by our church or denomination?

Rituals

One of the defining marks of denominations regards their rituals or traditions. The apostle Paul frequently spoke of traditions (rituals). However, his understanding of tradition, or *paradosis*, focused on core doctrinal beliefs, such as in 1 Corinthians 15:3, where Paul reminds them of a tradition "of first importance" about the death, burial, and resurrection of Jesus.[37] As Derek Tidball explains in *Ministry by the Book*, "These traditions soon stood for what was authoritative in Christian teaching as it was transmitted to others."[38] My approach here for rituals/traditions to further our cultural intelligence is more akin to James White's definition in *Protestant Worship: Traditions in Transition*: "Worship traditions, then, are specific ways of and attitudes toward doing worship that are passed on from generation to generation."[39]

Rituals/traditions can be observed poignantly in the ways the worship service is conducted. What is incorporated and what is excluded in the order of worship, and why? Does your congregation "pass the peace of Christ" to one another or read professions of faith aloud, such as liturgies, confessions, or creeds? How regularly or irregularly does your denomination celebrate Communion? Is there an altar call at the end of each worship service for nonbelievers to step forward and accept Christ as their Lord and Savior? Do you recite the Pledge of Allegiance during your Memorial Day weekend service? Rituals play an unspoken but profound role in the worship service and have an impact on our preaching ministry. For example, having visited churches from many different denominations, especially those that practice weekly Communion, the entire service represents a precursor to the main event, which is celebrating the Lord's Table together. While Jesus places heavy weight on Communion, oftentimes the preacher's big idea in the sermon affixes itself to the event of Communion rather than on what the biblical author was communicating in a given text.

Learn about the rituals/traditions in your congregation and denomination. Ask yourself the following questions: When and why did this ritual become adopted? Is the ritual biblical? Does this ritual promote unity or segregate the body of Christ? Moreover, to increase unity with fellow Christians, try to become informed about other Protestant denominations' rituals. David Buschart observes: "Protestants simply do not know, understand or learn potentially valuable lessons from one another."[40] In what ways are we actively growing in cultural intelligence about our fellow Protestant denominations? Or have we mentally discarded those who do not uphold our traditions?

Idols

Pastoral ordination and congregational membership in a denomination have benefits and limitations. For many, the benefits include accountability for the pastor and the church under the umbrella of a larger pastors' network and church network. The independent church where I served as pastor joined the Evangelical Covenant Church, a denomination that welcomed us with open arms. Once or twice a year the troops, meaning church leaders, gather as an assembly regionally and nationally to remind one another of core doctrines and denominational traditions. Denominational meetings can be seen as rallying events to bolster denominational "correctness" about theology and ministry philosophies. Influential and well-known guest speakers are brought in to celebrate and affirm the denomination's goals for the future and to seek hearty "Amens" to forge ahead with agendas.

At the same time, however, the ability to be patient with Others and their "highly egregious" teachings is tested regularly on social media and other outlets. In his book *The Imperfect Pastor*, Zack Eswine writes, "We take on late-night banter, blogging attacks, and tweeting daggers as if the culture, rather than Jesus, is our master. So Dr. Well-Known Preacher and Mr. National Blogger immediately and publicly castigate Rev. Famous Author and relationally dissociate from him."[41] One of the greatest idols we face in denominationalism is the idol of being right. Our self-congratulatory banners read: "We have the right doctrine. We worship in the right way. We have the right ministry goals, practices, and programs. We teach the right preaching models. Everyone else is driving in the wrong lane." A colleague of mine likes to say, "Hold on to the Bible tightly and your theology lightly." The need to be right is the very impetus for disunity in the body of Christ and the cause for more and more divisions.

One of the limitations of denominational affiliation, to put it bluntly, is that we (church leaders) simultaneously forfeit total control over how ministry is done in our local church context. The denomination can swoop in as the big-brother figure and try to curtail or modify our well-conceived ministry plans. This can be frustrating for preachers and church leaders who idolize control. When the denomination's philosophies and practices differ from our own, we are seized with the need to be in control and execute ministry our way. Preachers, especially in turbulent denominational circles, need to become mindful of the temptation for power and control. Among the 43,000-plus denominations around the world, I wonder how many were formed simply because of some leader's need for control. Consequently, in our preaching and teaching, be careful not to abuse authority in the pulpit and to set up the denomination as a straw man to get what we desire. When it comes to denominational concerns, the idols of being right and being in control stand out as primary temptations that exacerbate Christian disunity. Search your heart and your next sermon to see how these idols may be slowly creeping into your preaching and ministry philosophies.

Dreams

Denominational dreams are elastic in their spectrum. While some denominations are in survival mode, others are launching endless streams of new initiatives and planning long-term vision strategies. The first half of Proverbs 29:18 in the King James Version reads: "Where there is no vision, the people perish." Heeding the warning of this proverb, several denominations have published new books that articulate visions and dreams for the future.[42] For example, Sharon A. Christopher Brown relays the sevenfold denominational vision of the United Methodist Church:

- Teaching the Wesleyan model of reaching and forming disciples of Jesus Christ
- Strengthening clergy and lay leadership
- Developing new congregations
- Transforming existing congregations
- Ending racism as we authentically expand racial and ethnic ministries
- Reaching and transforming the lives of new generations of children
- Eliminating poverty in community with the poor[43]

The seven visions of the UMC are highly historic of the Wesleyan tradition, and yet they concomitantly reflect the current context and burgeoning needs of our growing diversity in American society.

David Dockery explains, "Throughout most of the twentieth century, being a Southern Baptist had a cultural and programmatic identity to it unlike anything else. This kind of intactness provided Southern Baptists with a denominational stability unmatched by any other denomination in the country."[44] However, Dockery reports that over the last thirty years, the Southern Baptist

Convention (SBC) has become increasingly fragmented, with a decreasing understanding of its denominational heritage, history, and theological identity.[45] The SBC desires to retain the historic roots of the denomination, but it also recognizes that the denomination's outlook requires a more ecumenical spirit to work alongside those of other Protestant traditions.

What are the specific dreams of your denomination? These denominational dreams and visions will influence your preaching. They may steer the direction of your preaching calendar and influence your selection of topical sermons. Communication of denominational dreams provides hope for all congregations but especially for churches in denominations that are experiencing decline. We do not want to act independently as rogue agents within our denominations. Prayerfully consider how your pulpit ministry can contribute to the overall health of your Protestant tradition and promote and reinforce these dreams in your preaching and teaching.

God

Every denomination latches onto particular characteristics of God that shape its theology and practice. In essence, what we believe about God in theory influences our entire view of Christianity and ultimately how we respond to him in obedience. I grew up in a very conservative Korean Presbyterian church, which belonged to the Korean American Presbyterian Church denomination. In those formative years of Christian development, I heard countless sermons that pontificated on the theological directives of Augustine and Calvin regarding God's sovereignty and predestination of "the elect." Calvin's well-known acronym TULIP was bored into our young consciences like a drill sergeant. Everyone knew that there was nothing that we could do to merit the favor of God; however, the preacher's recurrent sermonic thrust left listeners with a list of moralistic/legalistic instructions. The sermon became a catalog of dos and more frequently don'ts—referring to things like not shopping on Sunday and not attending prom.

Over the years I have discussed the preaching ministry in conservative Korean American Presbyterian churches with fellow believers. The common takeaway from these conversations has been that they too heard contradicting messages about the character of God and expectations for his children. Many children of Korean immigrants, the second generation, have left the church altogether because of this distorted and confusing teaching on who God is.[46] In their minds, God is a sovereign King who is omniscient and loving, but also a stickler for rules and impossible to please. As Abraham Kuruvilla expresses in his book *A Vision for Preaching*, preaching is indeed theological.[47] In every sermon, the text communicates theology: something definitive about who God is in his nature, character, and will.

Who is God according to your denomination? What view of God is most regularly communicated in your proclamation that your listeners visualize throughout the week? Is God purely the one who provides with material blessings? Is God a missionary God who longs for the gospel to be heard throughout the earth? Do we emphasize the holiness of God to the extent that his creation becomes too fearful of him? Are we so enamored with getting theological concepts conveyed such as the "double imputation of Christ" that we forget to communicate the simplicity of the gospel message to a lost and hurting world?

God is not one-dimensional or two-dimensional or even three-dimensional. His characteristics are bountiful. Some common attributes of God that denominations typically accentuate include the following: supreme, sovereign, holy, powerful, immutable, faithful, patient, merciful, gracious, loving, good, and numerous others.[48] In the words of Thabiti Anyabwile, "Members of Christian churches continue to think small thoughts of God and great thoughts of man. This state of affairs reveals that too many Christians have neglected their first great calling: to know their God. Every Christian is meant to be a theologian in the best and most intimate sense of the word."[49] Might we, by wearing our denominational caps, be reinforcing "small thoughts of God" in our preaching by focusing on a few select characteristics of God? Cultural intelligence in preaching within denominations encourages preachers to explore how our denomination and our church membership view God. If we are not already doing so, our joy and responsibility is to present a holistic and balanced view of God.

Experiences

In his book *Loving God When You Don't Love the Church*, Chris Jackson makes this confession: "I love the church—but I hate certain parts of it. I adore the people of God—but I've also been hurt so deeply by some of them that I almost lost my faith. In church I've met some of the sweetest saints to ever grace the planet—but I've also been lied about and slandered behind my back."[50] Perhaps comparable statements could be made about our experiences within denominational circles. For various reasons, denominations are cherished by some, tolerated by others, and despised across our Christian landscape. As we can already attest, denominational membership has its pros and cons, its joys and frustrations.

Here are some positive experiences produced by denominationalism that many of our congregants appreciate and enjoy today. First, denominations provide an expedited way to locate a place of worship. When moving to a new location, it can be daunting to find a new church to call one's *family*. Typing the name of a denomination into a search engine will call up any and all member churches of a given denomination in the area. Second, denominations provide human and financial resources to equip and empower congregations to accomplish more collectively than they can on their own. Roger Olson says, "Most denominations have charitable agencies that are involved in feeding the hungry, training people for jobs, community development, etc. And, of course, most have mission-sending agencies. Small churches that cannot afford to do these things (e.g., found a college or hospital or even support a missionary family) pool their resources better to do them."[51] Third, denominations provide congregants with a general rubric for what to expect for Sunday worship, congregational beliefs, and ministry programs. Fourth, denominations offer congregations emotional, relational, and spiritual support, especially during difficult and sometimes lengthy pastoral transitions. Fifth, listeners benefit from a denominational history, legacy, and traditions passed down from previous generations.

On the flipside, Thom Rainer provides eight reasons why people are moving away from denominational churches in favor of nondenominational ones:

1. Denominational churches have a negative reputation.
2. Denominations are known more for what they are against than what they are for.
3. There is too much infighting and politics in denominations.
4. The denominational churches are too liberal.
5. There is a general waning of institutional loyalty in institutions such as denominations.
6. Denominations have inefficient systems and organizations. They are too bureaucratic.
7. Some of the respondents could see no perceived benefit to belonging to denominations.
8. Denominations are not good stewards of their financial resources.[52]

Moreover, Roger Olson states that this exodus from denominationalism is increasingly the trend among younger Christians. He writes, "Many young Christians consider denominations old fashioned, divisive, top heavy, always embroiled in controversies, etc. They prefer what I call 'plain label' churches, often newly founded, meeting in rented spaces, grassroots-oriented, etc."[53]

What do these diverse denominational experiences mean for the preaching task? First, it means that our preaching cannot be monolithic with respect to denominations, because our listeners do not share identical experiences. We should avoid universal statements like "All of us believe . . ." or "We all think that . . ." Second, our listeners' positive and wounding experiences within a particular denomination need to be heard and respected, especially from the pulpit. Be extra sensitive not to be defensive about your denomination's decisions or behaviors that have upset certain listeners. Third, listeners need to hear from their pastor that they don't have everything figured out and that in God's kingdom there is room for flexibility on certain nonessential doctrinal matters and ministry practices. Many preachers convey a compulsive message: "This is the only proper way to interpret this passage. If you don't agree with me, find a new church that believes what you do." Fourth, we want to preach in such a way that our listeners' experiences within a denomination positively add to congregational diversity. The temptation is to scold and expel those who fail to agree with us on every single tenet of our tradition. Speaking positively of other Protestant denominations will only endear us to our listeners who frequently experience fragility and wariness when it comes to denominational differences in churches.

Stage 3: Speak Their DIALECT

Delivery

I have commonly heard it said that it takes the preaching of at least five hundred sermons before a novice preacher begins to find one's preaching "voice."[54] Although I am not convinced that there is a magic number for becoming comfortable in one's skin, how we deliver the sermon is in many ways context-specific and denominationally located as well. Simply put, denominations have their own preaching styles. For example, Charles Bugg says about the Baptist preaching tradition that "there exists a formulaic Baptist preaching style. In the pulpit, the minister becomes the 'preacher' who sounds like every other preacher. . . . We do not know ourselves as unique children of God and, therefore, our insecurity motivates us to become a caricature of our favorite preacher."[55]

In delivery, we tend to mimic the styles of preachers whom we appreciate and learn best from within the denomination or irrespective of it. Seminary preaching courses often require a homiletics textbook, frequently with denominational ties, that provides step-by-step methods for sermon construction and guidelines for effective sermon delivery within *that* Protestant tradition. Depending on how formal or informal your denomination is with regard to preaching, listeners may be expecting to hear a particular sermonic style. For instance, we can preach verse-by-verse exposition through a text, general studies of Bible books, narrative storytelling, didactic (lecture style), homily (a brief sermon with a devotional flair), topical sermons on life situations, motivational-inspirational talks, and so forth. In addition, a longer and more influential previous senior pastor's tenure will limit our ability to expand the preaching style to accommodate our idiosyncrasies. At the same time, David Dunn-Wilson writes, throughout the history of Christian preaching, "preachers had to adapt their style and themes to congregations' changing needs. Consequently, in every age, the sermons that are preached reveal the preoccupations both of those who preach and those who listen, illuminating the interaction between them."[56] In this section on delivery, be respectful of one's denominational preaching tradition, but at the same time create avenues to display one's own homiletical flavor.

Lawrence W. Wilson provides a helpful diagram describing four types of preachers and how denominational affiliations may have an impact on preaching styles (see fig. 5.1). We may find that our preaching style is modeled after one or more of these four "types" of preachers.

In his book *Refining Your Style: Learning from Respected Communicators*, Dave Stone uses the following metric to describe thirteen distinct preaching delivery styles: the creative storyteller, the direct spokesperson, the scholarly analytic, the revolutionary leader, the engaging humorist, the convincing apologist, the inspiring orator, the practical applicator, the persuasive motivator, the passionate teacher, the relevant illustrator, the cultural prophet, and the unorthodox artist.[57] Not mutually exclusive, the classifications above provide novice and veteran preachers with a template to assess and evaluate one's preaching ministry. In many ways, your denominational affiliation will steer you toward one or more of these styles. However, the goal is to be yourself in the pulpit while keeping your denomination in view.

Which type of preacher best represents your particular delivery? Whichever style of delivery is most comfortable to us, there is freedom within denominational preaching to embody our own style, or as Phillips Brooks once put it, to view preaching as "truth through personality."[58] We don't want our

Figure 5.1
Four Types of Preachers

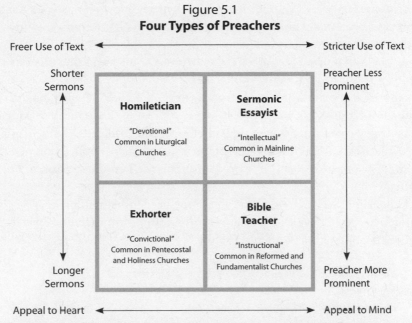

Freer Use of Text ←——————————→ Stricter Use of Text

Shorter Sermons ↑ | Preacher Less Prominent ↑

Homiletician

"Devotional"
Common in Liturgical Churches

Sermonic Essayist

"Intellectual"
Common in Mainline Churches

Exhorter

"Convictional"
Common in Pentecostal and Holiness Churches

Bible Teacher

"Instructional"
Common in Reformed and Fundamentalist Churches

Longer Sermons ↓ | Preacher More Prominent ↓

Appeal to Heart ←——————————→ Appeal to Mind

preaching tradition to make us robotic sermonizers to the extent that we lose our personality to fit into a specific denominational mold.

Illustrations

Preaching in denominational circles tends to encourage the use of certain types of illustrations. For instance, some traditions prize the use of quotations. That is, some preachers will draw illustrative material from their readings of well-known authors, pastors, theologians, or champions of the faith in church history (e.g., Reformed, Presbyterian, Baptists, Wesleyans, etc.). In nondenominational congregations, preachers tend to rely heavily on personal anecdotes and narratives of recent events in the life of the preacher, show movie clips, or play sound bites from social media. For other denominations, preachers have a proclivity toward reciting poetry or using various art forms (e.g., Anglicans, Episcopalians). In certain denominations, the preacher may adopt cookie-cutter illustrations lifted from sermon illustration books or sermon-made-easy websites. Rather, across the denominational spectrum, the hope for preaching with cultural intelligence is that illustrations would incorporate a variety of sources instead of a hyperemployment of a particular genre of illustrations. Employing the same kind of illustrations repetitively can make every sermon sound identical.

Wayne McDill provides a helpful rubric for connecting illustrations to the lives of our hearers in his book *12 Essential Skills for Great Preaching*, recommending what he refers to as "natural analogies": family, business, animals, athletics, common objects, world affairs, nature, children, education, history, travel, friendships, and other.[59] McDill advocates brainstorming by using these categories toward "picturing the idea for your audience."[60] What is the purpose of this illustration? Is this the best illustration to meet that end?

This chapter has focused primarily on the need for Christian unity across denominations. Consider the following illustration from Derek Penwell regarding denominational differences:

> "*Um, excuse me. You can't wear green socks in here.*"
> "Why not?"
> "*It's the Lord's house.*"
> "I'm not following."
> "*In our tradition, green socks are a sign of disrespect to the God who created the earth green.*"
> "Where does that come from? I'm pretty sure it's not in the Bible."
> "*Well, it's our reading of the Höckenstengel creed, produced at the council of the same name in 1737.*"
> "But see, from where I sit, that sounds arbitrary . . . and well, frankly, made up."
> "*Please don't say that too loudly. We've just come through a serious fracas with the no-blue-socks-wearing schismatics, and we really don't need another round of sock wrangling.*"
> "Blue socks?"
> "*For the sky.*"
> "Yes, of course."
> "*So, if you're willing to take off your green socks and acknowledge God's __true__ will, we'd be happy to have you commune with us. Oh, and lose the chin beard. God created the billy goats. You understand.*"[61]

Penwell's hypothetical example may be a perfectly acceptable illustration to confront disunity in the church in some denominations, but entirely inappropriate in others. In congregations where division is sorely festering, listeners may frown on such an illustration, which appears to make light of theological and ministerial differences. My point here is that we must know our denomination and congregation well to ascertain which illustrations will work most effectively.[62]

Application

Application, as already mentioned, is one of the most difficult elements in sermon construction. To apply the Scripture well takes prayer and guidance from the Holy Spirit and sufficient knowledge of one's congregation—members' joys, concerns, and struggles. A common tendency is to apply the text in ways that underscore the preacher's values or congregational/denominational concerns irrespective of what the biblical author intended. Years ago, David Bebbington articulated his quadrilateral with regard to biblicism, conversionism, crucicentrism, and activism, making four broad brushstrokes to define an evangelical Christian.[63] For many preachers, whether consciously or not, Bebbington's quadrilateral has served as an applicational grid, focusing on one or more of these four quadrants. That is, the application may center on the conversion experience, the atoning work of Christ on the cross, obedience to the Scriptures, or practicing Christian activism through social and missionary activities.[64] At times, applications reflect the traditions of our particular denomination more than the thrust of the original author's intention, to our listeners' peril.

Draw out thirst-quenching application directly from the same textual stream. Sadly, preachers in many denominational cross-sections travel down one of three applicational boulevards: (1) *tangent street*—substituting the main textual application with a tangential application or possible implication (what is implied in the text); (2) *break away trail*—leading listeners to an entirely different Scripture text to draw out an application; or even (3) *good luck highway*—abandoning listeners to come up with their own application. As an aside, implications in the passage are worthy for the listener to explore; however, they are secondary to the primary application in a given text. Therefore, explain the application first and then spell out what the implications might be. Don't substitute implication for application.

A growing trend in some denominations is to swap out a genuine application *in the text* with a closing denominational tradition at the end of the worship service, such as an altar call or celebrating Communion together. Though these are important observances in congregational life, remember that our responsibility as preachers is to do the hard work of serving tangible applicational morsels for our listeners to digest and implement each day. To put it succinctly, find the application *in the text*.

Language

Every congregation and denomination speaks its own language. Just because the preacher uses certain phrases, terminology, catchy names, or acronyms for ministry programs does not automatically denote mutual understanding. Language that is unfamiliar to the people invariably produces distance between us and our hearers. We want to build a bridge. Michael Brothers explains, "*Distance* in preaching can be described as a 'psychic' separation, holding hearers 'at bay,' keeping them from 'direct participation' in a biblical text via the sermon's form, technique, style, and delivery. Distance can be contrasted with 'nearness,' or 'participation,' which draws the hearer into the sermon."[65] I suggest that disconnected language can be another barrier that creates an unwanted sense of distance. This distance is acutely felt in the area of theological language. Oftentimes preachers use theological language without clear explanations. A preacher will assume that the listener will already be cognizant of and even conversant in the particular doctrine under discussion. Visitors or even regular attendees who feel left behind may wonder if this church is really for them. Just as biblical literacy cannot be assumed in today's culture, familiarity with "rudimentary" theological concepts, such as the incarnation, atonement, or the Trinity, which can be tricky terms to explain clearly, should not be taken for granted either.[66]

Perhaps we have preached sermons where highfalutin "seminary" terms like justification, sanctification, transubstantiation, imputation, eschatology, soteriology, penal substitution, and the like are flung freely into the sanctuary like a Frisbee, without providing listeners with the handles to receive their meaning and significance for the Christian life. If using these terms, provide a lucid definition of the term and also a clear illustration that provides further coherence and adherence. After saying a theological term like "atonement," give your listeners a real-life example or illustration of what atonement looks like today. Going a step further, help your listeners see why the concept of atonement matters in daily life to the single father or the CEO of a hedge fund company. Make theology practical for them. In many ways the ability to articulate theological language in the lingo of the listeners compels the preacher toward a more textured understanding of these important theological concepts.

Embrace

Unity is a key theme of our Scripture text. However, embracing all listeners is taxing and challenging. What visceral response do we have toward listeners who differ from us theologically or denominationally? How do we embrace them in our proclamation? What biases do we hold against them? During my years as an undergraduate student at Carleton College, I took a liking to the subject of history and eventually landed on a history major. I decided to major in history, specifically medieval and Renaissance studies. Like my family members, I can detect what you are thinking: What do you do with that degree? History appealed to me as a major because of the profound influence of Professor Philip H. Niles. In each of his courses, we were tasked with writing four papers responding to a singular question of his choice. In my first trimester, I took his peculiarly titled course Medieval Monks and Nuns. On the last page of each of these four papers, Professor Niles wrote iterations of the following: "Matt, you didn't answer the question." I thought I had answered the question clearly and convincingly, even with ample ammunitions of quotations and footnotes.

Through many visits to his office, I eventually caught on that we do not fully answer a question if we only respond to the question from one perspective—what *we* believe is the correct view. To truly answer a question, Niles explained, the student must also consider and wrestle with the ideas from an alternate angle, in this case, an opposing or contrasting argument. Likewise, in the task of preaching, many preachers proclaim the message from only one theological or denominational viewpoint. Using an argument of silence, we hope that no one listening out there will challenge our views of Scripture, theological presuppositions, or ministry philosophies. However, it is only when we truly acknowledge and wrestle with the other side of the argument that we begin to answer their questions, demonstrate cultural sensitivity and intelligence, and most significantly embrace them.

As mentioned earlier, to embrace our varied listeners means that we take into account their point of view, their interpretation, their theology, their very existence. In preaching a topical sermon series called "What Do I Believe?," I led the church in considering a number of theological topics that commonly divide Christians, such as predestination/election, environmental concerns, baptism, women's roles in ministry, and a few others. In each sermon, I presented both or multiple sides of the argument, with scriptural support for each. I challenged the congregation to follow the example of the Berean Christians in Acts 17:10–15 to test their beliefs according to the teachings of Scripture. To my surprise, the congregation was divided on all the theological topics addressed in the series; based on this experience, some surprisingly switched their belief to the other perspective. At the end of the sermon series, several congregants thanked me for taking the time to explain and show them the other side of the argument.

In much preaching today, denomination-centric language is employed, which puts those who disagree with the majority view on the defensive. To embrace our listeners well means that we are able to see beyond their "flawed" theological perspective and show care for them as individuals and humans. If I can be blunt, sometimes we place those who disagree with us in the inhuman category. For instance, pastors are publicly chided on social media by other pastors who hold differing points of view, particularly regarding nonessential issues. Embracing all listeners is the type of unity that Paul suggests in Ephesians 4. Unity encourages us to avoid us-versus-them language. It brings a sense of balance to our preaching rather than simply steamrolling our listeners with our denomination's doctrinal positions as being the only valid expression of Christianity.

Content

What is the content of the sermons within our denomination? On what themes, Bible books, doctrines, visions, and so forth does our particular denomination focus its messages? How do preachers in our denomination (or nondenominational church) plan their preaching series? Perhaps, in your denomination, a sermonic goal is to expound on the congregational vision. For instance, as Charles Bugg recounts, "Baptist preachers tend to be pragmatic in their preaching, often tying their preaching to a 'vision' for their church."[67] In other denominations, sermons are heavily geared toward reminding listeners of their theological positions and doctrinal beliefs by way of homiletical blueprints, such as law-versus-gospel preaching among Lutherans or the fallen-condition focus in Reformed/Presbyterian circles.[68] Some Protestant traditions utilize the weekly sermon to stir the pot each Sunday for serving the needy as Christ's hands and feet or to share the good news of Jesus Christ with one's neighborhood, friends, and family. The key is providing a balanced diet in our sermonic entrées. As Anthony Robinson bemoans, "We have forgotten how to be theological, and not even noticed that our sermons are by and large anthropological, . . . less about God and what God has done and is doing, and endlessly about us, about who we are, and what we have done or might possibly consider doing."[69]

How does cultural intelligence inform our sermon content? Scott M. Gibson states, "Too many preachers have their needs, their concerns, their pet theological positions, and their darling texts to promote or emphasize when they choose texts for preaching."[70] Some preachers might object by asking: "What's wrong with my text selection?" Do not misunderstand me: all Scripture is worthy of being preached. As Paul rightly explains in 2 Timothy 3:16–17, "All Scripture is God-breathed and is useful for teaching, rebuking, correcting and training in righteousness, so that the servant of God may be thoroughly equipped for every good work." Yet at times our preaching is more self-interested than maturity-oriented. Remember, we have only a set number of years with our congregation. Some denominations like the United Methodist Church have pastoral rotations, where preachers serve one congregation for a select number of years. How can we mature our listeners in the time that we have with them?

Regardless of our denominational affiliation, here are two reflections about sermon content. First, could we be more balanced in our preaching with respect to using texts from both the Old and New Testaments? Michael Horton observes that "our Christian growth depends on a lifetime of such sermons, and we need the full counsel of God's Word to help us grow and mature in our obedience to Christ."[71] You may agree that the New Testament is preached with much more urgency than the Old. Quickly take an inventory of your sermon text selections over the last year or two. The unintended consequence may be that our listeners believe the Old Testament has little to say about their lives as twenty-first-century Christians.

Second, can we be more intentional about prayerfully discerning what our congregations need to hear in order to mature in Christ over the next year, three years, five years, and so on?[72] Driving home doctrinal truths is a focal point of our ministry calling, but such didactic coaching must be coupled with the ability to embrace suffering, sharing the gospel, and other Christian service. Like so many congregations, churches corner the pastor for feeding and nourishment without honoring deep inklings to exercise their faith in the real world. Preaching with cultural intelligence involves knowing our flock and preaching in a balanced fashion that promotes maturity for all faith levels.

Trust

Last, how do we gain the trust of our listeners with respect to denominational matters? Trust is hard to come by in our society. Mark Meynell writes in *A Wilderness of Mirrors: Trusting Again in a Cynical World*, "Because power has been so abused so appallingly, we must now be suspicious of *any* who wield it. Nothing can ever be taken at face value."[73] In some denominations, pastors are still bestowed with substantial power. Julius Kim highlights the importance of a preacher's character for the listeners: "If the speaker is considered credible and the speaking environment is considered safe, the levels of attention and retention in the hearers increase. Conversely, if the hearers perceive the speaker to be arrogant, untrustworthy, or insincere, it will be a long thirty minutes for both parties."[74]

Congregations today are in dire need of positive examples of unity across denominations and traditions. How are we doing with respect to forging ministry partnerships with various churches in our community, especially interdenominational relationships? One approach to gauge denominational territorialism is whether we can share the pulpit with preachers from other traditions. Are preachers hearing from the voices of those who possess a different view of baptism, church polity, the handling of sacraments, and other nonessential theological strands? Or are we too insecure to invite preachers who hold a different theology and might corrupt "my" flock?

Another method to earn trust is to speak favorably of other denominations or at least minimize our disparaging comments about them. Preachers can rapidly lose the trust of listeners when they belittle the previous denominations of their listeners or the current denominations of listeners' loved ones. Over the years, I have heard numerous sermons where preachers have made offhand jokes and comments about other denominations, their beliefs, and their practices. These haphazard comments damage our pastoral reputation and even unintentionally escort some congregants out the door.

Third, we gain a wider hearing by confessing that some nonessential truths are, in fact, nonessential and up for debate because Scripture is inconclusive. In other words, it is permissible and perhaps necessary to admit, "I am not absolutely certain about this interpretation." In *No Perfect People Allowed*, John Burke says, "Creating a culture where questions and doubts can find voice is not only healthy, it's thoroughly biblical."[75] In the pulpit, let us nurture trust among the hearers by safeguarding at all costs the unity in Christ that Paul pursues for all Christians in Ephesians 4:1–6.

Conclusion

Denominational differences are inevitable, and they are not going to go away. We joined a particular denomination because we affirm most, if not all, of its beliefs and practices. Some of us have been raised in a specific denomination. We've decided to weather the storms and stay the course. Differences in interpretation are notable, and church history reminds us that many have given their lives on account of these theological issues. While denominational and theological differences matter, cultural intelligence is gained by having an attitude of unity over disunity. How can we preach in such a way that our varied denominational listeners experience oneness in Christ rather than feel like second-class citizens? How can we be respectful of our denomination's beliefs and practices and yet make room for others? *Yes, sin is still sin!* Erwin Lutzer observes this about the human condition:

> Prejudice dies hard. We've all met people who would never give up cherished doctrines even if they became convinced that such teachings were unscriptural. "I was raised a [choose one] Catholic, Anglican, Presbyterian, Baptist, Calvinist, or whatever, and I will die one!"
>
> The hidden assumption is "I'm not open to rethinking what I believe. Whether my beliefs are true or not is not of primary importance. I like what is familiar; I don't want to deny my upbringing. I'm comfortable, so leave me alone."[76]

Denominational ties and identity do not die hard. Someone once put this denominational cleaving into this humorous rhyme: "I was Baptist born. I was Baptist bred. And when I die, I'll be Baptist dead."[77] To have this myopic tunnel vision as a preacher can lead to divisions even in a denominational church setting where we believe everyone thinks like us. Cultural intelligence with regard to denominations seeks unity at all costs so that preachers might not add to the partitions that so often have marred Christianity. In the next chapter, our conversation on unity will shift to what preaching with cultural intelligence looks like regarding ethnicity.

6

Preaching and Ethnicities

Popular terms like "postracial America" presume that we, as Americans, have overcome racial hostilities and now live in a society of racial parity. Quite the contrary, racial and ethnic divides linger on across America. Even in our preaching ministry, we are either perpetuating prejudice with our silence or making progress toward peace, healing, and reconciliation in our churches. Many evangelical Christian leaders have been sluggish in exhibiting the ministry of reconciliation across racial and ethnic lines. As culturally intelligent preachers, it is paramount that we lead the charge in helping our congregations embrace and celebrate ethnic and cultural differences.

In this chapter I am purposefully writing from the perspective of ethnic minorities (in my case, Korean American) and will concentrate on strengthening cultural intelligence for all but, in particular, for white, European American preachers. By this, I am by no means implying that *only* Caucasians require greater cultural intelligence in understanding ethnic minority congregants. Nor am I arguing that all ethnic minorities share identical experiences of discrimination while living in the dominant culture. However, since the majority of this book's readership will be preachers from the dominant culture, my hope is to guide white preachers to be more informed about ethnic minority listeners and preach to all with cultural intelligence.

The elephant in the room is that, to varying degrees and on various occasions, *all* humans struggle with racist, prejudiced, and ethnocentric thinking. As David Anderson observes, "Racism is not reserved for one color or culture of people. The sin of racism is an equal opportunity employer."[1] You may object to this hypothesis, but if you think back to all of your encounters with people from a different ethnic background, my assumption is that we have found ourselves thinking a range of sinful thoughts including superiority, pride, hatred, animosity, deprecation, loathing, anger, suspicion, misgivings, and a host of other pejorative thoughts toward those of a different ethnic or racial group.[2] We can be honest with ourselves about how we view or omit consideration of other races and ethnicities in the task of preaching. Unspoken challenges abound when we think about preaching to unfamiliar people.[3] Our cultural ignorance can brood feelings of trepidation, awkwardness, and perhaps even distrust. However, increasing our cultural intelligence will calm some fears and concerns when communicating across ethnic differences.

Ethnicity versus Race

For this chapter, our nomenclature will be to use the term "ethnicity" whenever possible rather than "race." Here is the primary difference, as explained by Kenneth Mathews and M. Sydney Park: "'Race' and 'ethnic' are often used as synonyms, but each has a different nuance. 'Race' refers to inherited physical traits that characterize peoples, such as facial features and skin color. On the other hand, the term 'ethnic' (Greek, *ethnos*) identifies an affiliated 'people group' who share history, traditions, and culture, such as familial descent, language, and religious and social customs."[4] Sociologically, ethnic groups represent "groups set apart from others because of their national origin or distinctive cultural patterns."[5] Although I will mention broader racial classifications such as African Americans, Hispanic Americans, and Asian Americans throughout the chapter, we will try to think in terms of specific ethnic groups (e.g., Haitian Americans, Puerto Rican Americans, and Chinese Americans) when we consider preaching to the people in our church. All people of the same race are not culturally monolithic. This is the fundamental problem with the social construct of race that enabled the US government to categorize Others into five neat racial classifications in the US Census based on their physical features and the color of their skin (e.g., white, black, Asian/Pacific, Native American, and Hispanic).[6]

Ethnicity versus Culture

At the same time, ethnicity is also markedly different from culture. How are they different? "Ethnicity" refers to a people group, while "culture" as we have defined it is *the way of living, way of thinking, and way of behaving* within the parameter of cultural norms in the society in which one resides.

Here is a common example of this distinction. You may encounter a visitor at church who on the surface looks to be Chinese. Let's say that he is Chinese. Being Chinese is his ethnic heritage. However, that same person may actually have grown up in Latin America. His ethnically Chinese parents immigrated to Colombia when he was nine years old. He and his family members speak fluent Spanish in the home. Therefore, the first language of your new visitor is Spanish, not Chinese. He is ethnically Chinese but culturally Colombian. Furthermore, some of your Asian, Latino, or African congregants who are ethnically Japanese, Cuban, or Ghanaian may actually be culturally American, Canadian, or Australian, making these persons Japanese American, Cuban Canadian, and Ghanaian Australian. Be careful not to automatically equate ethnicity with culture. They are often distinct elements in a person's life in Western societies.

Ethnocentrism

The primary sociological concept undergirding our discussion regards the concept of ethnocentrism. By dissecting this word, it becomes clear that ethnocentrism is the belief that one's ethnicity is the center of the universe, the most important, and thus ethnocentrists believe that all other ethnic groups are inferior to their own ethnic group. When we are ethnocentric, we look down on others and expect them to become just like us (i.e., forced assimilation). Ethnocentrism becomes exacerbated whenever there is a clear majority of one ethnicity or race in a church context. The assumption is that Others will simply conform and assimilate to the traditions and cultures of the dominant group. Little or no effort is made by members of the dominant group to familiarize themselves with the cultures of the Others.

Racial and ethnic demographics have been changing rapidly in the United States. The National Center for Education Statistics states that in US public schools, for the first time, nonmajority students represent more than 50 percent of students in the classroom due to the increase of Latino and Asian American populations.[7] Projections for future demographic shifts are even more staggering. The US Census Bureau reports that "by 2044, more than half of all Americans are projected to belong to a minority group (any group other than non-Hispanic White alone)."[8] Demographic shifts in public education reveal changing demographics in our neighborhoods, which raises the question: Are preachers willing to make necessary adjustments to preach across cultures? To cultivate cultural intelligence in our congregations, the onus is formidably on the preacher to lead the charge in authorizing and shaping a church culture that embraces all ethnicities and cultures.[9] How will we respond to preexistent or perhaps budding racial and ethnic diversity in our preaching ministry?

Let's begin to explore the topic of ethnicity by working through the three stages of the Homiletical Template.

Stage 1: Follow Your HABIT

Scripture Text
Acts 15:1–21

Historical, Grammatical, and Literary Context

Historical Context

Our Scripture passage comes from Acts 15:1–21, known as the Jerusalem Council. In many ways, this text represents a pivotal moment in the history of the early church relating to the themes of ethnicity and culture. The question is raised about whether Gentile believers must adhere to certain requirements of the Old Testament laws of Moses.[10] According to F. F. Bruce, "The Council of Jerusalem is an event to which Luke attaches the highest importance; it is as epoch-making, in his eyes, as the conversion of Paul or the preaching of the gospel to Cornelius and his household."[11] The primary issue at hand pertained to the Jewish rite of circumcision. Division occurs between Paul and Barnabas and these men of Judea who instill this belief in Acts 15:1: "Unless you are circumcised, according to the custom taught by Moses, you cannot be saved." Did Gentile Christians need to keep the Mosaic law by being circumcised (i.e., become religiously and culturally Jewish) in order to become saved members of God's family? Or was it that the "church's captivity to Jewish culture had to be reconsidered"?[12] The remaining verses in this section narrate the conflict and resolution.

Grammatical Issues

A couple of grammatical issues are worth mentioning here. First, David Williams highlights the significance of Luke's use of a perfect participle to describe who these believers were who required circumcision of the Gentiles. Williams maintains, "They were believers, where the perfect participle is intended perhaps to emphasize the reality of their faith (see disc[ussion] on

14:23), that is, they were fully convinced that Jesus was the Messiah, though they thought of him still as the king of Israel from whose kingdom the Gentiles would be excluded unless they accepted its law (cf. 1:6)."[13] Studying who those of the "party of the Pharisees" (15:5) were with greater cultural depth is important because it enables us to appreciate believers who come from different cultural and theological perspectives. In every congregation, some parishioners hold conflicting views on cultural and theological matters, and we want to become acquainted with their rationales and practices.

Second, another worthwhile sentence to explore further is Peter's statement in verse 9: "He did not discriminate between us and them, for he purified their hearts by faith," which is the central lesson that Peter learned from God in his vision in Acts 10. What does it mean for this leadership council to comprehend that God makes no distinctions between Jewish and Gentile believers? How do we make ethnic, cultural, and personal distinctions in the body of Christ? As we come to greater awareness of what these distinctions are in this text, we will find more talking points to address in the sermon. The reality is that preachers also make ethnic and cultural distinctions.

Literary Study

The literary genre of the account in Acts 15:1–21 "is a *historical narrative* that includes *direct speech*" and "a *quotation* from the Old Testament (vv. 15–18)" that James employs from Amos 9:11–12.[14] Luke records Peter's speech in verses 7–11 and later presents James's speech in verses 13–21. With respect to this historical narrative, Eckhard Schnabel helpfully points out: "The Apostles' Council in Jerusalem (15:1–33) completes Luke's shift from his focus on Peter's mission (chs. 1–12) to Paul's mission (chs. 13–14; 16–20)."[15] In the first half of Acts, Luke reiterates in narrative form (especially in Acts 10–11) the dramatic shift in Peter's realization of God's plan to include Gentiles in the kingdom of God.

The remaining chapters in Acts illustrate Paul and Barnabas's desire to champion Peter's cause by proclaiming salvation through faith in Christ Jesus to the Gentile world. Paul and Barnabas travel to various Gentile cities and cultures, where their cultural intelligence for Jewish and Gentile contexts is put to the test. Stephen Um and Justin Buzzard write, "Note Paul's hope-reinforcing and idolatry-challenging method of restabilizing a city's story line with a Jewish audience in Antioch of Pisidia (Acts 13), a Gentile audience in Lystra (Acts 14), a predominantly Gentile audience in Philippi (Acts 16), and a mixed audience in Thessalonica (Acts 17), Athens (Acts 17), Corinth (Acts 18), Ephesus (Acts 19), and Jerusalem (Acts 21)."[16] While historical narrative is descriptive and not always meant to be prescriptive, our cultural knowledge of Jewish laws and the Pharisees' arguments to observe these laws enlarges as we take in each development of the narrative. To formulate a more holistic perspective of this narrative, we might venture into the epistles in Galatians 2, where Paul makes reference to Peter's visit to Antioch and his emphasis on Gentiles adopting Jewish practices with respect to food.[17]

Author's Cultural Context

In Luke's cultural context, two primary practices merit discussion from this passage. The first is the cultural and religious practice of circumcision. The immediate concern up for debate in this council regards the process by which one comes to be saved.[18] For certain Jewish Christians, especially from Judea, the ethnic and religious tradition was steeped in total surrender to the Torah, which included circumcision as a prerequisite for salvation.[19] In contrast, Peter, Paul, Barnabas, and James articulate the requirements of faith and belief in Jesus Christ and the Lord's grace that one is saved in Acts 15:9 and 11. How do congregations in the twenty-first century make analogous versions of salvific requirements based on ethnicity, culture, or theology? Even today, it is not uncommon for Christians to espouse certain rubrics that test and prove whether a person is truly saved according to their own perspective.

As already mentioned, ethnocentrism is a dominant belief in this text regarding the cultural practices of the Jewish believers. Throughout the narrative, Jewish Christians demand circumcision for Gentiles, but we also clearly witness ethnocentrism toward the end of the passage, in verses 20 and 21. In these latter verses, James, the half brother of Jesus and a leader in the church, calls for ethnic purity among Gentiles to adhere to culturally bound stipulations regarding food. Specifically, William Willimon observes:

> Out of care for the sensibilities of Jewish Christians (a major concern of Gal. 2:11–21), Gentile Christians are asked to observe four things: eat nothing sacrificed to pagan gods, abstain from incestuous marriages, eat no meat of strangled animals, abstain from partaking of blood (15:20–21). Leviticus 17–18 applies these rules to both Jews and the aliens who reside within Israel. James seems to regard these Gentiles as analogous to "strangers" in the Hebrew Scriptures. Thus, Gentile Christians are compelled to observe the minimum requirements that had been set for strangers wanting to enjoy fellowship with conscientious Jews. At the table of the Lord, we Gentiles continue to be the guests of a Jewish host.[20]

Connecting with Luke's cultural context, think about your own ethnic context. List several ways that your congregation expects acquiescence of Others to accommodate your own culture's rituals. This text will naturally concentrate on ethnic food practices, which connect so well with many, if not all, of the ethnic groups represented in your local church. Food is important across all cultures. However, as you explore your congregation more broadly, other cultural forms of ethnocentrism will emerge.

Big Idea of the Text

Subject: What is demonstrated in Luke's account of the Council at Jerusalem regarding the disagreement on whether Gentiles need to be circumcised for salvation?

Complement: God makes no distinction among persons, and salvation is by faith through belief in Jesus Christ.

Exegetical Idea: Luke's account of the Council at Jerusalem regarding the disagreement on whether Gentiles need to be circumcised for salvation demonstrates that God makes no distinction among persons, and salvation is by faith through belief in Jesus Christ.

Homiletical Idea: Salvation is not based on cultural practices, but based on faith in the Christ in whom we believe.

Interpret in Your Context

Assumptions

Due to our ethnocentrism, the natural inclination of every person is to expect the Other to follow our cultural practices. Just as the Jewish Christians sought the enforcement of circumcision as the rite of passage for Gentiles to become like them first in order to be saved, we may have our own nonnegotiables that determine who are truly insiders and outsiders. Interpreting this passage in our own context informs our historical consciousness in light of the historic experiences of Others in American society, a scene that correlates with the church as well.

I once spoke at a men's retreat in northern California. Being an Asian American, my race naturally sparked conversation regarding cultural differences between Anglo Americans and Asians—in this case, what this individual thought of Japanese businessmen. A white member of the church approached me and expressed his cultural distaste on coming back from a recent business trip to Japan. He initiated our talk with this striking question: "Why can't *you people* make decisions?" "Excuse me," I thought to myself. He proceeded, "I just spent several days with Japanese businessmen, and none of them could make a decision on anything. All they did was stare at me. You people can't make up your mind." His first assumption was that I was ethnically and culturally Japanese. His second assumption was that everyone should make decisions like him—a white, male businessman—to study the facts, assess the situation, and decide right away. Perhaps for these Japanese clients, other factors were involved in the decision-making process that the American businessman could not understand because both sides were coming from their own cultural perspectives.

Likewise, our Scripture text presents a similar obstacle because assumptions are made only from one culture's vantage point. While James recognizes that salvation for Jews and Gentiles alike is by faith alone, the food stipulations in verses 20 and 21 require the Gentiles to alter their ethnic and cultural practices as a necessary condition to join in table fellowship with the Jewish believers. It would have been unthinkable for the Jewish Christians to disregard food laws in the Torah to eat with the Gentiles and taste their impure cuisine. A fundamental lesson in cultural intelligence across ethnic groups is to release one's grip on ethnocentric thinking. Of course, this is much more difficult to do in reality, but the culturally intelligent preacher will increasingly take time to consider the other person's ethnic and cultural perspective and ask questions as needed.

Conflicts

The tension when ministering and preaching cross-culturally is that we are constantly dealing with historic and systemic issues that can create sizable barricades between members of different ethnic groups. A minority culture is not simply determined by numeric disparity in being outnumbered by the dominant society. Richard Schaefer explains, "Members of a minority experience unequal treatment and have less power over their lives than members of a dominant group have over theirs. Social inequality may be created or maintained by prejudice, discrimination, segregation, or even extermination. . . . When a group is the object of long-term prejudice and discrimination, the feeling of 'us versus them' can and often does become extremely intense."[21]

With a long history of segregation and even deportation, ethnic minorities in American society on a consistent basis feel as though they need to fight for dignity, respect, and equality. Many minorities are hoping for acceptance from members of the majority culture. Others seek the ability to have ideas implemented and receive decision-making rights by the dominant culture. The default position is that the dominant culture gets its way because of their upper hand numerically and concurrent hegemony. The same types of ideologies permeate our churches that perpetuate conflict between majority and minority groups. When it comes to matters nonessential for salvation, our cultural intelligence enables us to build a bridge not only to see life through the eyes of the Others but also to enrich our congregations by incorporating ethnic and cultural practices into our church's culture.

Think about a "minority" person in your congregation. Is this person ignored, acknowledged, or valued? Do we introduce this person to others the same as we do by second nature for those who are like us? Are opportunities presented for this "minority" person to voice ideas, and are those contributions taken seriously in the church?[22] If you suspect that this person may not be resonating with your preaching, a major consideration would be to listen intently to this person's thoughts, opinions, and ideas that may differ from *your* ethnic and cultural background. Since so much of preaching involves connectivity, especially with ethnic minorities, the preacher's ability to notice, value, appreciate, respect, and encourage them will prove invaluable.

Questions

Many of the questions pertaining to the Scripture text have already been addressed in our discussions about ethnocentrism and circumcision. In summary and based on Acts 15, Soong-Chan Rah asks tough and direct questions to majority group members: "How do we encourage all cultures to perceive themselves as bringing a legitimate voice emerging out of their own experience and history? How can the church replicate the Jerusalem Council two thousand years later so that the church may be freed from Western, white cultural captivity in the same way it was freed from Jewish cultural captivity two thousand years ago?"[23] Depending on our ethnic context, we may want to probe further the ways in which our congregation promotes or experiences cultural captivity and find opportunities for a healthy dialogue across ethnic boundaries. Part of our responsibility will be to persuade members of the dominant culture that having this conversation of appreciating and empowering "ethnic minority" persons is important and even necessary in the body of Christ. This Scripture text will naturally spawn queries about your church's leadership structure, decision-making processes, cultural values, rituals, and more.[24]

Theological Presuppositions

The overarching but perhaps unnamed theological topic regarding ethnic minority persons in your congregation is the *imago Dei*. What does it mean to be made in the image of God? Why does it seem that in certain Christian contexts some ethnic groups are created more in line with God's image than others? Fifty years removed from the civil rights movement in America, we are still confronted by the hideous attitude that not all lives are equally valuable.

Daniel Carroll presents three common views regarding the image of God. He summarizes, "Each one in its own way underscores the particular value of all persons: what they inherently are, their potential relationship with the Creator, and their capacity and privilege as rulers. Everyone is made in God's image and therefore has a singular standing before God and in the world."[25] Whichever definition of *imago Dei* the preacher espouses, the implication is that we will promote the value of all persons based on our bearing the image of our common Creator, regardless of one's ethnic heritage, nationality, race, skin color, language, and other differences that typically divide people groups.

For many ethnic minorities, the recurrence of denigration and rejection based on affiliation with one's ethnic group conjures up innate questions of self-worth. While not overtly stated, ethnic minorities in the United States may wonder why God chose to create them as nonwhite persons, who seem to be "God's gold standard." Bruce Milne comments, "The 'different' stranger is commonly a threat to be resisted rather than a friend to be embraced."[26] This should not be so in the body of Christ. Ultimately, one of our responsibilities as preachers, especially in ethnically diverse church contexts, is to befriend the Other and instill the corporate value of self-love and celebration of all ethnicities and cultures. We remember that in all situations we befriend the Other, but in certain situations we recognize our Otherness as well.[27] No person is invariably a majority-culture person in every single cultural context. Therefore, a target goal in this chapter is to learn how to appreciate and celebrate ethnicity in our proclamation.

Stage 2: Build the BRIDGE

Beliefs

The Cultural Intelligence Center shares seven common cultural beliefs or value orientations that can cause tension in any institution or organization and even in our churches: (1) individualism versus collectivism; (2) low power distance versus high power distance; (3) low uncertainty avoidance versus high uncertainty avoidance; (4) cooperative versus competitive; (5) short-term time orientation versus long-term time orientation; (6) low context communication versus high context communication; and (7) doing versus being.[28] Preachers can become easily frustrated with listeners who come from ethnic cultures that hold the opposite cultural belief system. Typically, members of Western cultures follow more closely to the first (or left) descriptor, whereas non-Western ethnic groups will lean toward the second (or right) characteristic. However, we must remember that there are always exceptions to the rule.

Due to limited space, I am unable to unpack each of these categories. However, let's spend a few moments on differentiating *doing* cultures versus *being* cultures. In North American congregations led by majority-culture pastors, *doing* ministry and being actively involved in quantifiable programs and services are preferable to immeasurable ministry activities such as building relationships. Members of *being* cultures may find it natural and reasonable to meet with the pastor for hours on end, while doing-oriented pastors are happy to meet for a limited period of time for the purpose of future ministry productivity (i.e., to ascertain how this person will serve the church). For instance, a pastor from Kenya may visit a parishioner for several hours of conversation: to leave early would be an insult to his hosts. For a Euro-American pastor, having coffee for an hour at Starbucks is his expectation, and his packed schedule does not permit any additional time. At the end of the conversation, the Kenyan relationship is built up without concrete ministry plans developed, whereas the Euro-American pastor may hope that his conversation will lead to increased ministry service for the person in whom he has invested this time. Thus people from doing cultures and being cultures frequently misunderstand each other.

At first glance it should be apparent that these and other cultural differences warrant understanding and sensitivity as we minister and preach across ethnic groups. Our homiletical tendency is to communicate from our cultural perspective alone (i.e., ethnocentrism). What would it look like in our preaching to acknowledge Others' cultural perspectives and then even validate the other perspective as being both legitimate and beneficial? Going back to Acts 15, what parallels do we see in today's cultural beliefs with the Jewish/Gentile debate over circumcision and food requirements? Any of the seven cultural beliefs above could be highlighted in the sermon to make connections with the author's cultural context. Perhaps the most immediate of concerns would be the category of low-power and high-power distance: Who ultimately gets to make the final decision, and why? Here the expectation is that if the Gentiles want to share a meal together with Jewish Christians, they are required to obey the four Jewish food stipulations. In strategic places in the sermon, the culturally intelligent preacher would reflect on the various cultural beliefs being circulated among congregants from the different ethnic backgrounds represented.

Rituals

A dominant ritual that permeates American Christianity is Western evangelicalism. Michael Emerson and Christian Smith accentuate the tight-knit relationship between American and evangelical values: "Many American values—freedom, individualism, independence, equality of opportunity, privacy, and the like—derive largely from the confluence of evangelical Protestant Christianity and Enlightenment philosophy, within the context of conditions encountered in the new world."[29] As an evangelical Christian, I am the beneficiary of a rich Protestant legacy dating back to the Protestant Reformation. I ascribe to the Five Solas of the Reformers: Sola scriptura, Sola fide, Sola gratia, Solus Christus, and Soli Deo gloria. In addition, I hold to a Reformed confession of faith. In short, I am a Western evangelical.

However, a theological/cultural difference with American evangelicalism for various ethnic groups (especially immigrants and those with strong ties to their ethnic heritage) pertains to awareness and understanding of indigenous theologies, such as black theologies, Asian theologies, and liberation theologies. The common denominator across non-Western theologies is the experience of pain, suffering, and oppression from living as minorities in a majority society. For Western evangelicals, non-Western theologies are immediately discarded as being heretical and antithetical to the ideals of the true Christian faith (i.e., Western evangelicalism). Why are we so afraid to engage the Other? Little attempt has been made by evangelicals to understand why these theologies emerged and persist.[30]

Yet it is in the purview of every culturally intelligent preacher to unmask and sympathize with our listeners who have experienced deep-seated wounds as minority group members and to provide avenues for authentic healing and reconciliation, especially with injuries from the dominant culture. While I acknowledge that real theological differences exist and elements of non-Western theologies are biblically misaligned, our cultural intelligence engages in active listening to place ourselves in the shoes of those who have encountered discrimination and affliction on account of their race and ethnicity and to identify with their pain.

In their sermons, for example, many Korean preachers emphasize "the national and collective experience of suffering, oppression, and injustice" at the hands of cultural oppressors, especially from neighboring China and Japan.[31] Similarly, in African American preaching, sermons commonly integrate the themes of slavery, suffering, and hope for black Americans, because these experiences are ubiquitous among African American Christians.[32] Likewise, Hispanic American listeners resonate with "biblical themes that speak to the issues of marginalization, poverty, and liberation" in light of the social and economic conditions of the Hispanic American people.[33] Before Jesus preached and instructed the people to win their souls, oftentimes he met the people where they were and assisted them with their immediate needs first. Remember the ten lepers, the woman at the well, blind Bartimaeus, and the woman suffering from bleeding? A key ingredient in our sermon preparation can be learning more about non-Western theologies and how they are similar and divergent from the tenets of Western evangelicalism.

Idols

Although some expressions of idolatry are omnipresent in every ethnic group—as named by the apostle Paul in Colossians 3:5, "sexual immorality, impurity, lust, evil desires and greed"—we recognize that there are more ethnic-specific types of idols.[34] We can probably list a number of idols that are commonplace, especially in Western cultures: materialism, homes, cars, sex, control, comfort, food, games, gadgets, beauty, children, sports, education, occupations, titles, equality, intoxication, and so on. However, certain ethnic groups tend to give prominence to some idols more than others. Dwell on your congregation and the different ethnic groups it includes. Timothy Keller and Katherine Leary Alsdorf observe, "While we are usually blind to our own idols, it is not very hard to see them in others, and to see how others' counterfeit gods fill them with anxiety, anger, and discouragement."[35]

What do your listeners idolize? Put another way, what do your listeners seem to love more than they love God? One way to determine what is an idol for an ethnic group (not your own) is to answer this basic question: Why do they seem to care so much about *that*? While some overlap exists, different ethnic groups focus on different spheres of life primarily based on their marginalized experience of living in American society. For instance, many Asian ethnic groups in America (especially more recent immigrants) have created idols out of the things of life that might, in their minds, mitigate discrimination against Asians as being inferior people through educating their children at Ivy League universities or encouraging white-collar careers in medicine, law, engineering, or business. Indeed, some of this idolatry has spilled over from the cultural ideologies in one's home country, such as Confucianism, which highly emphasizes education and social standing based on earned degrees, particularly in East Asian countries like China, Japan, and South Korea. African American and Hispanic American ethnic groups will make idols out of these and other life constructs with the hope of improving their perception and social standing in the eyes of the dominant culture.

As we discern what cultural idols consume our listeners from other ethnic groups, this process naturally invites reflection on our cultural idols. Rodger Woodworth writes, "Only when we allow the relationship with another culture to honestly critique our cultural expressions of faith can we see our prejudices. We need our brothers and sisters from across the cultural divide to help us identify potential idols. Especially for us Eurocentric Christians, the danger is to put our cultural identity above our Christian beliefs without even knowing it."[36] Cultural idols for ethnic groups vary, but many of these idols are shared across the ethnic spectrum. Asking questions and listening to others will enhance our ability to establish which idols are most captivating and in due course have us reveal and extinguish these cultural idols.

Dreams

While, no doubt, the spiritual dreams and possible selves of all Christians, regardless of ethnicity, is to become a disciple who makes disciples, as Jesus commands in Matthew 28:18–20, lingering obstacles on earth stymie this pathway to discipleship. Every race and ethnic group possesses its own set of dreams that beget hope to make a difference in the world. And yet these dreams are often snagged by elements out of their control. In ethnic minority circles, a basic and yet fundamental dream is to simply become visible. Ralph Ellison wrote about this struggle in the middle of the twentieth century in his award-winning book *The Invisible Man*. The prologue begins with these indelible words: "I am an invisible man. . . . I am invisible, understand, simply because people refuse to see me. . . . When they approach me they see only my surroundings, themselves, or figments of their imagination—indeed, everything and anything except me."[37] Ellison's story about the black man's experience in America takes root in the lives of all ethnic minorities in the United States, even today.

Familiar experiences of invisibility include being ignored, being cut off in line, not being greeted or acknowledged, not being asked to speak up and express one's opinions, experiencing a glass ceiling at work, "an invisible but very real, barrier for even qualified women and people of color to move upward into managerial ranks (especially upper management) within both private and public institutions,"[38] and even in the church—these are symptoms of invisibility. Most, if not all, of your ethnic minority congregants have already experienced and still experience gradations of being unseen.

Likewise, in Acts 15 the Gentiles represent invisible persons whose cultures and ways of living are ignored by some Jewish Christians. The Gentile believers were expected to become Jewish and to act like the majority in order to fit into this newly merged church's mold. I imagine that the early Gentile Christians felt much like ethnic minorities living today. Visibility has ministry implications that include and far exceed the task of preaching. How can we in the church validate and empower those who reside at the margins? Encourage invisible persons and make their presence known. In most cases, their cultural reserve will prevent them from jumping into the light. In many ethnic cultures, congregants remain silent until someone in authority asks them to share their thoughts. You, as the preacher, will need to take the onus to integrate them into new dimensions of church life. Many will not approach you first.

God

A corollary to ethnocentrism regards partiality and favoritism in the Bible. The ethnic minority person may be dubious about God's impartiality as expressed in Acts 15, because it seems that God still shows favoritism to certain types of people (such as Jewish Christians who maintain their Jewish food rituals or white Americans who wield societal influence and power today). Living in American society, many ethnic minorities have the perception that God must favor whites on account of their hegemony. Another popular sentiment among people of color concerns the *imago Dei* and whether God made a mistake by creating nonwhite persons. Those categorized as have-nots question God's equity because minority persons are so commonly misunderstood, misrepresented, and left to fight "the system" in a highly racialized[39] culture marked by inequality. As mentioned, non-Western theologies are a direct response to the oppression and marginalization experienced by members of minority cultures. Non-Western theologies are directed less toward God and targeted more toward the societal powers that restrict freedom and power for minority groups. In our preaching, how can we respond positively to encourage a sensitive and yet affirmative view of God and ethnic differences?

Understanding the impartiality of God is complex. God's impartiality is reflected in how God is no respecter of persons. Caleb Colley writes, "God's impartiality does not mean that everyone will have exactly the same amount of money, exactly the same amount of influence, exactly the same number of children, or exactly the same number of years upon the Earth."[40] God blesses all people uniquely and differently. Remind your listeners of these blessings that transcend ethnicity and race. Yet the dual reality is that God is impartial but humans are not. We must deal with human sin and racial privilege, and more specifically the white privilege that exists in America. For instance, Mark Labberton writes, "Every person of color I know—and especially Blacks—have daily experiences that tell them their lives do not count as much as white ones do. As a white follower of Jesus, I cannot be blind to the fact that white privilege negatively shapes and defines the experience of being black."[41] How can those seated in places of power and privilege lift up those who cannot get off the ground?

Experiences

Cultural Assimilation Categories: C1, C2, and C3

Historically, the United States has required assimilation of all its citizens. That is, rather than embracing, celebrating, and retaining ethnic and cultural differences, new immigrants have always been expected to become "American" and jettison the language and customs of their ethnic/immigrant country in order to fuse themselves into the dominant culture.[42] Bryan Loritts articulates a helpful mode of thinking about the range of cultures within a single ethnic group through pop-culture references. Labeling these three cultures as C1, C2, and C3, Loritts explains the range of cultural diversity among African Americans and proposes that ethnicity be classified into three categories:

> C1, C2, and C3. . . . C1's are those who have assimilated into another culture, typically the majority culture. This is what we would call Carlton Banks from the television show "The Fresh Prince of Bel Air." He's a Black guy who is really White. In Acts 6, these are the Hellenists. On the other extreme are C3's. . . . Sticking with the acting theme, this is the actor and rapper Ice Cube. In Acts 6, these are the Hebrews. Finally, in the middle are C2's. These are people who are able to connect across different ethnicities and cultures. . . . This would be someone like the actor Denzel Washington. . . . The most effective multi-ethnic preachers are those who are C2's.[43]

In the United States, we can find parallel examples for all racial/ethnic groups. For instance, in the Asian American community, C3's are represented by Randall Park's character Louis Huang on the television sitcom *Fresh Off the Boat*, with a Chinese immigrant trying his best to help his family navigate their strange new American surroundings. C1's would be Hollywood actors like Ken Jeong, a medical doctor turned actor, who is completely Westernized in his cultural affinities and his speech. In some movies and shows, Jeong is so Americanized that he even speaks what sounds like a form of Ebonics. Finally, a C2 would be an actor like John Cho, who can play the role of the immigrant as well as the lead American character in a movie.

Our homiletical homework is to discover whether our congregants from a certain ethnic group are C1, C2, or C3. For C1 and C2 (Loritts's designation for the bicultural) listeners in our churches, our preaching ministry will require little adaptation because our listeners will be familiar with our use of cultural references, American customs and norms, and the range of expressions in the English language. However, the more C3 congregants we have in our congregation, the more we will want to be sensitive to their cultural and linguistic differences.

Liminality and Shame

Depending on where your listeners find themselves on the C1, C2, and C3 continuum, they will have internalized feelings of liminality and shame. When I ask white Americans to tell me about their ethnic heritage, the typical unabashed response is "I'm American. But I know that I have some German, English, and Italian in me." Most Anglo-Americans rarely think about their ethnic background unless they prescribe to a symbolic ethnicity where one chooses to celebrate some ethnic heritage through symbolic forms, such as observing national holidays like Saint Patrick's Day for those of Irish descent or eating ethnic foods like haggis for the Scottish.[44] However, being reminded by others that one is Irish or Scottish or different as a daily occurrence is not the norm for white Americans. For ethnic minorities, however, one's ethnicity is inescapable and regularly pointed out by those of the majority culture (who ask, "Where are you from?," hear "Chicago," yet persist, "No, where are you *really* from?"), which exacerbates feelings of in-betweenness, liminality, and shame. In contrast, white Americans are rarely asked where they are from in terms of ethnic background apart from their geographic location of where they grew up, unless they speak with a noticeably non-American accent. George Yancey writes,

> Many of my white friends have confessed to me that they have never considered racial issues before in their life. This is to be expected since it is very

possible for white Americans to go through life never having to deal with racial prejudice or discrimination in any meaningful way. They don't have to deal with these issues unless they choose to do so. Racial minorities, however, must not only often confront the hatred and bias of whites, but they must often contend with situations where those who put them down also have power over them.[45]

Living in New England on Boston's North Shore, I internalize feelings of shame regularly when I walk into stores and restaurants where I am the only Asian person. Sadly, all eyeballs turn to stare at me, and this makes me feel unwelcome.

Noel Castellanos puts words to the common ethnic minority feeling of liminality or in-betweenness, even as a third-generation Mexican American: "I often felt like a piñata torn right down the middle by a kid desperate for his candy. I was neither Mexican enough nor *Americano* (from the US) enough, depending on where I was or who I was with. I was a *Pocho* (Mexican American) through and through. . . . And living and existing between these worlds often created conflict in my soul."[46]

Cultural intelligence with respect to ethnicity and preaching involves recognition of liminality and shame among ethnic listeners. Ethnic minority listeners question their ethnic or racial identity regularly as they try to make sense of who they are as Others. Members of the dominant culture would be well served to realize that ethnic minorities live under a cloud of shame because we are continually reminded that we are different and do not blend in.

One of the greatest gifts we can give our listeners is to help release ethnic minorities from feelings of shame by simply welcoming them and not referring too quickly to their ethnic differences. While ethnicity will become a conversation piece at some point, and congregations will ask about differences in "greeting practices, music, foods, worship styles, comments, [and] expressions of welcome," among other topics,[47] suspending acknowledgment of a person's ethnicity or race will enable this individual to feel fully invested as a member of the church family—who just *happens to be* from a particular ethnic group. No longer are they seen as outsiders and treated as Others. Once they feel embraced initially, inevitably discussions about ethnic and cultural diversity will transpire over time. However, we do not want to always commence the relationship with Others by talking about ethnic and cultural differences. Begin by acknowledging them as people.

Another homiletical challenge for the twenty-first century will be navigating cultural sensitivity for racially/ethnically mixed persons. The ethnic and cultural diversity of America has concomitantly increased the number of racially mixed children. Gretchen Livingston presents the following statistics from the Pew Research Center: The percentages of those younger than one year of age who are identified as white-black, 36 percent; white-Asian, 24 percent; white-American Indian, 11 percent; and black-American Indian, 1 percent. Those eighteen years or older identified as white-black, 18 percent; white-Asian, 18 percent; white-American Indian, 25 percent; and black-American Indian, 5 percent.[48] Emerson and Smith comment, "The development of mixed-race relationships has an important pragmatic function. Ideally it exposes whites, typically unable to understand or see the depths of racialized society, to a United States seen through the eyes of those experiencing its injustices."[49]

Liminality and shame may be heightened for mixed-race persons as they navigate the cultures of each race/ethnicity. Biracial and multiracial persons may identify with or align themselves with one race more than the other. In conversations, as people open up about their biracial or multiracial experiences, we can encourage them to embrace the inherent traits in both or multiple cultures.

Stage 3: Speak Their DIALECT

Delivery

As we consider the topics of preaching, ethnicity, and delivery, our focus will be on the third triad (ethos, logos, and pathos) of Aristotelian rhetoric: pathos. Preaching in an ethnically diverse context requires pathos, from which we get the word "empathy." Empathy comes in many shapes and sizes. Let's view empathy through the lens of the psychology of race and ethnicity. When we begin to understand how one's race/ethnicity affects the mind, we will grow in empathetic communication. Jenell Williams Paris contends that in "racialized" societies like ours (as well as in the ancient Roman world), humans have learned to live within racial norms that expect conformity to the majority culture.[50] As such, Paris makes this helpful observation:

> Race affects our minds deeply. Though we are born without knowledge of race, we are socialized from birth to perceive the world in racial terms. Each of us is assigned a race, and accepts it as part of personal identity. We learn to perceive

others as belonging in race categories, and learn the stereotypes associated with the categories. In this way, race affects everyone, not just people who experience discrimination.[51]

Our race and ethnicity also impact the delivery and reception of the message. My preaching experience in these years as a seminary faculty member includes supplying pulpits in white, New England congregations. This too requires homiletical empathy. I must remind myself that my listeners read my name in a bulletin and see my face in the pulpit as they make internal evaluations about whether they're going to listen. I can't hide the fact that I am Korean American. Ethnic empathy as a preacher reminds me to think consciously what it means to hear and receive the sermon from the majority of my listeners' perspective (i.e., European Americans).

To disarm listeners and diffuse some of the unspoken assumptions they may have about me based on their cultural stereotypes, I have developed a helpful practice at the outset of my sermons. In the opening minutes, I state the obvious and mention that I am Asian American. Next, I explode any stereotypes that they may have about me and my people. Usually this means sharing a story about my ineptitude with math, which blasts the stereotype that all Asians are good at math. The congregation erupts in laughter, and we can now get down to business in expositing God's Word and seeing how it relates to our lives. I have tried preaching in similar contexts where I did not begin with this moment of ethnic empathy in the sermon. In such scenarios, I sense that many listeners are still hung up on the fact that I do not look like them, and they seem restless throughout the sermon.

Preaching in ethnically diverse churches will benefit from our ability to offer ethnic empathy. We, ethnic minorities, display our share of foibles in this regard as well. I still remember vividly the time when I asked an African American visitor to our church when we could play basketball together. Since I enjoyed playing basketball, I usually asked male congregants if they played as well. Although I always invited newcomers to play basketball with me, this African American visitor may have taken this question the wrong way, assuming that I asked the question on account of his race since the stereotype exists that all blacks are good at basketball.

How does my race or ethnicity impact the way my listeners hear me? How do the races and ethnicities of my listeners impact the way they hear me? What barriers exist between my ethnic/racial group and others? What would ethnic empathy look like in your congregation? Who in your church would benefit from increased ethnic empathy? Cultural intelligence invites empathy in all hues, especially ethnic and racial empathy.[52]

Illustrations

Addressing Racism

Stated bluntly, our human nature assumes the worst in other people, especially those from other ethnicities. Christena Cleveland observes that Christians continue to find ways to divide themselves and persist in this disunity.[53] Specifically, our modus operandi is to stereotype persons from other ethnic groups or races by "making an observation about members of another group. . . . It allows people outside the group to decide who the others are without having to consider who that individual person is. Ethnic jokes and nicknames develop from these stereotypes."[54] Jenell Williams Paris explains the historic stereotypes associated with three different racial groups: "'Whites' were viewed as civilized, intelligent, capable of self-government and self-restraint. 'Blacks' were seen as dependent, childlike, and lazy, thus needing slavery to provide order in their lives. 'Asians' were viewed as intelligent, similar to whites, but also crafty and devious."[55] With respect to various immigrants, "Protestants began to stereotype immigrants as poverty stricken, relying disproportionately on public assistance, and exhibiting gross immorality, violent crime, and drunkenness."[56] When we see a person of a particular ethnic group, what immediate prejudices ("beliefs or feelings, usually negative, held toward an individual or a group")[57] do we hold against that person? Again, ethnic minorities are not exempt from answering this question, because stereotypes undergird our thinking toward whites and other minority groups as well.

Jesus upset the cultural equilibrium of his day when he used a Samaritan as a positive example (protagonist) of what it means to be a bona fide disciple and a person whose actions please God. The story of the good Samaritan shocked Jewish listeners as they heard Jesus make a hero out of someone they thought to be their ethnic and religious inferior. When listening to sermons that reference ethnicity, I typically hear common stereotypes that are less than positive for ethnic minorities. For instance, the protagonist in stories is typically a white male. White characters are often portrayed as successful white-collar professionals; African Americans are characterized as blue-collar workers; Asian Americans are often referred to as owners of restaurants and dry cleaning businesses; and Hispanic Americans are stereotyped as "the help," manual laborers, and nannies. While some stereotypes may be true of some individuals in a particular ethnic group, what if we realigned our illustrations closer to what Jesus accomplished in the good Samaritan story, by making a protagonist out of someone the congregation doesn't expect—that is, someone from a completely different culture?

The topic of preaching and ethnicity warrants addressing the sin of racism head-on, even in our illustrative material. Rather than using direct imperatives like "You are a sinful racist, so confess and put an end to your racism," a more gracious and nuanced approach might be to employ illustrations from movies or magazine/journal articles that speak to the issue. For instance, the movie *Remember the Titans* looks at the issue of race in American society in a humorous but honest way through the cultural lens of high school football. Based on a true story of a high school football team in Virginia, Denzel Washington's character, Coach Herman Boone, takes over as the head coach of a high school team divided by black-and-white racial lines. The story line paints a portrait of racial stereotypes that exist in America and what can happen positively when the leader of any sport or organization overcomes those racial prejudices. Numerous scenes from this movie could be incorporated into the sermon when addressing the issues of ethnocentrism and racism.

A rather surprising example of racial reconciliation from magazine articles is found in the January 1971 edition of *Christianity Today*. Racial reconciliation comes in the form of a letter written to whites from the perspective of a black person. Here is an excerpt:

Dear White Person:

I, the black person, feel I know more about you because I had to. My will to survive forced me to learn about you. I was forced to learn your ways of doing things, forced to accept your concepts and values, and yet denied the right to share them. . . . Evaluate your life experiences and see how they may have given you your views of the black person. . . . If that happens, it will enable us to love and to live together and enjoy the blessing God intended us to share.

In response to this letter, a white evangelical woman wrote in the March 1971 edition of *Christianity Today*:

Dear Black Person:

For many years I was guilty of ignorance. . . . I did not know that black men were routinely but rudely questioned for just walking along the street, or that black homes were frequently invaded without benefit of warrant. . . . I admit my guilt. But more importantly, I have repented. . . . God forgive us. And please, Black Person, give us your forgiveness too.[58]

Reconciliation in Christ extends beyond simply sitting next to people from different ethnicities and cultures in the pews during Sunday morning worship. Racial and ethnic reconciliation, in particular, is manifested by unrelenting and conscientious acts of *metanoia*—seeking repentance, asking forgiveness, and experiencing changed attitudes toward Others. Racial and ethnic prejudices do not escape us completely. Rather, like dormant viruses, they break out in moments of fleshly weakness. So find creative, palpable, and everyday illustrations that will address racism and provide opportunities in congregational life for all members of the church to be reconciled to one another.

Addressing Ethnicity and Class

Not only does preaching and ethnicity invite reconciliation across ethnic barriers; Anthony Bradley makes the insightful observation that Christian conversations related to race and ethnicity must also include discussions about economics and social class. Oftentimes segregation in churches occurs not solely based on ethnicity and race. It is frequently likewise a class issue. People of the same socioeconomic background may worship together to the exclusion of other classes, thus transcending race and ethnicity. Bradley believes that we must deal with race and ethnicity in tandem with race and class.[59]

The congregation where I served in Denver was primarily Asian American demographically. Our church was composed also of several white men who were married to Asian American women. Many visitors entered the sanctuary from various walks of life and from many ethnic groups. A trend that I noticed over the years was that those who remained as regular worshipers in the church were those who could keep up with the Joneses regardless of their ethnic heritage. Being an affluent church, what unified our congregation was not merely a common ethnic lineage, but perhaps more significantly a common lifestyle of leisure. If one could keep up financially with others, they would stay. If not, they would leave, never to return to our church again even if they were Asian Americans.

Sharing the same socioeconomic background on some level can overcome initial racial and ethnic barriers. Bradley goes as far to argue, "So if a church is full of Latinos and Asians and Blacks, and they are all of the same class, that is a white church."[60] While stated strongly, Bradley's point is well taken in that economic class matters significantly in how we view others. His point is that in many tacit ways affluence transcends skin color. Take a quick mental survey of your congregation. What income bracket would you say is most prevalent among your worshipers? Would you agree with Bradley that social class is a conversation your leadership should address along with race and ethnicity? How can we preach in such a way as to include others of all income levels in addition to all ethnic backgrounds?

Application

From Ethnocentrism to Gracism

Thus far in this chapter we have focused heavily on ethnocentrism. The opposite of ethnocentrism, according to David Anderson, is a new term: "gracism." Combining the words "racism"—which is "speaking, acting, or thinking negatively about someone else solely based on that person's color, class or culture"—and "grace," "the unmerited favor of God on humankind,"[61] Anderson writes: "I define gracism as the positive extension of favor on other humans based on color, class, or culture."[62] What does gracism look like in preaching?

Anderson lays out seven principles of a gracist heart by building on 1 Corinthians 12:22–26: "I will lift you up. I will cover you. I will share with you. I will honor you. I will stand with you. I will consider you. I will celebrate with you."[63] In many ways, gracism is our Christian response to receiving God's grace in our lives. It resembles a selflessness that Jesus modeled throughout his life and ministry. It acknowledges Others and then puts them ahead of ourselves. It means valuing the ethnicities and cultures of Others and celebrating all the beauty of God's creation together. Gracism in preaching will look different in each congregation. Perhaps you can apply each of Anderson's seven principles of gracism in your sermon preparation over the course of seven Sundays in your church's yearly schedule.

Conflict Resolution

Patty Lane documents five common strategies for conflict resolution in American and other Western cultures: (1) win-lose (competition), (2) lose-win (acquiescence), (3) lose-lose (avoidance), (4) lose-lose (compromise), and (5) win-win (collaboration).[64] Lane highlights the cultural differences in each approach in that strategies 1, 4, and 5 are more Western and individualistic, while strategies 2 and 3 are more non-Western and collectivistic. What this means is that in our preaching, teaching, and church practices, allow room for different expressions of resolution, since ethnic groups resolve issues differently. Bible scholars explain:

> It is helpful to see how the churches in Antioch and Jerusalem resolved their conflict: (1) the church in Antioch sent a delegation to help seek a solution; (2) the

delegates met with the church leaders to give their reports and set another date
to continue the discussion; (3) Paul and Barnabas gave their report; (4) James
summarized the reports and drew up the decision; (5) everyone agreed to abide
by the decision; (6) the Council sent a letter with delegates back to Antioch to
report the decision.[65]

In this biblical example from the Jerusalem Council, we witness primarily
"Eastern" approaches to conflict resolution, which tend to prefer conflict
avoidance. Conflict resolution in our congregations will require much cultural sensitivity as we navigate "Western" and "Eastern" philosophies. In
preaching, our cultural intelligence will dictate whether we speak directly
to issues from the pulpit or whether we choose to resolve conflict through
other channels.

Language

Idioms

To express meaning, the English language relies heavily on idioms, "a
manner of speaking that is natural to native speakers of a language."[66] These
idioms are perpetuated in daily speech as well as in television and movies.
But for those in our congregations who are more recent immigrants or who
did not grow up in the North American context, these cultural expressions
are confusing and do not make sense because they are taken literally and
not figuratively. Our cultural intelligence with respect to other ethnic groups
will present opportunities to demonstrate cultural sensitivity by limiting our
use of idioms and explaining what they mean for those who are not native
English speakers.

Here are some idioms that we use in daily speech and take for granted:
"Break a leg," "Let me be the devil's advocate," "I feel a bit under the weather,"
or "Let the cat out of the bag." Many immigrants and members of ethnic
groups unfamiliar with these phrases are utterly baffled by them. When using
idiomatic phrases in a church context where nonnative English speakers worship, we can be culturally sensitive and make the extra effort to find parallel
idioms in their native language.

Honorific Language

Western culture tends to be egalitarian in viewing others as equals regardless of age, gender, class, education, occupation, and so forth. This egalitarian
worldview is not the case in African American, Asian American, or Hispanic

American cultures. Whenever possible, ethnic cultures use respectful and honorific language to elevate the Other. For Korean immigrants the Korean church is the only place in American society where one can experience honor and respect by way of titles such as "elder" or "deacon." Six days a week many Korean immigrants work in menial jobs to put food on the table, even though they were originally trained as doctors and lawyers in Korea. However, on Sundays at the Korean immigrant church, they can become *somebody* even though never viewed as such by members of the dominant culture. Therefore it is unthinkable in the Korean church context to call someone by their first name. Rather, Koreans and others use titles such as Elder Park or Deacon Chung to honor the other person. When communicating with non-Western congregants, using honorific language and titles before their first names increases our rapport with them and will remarkably bolster our overall communication with members of cultures that value honorific language.

Embrace

Woosung Calvin Choi helpfully articulates a starting point for preachers to embrace their multiethnic church setting. He explains that the culturally intelligent "preacher is comfortable to be in the world of in-betweenness—to be among multiple cultures and yet recognize the uniqueness and value of different cultures by promoting a spirit of inclusion without losing [one's] own identity."[67] Choi identifies two important elements to preaching across ethnic differences. First, he observes that multiple ethnicities within a church context will naturally create a congregational dynamic of in-betweenness or liminality, as mentioned above. Second, this liminality is not amorphous or paralyzing, but rather can be the impetus to celebrate the various ethnic groups in the church.

Ethnic celebration can take many different avenues. First, we can celebrate ethnic differences with simple acknowledgment of the Other's presence. The conscientious preacher finds opportune moments to acknowledge cultural differences in the congregation without arousing unnecessary attention by saying, "I know that some of you may think differently on this issue," or "This looks different in different ethnic contexts, and both viewpoints are respected and valued." Verbal acknowledgment and validation of another's ethnicity and culture is rarely witnessed among ethnic minorities. To hear such recognition would greatly strengthen your listeners.

Second, James Nieman and Thomas Rogers point out that, particularly in ecclesial settings where immigrants are present, preachers can use ethnic words in the languages of the people represented in their congregation, whether in

Spanish, German, or Chinese, which can be contextualized to be more easily absorbed.[68] Oftentimes we see this approach reflected in ethnic churches where English words find greater reception than words from one's own language.

Third, celebration could involve inclusion of simple ethnic customs, especially in churches where C3's are prominent. As Michael Pocock and Joseph Henriques observe, "Asking the people in your multicultural fellowship the meaning of certain colors in their culture could reveal important, useful information. In the case of the Chinese, knowing that red is the primary color used in joyous and festive occasions, it would make sense to use red during any celebration that includes Chinese."[69] Here the preacher will want to remember cultural sensitivity with respect to generational differences and how long this particular Chinese American has lived in the United States. That is, if Chinese American congregants are C1s and C2s (second-, third-, or fourth-generation Americans and thus fully American), they may not appreciate the symbolism of the color red as much as a first-generation Chinese immigrant.

Fourth, we can share in table fellowship with one another across different ethnicities and cultures, something that was particularly challenging for the Jewish and Gentile Christians in Acts 15 to do. For example, Forest Hills Baptist Church in Raleigh, North Carolina, reserves six Sundays per year to join together four different congregations from four different cultures who other Sundays meet in the same building but separately due to language differences: the English-speaking congregation, a Mandarin-speaking congregation, a French-speaking African church, and a Farsi-speaking Iranian church. These ethnic or "mosaic" services bring together approximately six hundred people and "expose worshipers to different kinds of music, language, dress and ethnic traditions."[70] They can even eat together and learn about one another's cultures.

Fifth, embracing ethnic diversity, perhaps most crucially, manifests itself by inviting Others to a seat and offering their voice at the table. Can we learn from those of different ethnic backgrounds? This can be tested in the church by ensuring that Others are seated at the table and given maximum access to contribute their voice in the conversation. The concept of "roundtable preaching" endorsed by John McClure and Lucy Atkinson Rose is helpful in this regard.[71] They invite preachers to dialogue with their listeners presermon and postsermon. Here are some ethnic-related questions that we can explore together:

1. How would you describe yourself in terms of your ethnic identity?
2. In what ways does your ethnicity and culture influence how you listen to and interpret the sermon?

3. Has my preaching ever intersected with your particular ethnic and cultural experience?

4. Have there been any occasions where I have offended, omitted, or misrepresented your ethnicity and culture?

5. How do you think my sermons could improve in tailoring to the experience of nonmajority-culture members?

6. What do you wish I knew about your ethnicity and culture?[72]

Embracing ethnicities in our preaching does not need to be forced, nor does it need to be overly complicated. The suggestions above are not the only ways to preach with ethnic sensitivity. You are welcome to integrate your own helpful methods as well. In your upcoming sermon, locate organic moments for ethnic acknowledgment and celebration, and your listeners will appreciate and, I trust, benefit from this awareness and engagement.

Content

The Bible is God's story of reconciling work, both salvific reconciliation between God and humanity as well as racial reconciliation among human beings.[73] For Emmanuel Katongole and Chris Rice, "the language of reconciliation is not grounded in a historical or sociological reality, but in a theological one" because "a vision of reconciliation grounded in the story of God not only affirms diversity but also displays it as part of God's purpose in creation."[74] Mathews and Park also maintain from Scripture, "It is also clear from Ephesians 3:1–13 that the burden to preach racial reconciliation falls to the church and not to the secular world precisely because reconciliation stems from the cross."[75] A common misconception is that racial reconciliation automatically happens in the context of multiethnic worshipers. We errantly assume that sitting in pews during Sunday worship next to persons of different ethnicities and races will automatically transform us into "the reconciled," demonstrating mutual love, respect, forgiveness, grace, cultural understanding, and celebration.

True reconciliation tasks us to do uncomfortable things. It demands active reciprocity among all racial/ethnic parties involved. Emerson and Smith make the plea that "whites, as the main creators and benefactors of the racialized society, must repent of their personal, historical, and social sins. . . . African Americans also have a responsibility. . . . They must be willing, when whites ask, to forgive them individually and corporately. Blacks must repent of their anger and whatever hatred they hold toward whites and the system."[76]

Reconciliation in the United States begins with the black-and-white gulf but extends to members of all ethnic backgrounds.

I am commonly asked, "Why do Korean students always sit by themselves and not integrate with others in the seminary dining hall?" What if we asked the same question but the other way around: "Why do white students sit by themselves and not integrate with others in the seminary dining hall?" The latter question sounds strange because the cultural expectation in America is that those in the minority, of course, should make the first step to mingle with the majority. That is, the onus is on the minority to figure out a way to assimilate with the majority. In our case study of Acts 15, a similar phenomenon is taking place. Even at the end of the chapter, I am not convinced that racial reconciliation has truly taken place. While an initial resolution has been made in that Gentiles are not required to observe the Jewish rite of circumcision to become Christians, Luke makes no pronounced acknowledgment that the Jewish Christians have considered Gentile practices and customs as a legitimate way to express the Christian faith. Acknowledging that I will not resolve the issue of racial reconciliation in this chapter, my encouragement to all preachers is to learn about and pursue reconciliation by beginning with earning Others' trust.

Trust

Saying "I'm Sorry" and "Forgive Me"

When spoken from the heart, the words "I'm sorry" and "Forgive me" may be two of the most powerful phrases in the English language. In our culture of entitlement, apologies are seldom spoken to one another even when our actions and words have splintered relationships. Even in the pulpit, preachers veer away from saying sorry or asking for forgiveness in fear that these rueful phrases might somehow diminish their capacity for leadership. Yet when it comes to ethnic and cultural differences, overcoming misunderstandings, misplaced uses of humor, and attempts toward reconciliation, no words may possess greater weight and build more trust.

In their book *Forgive Us: Confessions of a Compromised Faith*, Elise Mae Cannon and colleagues lament, "Too often the church has proven a source of pain rather than a place of hope."[77] If we are honest with ourselves, preachers are no exception. Through our speech and actions, we may be complicit in aggravating the pain of our listeners, especially when we have offended them with respect to their ethnicity, race, and culture. The inability to say "I'm sorry" and "Forgive me" reveals the lurking "sin of pride [that] undergirds racism. Pride is a misdirected self-love that regards others as being inferior to the individual or race."[78] Anthony Bradley similarly writes, "In evangelicalism, there is a strange tendency to confess that we struggle with other sins, like materialism, anger, gossip, adultery, individualism, and the like and to rebuke American society because of abortion, homosexuality, alcohol abuse, and so on, yet to ignore the racial issues in our own midst."[79]

Racism is a systemic problem. As noted at the beginning of this chapter, every person struggles at certain points with racist thoughts and prejudiced actions, and that includes preachers. What would it mean for our listeners to hear a heartfelt apology from their preacher who has in some tangible or subconscious way revealed an ethnocentric or racist heart? Public confession and apologies, when warranted, are moments of timely grace for the congregation and opportunities for immense relational growth across ethnic waters. We can earn our listeners' trust through our apology and humble requests for forgiveness, even historic sins of one's own ethnic and cultural group toward another. For example, to this day many Koreans still harbor feelings of hatred and animosity toward the Japanese on account of the Japanese occupation in the early twentieth century. What strides in reconciliation could take place if Japanese and Korean clergy mutually requested the forgiveness of the Other?[80]

Love Language of Time

Another avenue to earn our listeners' trust is to extend the language of love in the form of time. What is more valuable in today's culture than a person's time? In America, time is money. A pastor in inner-city Detroit offers this word of advice in discipling and preaching to African Americans: "'Give yourself to them.' Let me clarify. It is easier to train people in theology than to labor with someone as they grow up in Christ. . . . Don't mistake giving yourself to them as making them like you. The goal is not to make them middle class, upper class, etc. The goal is always to show them the heart of Jesus."[81]

Spending quality time with persons of a different race or ethnicity can be challenging but also mutually enriching. By crossing ethnic lines, we are deliberately putting ourselves in situations where we cannot simply coast in relationship building as when we are with those of the same background. It forces us to consider the Other more thoughtfully and discern blind spots in our thinking. It encourages us to grapple with cultural beliefs and assumptions that are not common to all. In short, the language of love in spending time with Others increases our understanding of the heart of God in his creation of various ethnicities and cultures. And it draws us ever closer to the prayer of Jesus in John 17 that his disciples may be one.

Conclusion

The topic of preaching and ethnicity is expansive and complex. This chapter could not comprehensively discuss the various layers and textures it requires. Rather, I have focused on more fundamental issues with regard to ethnocentrism and racism. This is the launching point for all matters on ethnicity and preaching. Though the task before us will be arduous, David Livermore reassures us, "Nobody behaves flawlessly in cross-cultural interactions. And frankly, the mistakes we make are often the best teachers for improving our CQ."[82] Indeed, I have made my healthy share of unintended faux pas as well. My hope is that some of what I have presented in this chapter can be incorporated into our preaching ministry, yet more importantly, we will embody and integrate *gracism* and ethnic celebration into our Christian discipleship.

7

Preaching and Genders

Imagine yourself preaching to listeners of the opposite gender only. How would you feel? Would your sermon preparation change in any noticeable way? Would you alter your content, delivery style, language, facial expressions, tone, illustrations, or applications? Preaching to the other gender poses many questions as we think more intentionally about our listeners. In many ways, the goal (for male preachers) in this chapter is "to step virtually into the skin of a woman, to listen as she listens, to hear what she hears, and to think as she might think—about God, the Bible, and the Christian life."[1] Most readers of this book have been preaching to the opposite gender (in most cases women) for years and even decades. How are we doing? Are we connecting with both men *and* women in the church?

I confess that I am far from an expert on gender issues. I remain perplexed by what gender differences fully entail in the task of preaching. I was born into and raised in a hypermasculine family as the eldest of three boys. We grew up playing sports, wrestling and punching one another, and talking about guy stuff. As an adult, I am now the father of three boys of my own and daily observe yet another generation of budding manhood. I admit that the only women I have spent any modicum of time with are my mother and my wife. Speaking to women (apart from my mother and wife) terrifies me. I often freeze in awkward silence. I don't know what to say or how to say it. Perhaps you resonate with my male-centered universe. Preaching to or even conversing with the opposite gender can be intimidating.

Similarly, recent literature on ministry and congregational studies indicate a concern that churches and their pastors are not addressing the real needs of men or women. David Murrow's *Why Men Hate Going to Church* and Rebecca Jones's *Does Christianity Squash Women?* are a sampling of books that disclose likely symptoms of an unhealthy congregation regarding the issue of gender. Murrow's book provides the following statistic:

> The typical American churchgoer is a woman. The U.S. Congregational Life Survey pegged her as a fifty-year-old, married, well-educated, employed female. An ABC News/Beliefnet poll found that a worshipper is most likely an older, black female who lives in the South. Figures from Census 2000 and a study by Barna Research estimate a weekly gender gap of more than 13 million in America's churches [where adult women represented over 48 million worshipers and adult men over 35 million worshipers].[2]

Despite this ecclesial reality, homileticians like Haddon Robinson report the propensity for male preachers to disregard female listeners in their proclamation: "In virtually every congregation, 60 percent or more of regular attendees are women, but many male preachers seldom refer to them or use illustrations or applications specifically related to their experiences."[3] Even in homiletics textbooks, gender (particularly preaching to women) is often sidelined as a nongermane topic for preaching. It is to the chagrin of myself and my readers that we will not be able to discuss gender in any comprehensive manner. Yet we can still take a few proactive steps closer to communicating effectually to both genders. That will be the intended goal of this chapter.

Preaching and the Gender Spectrum

Gender carries a completely different connotation from one's biological sex. In her helpful book *Preaching That Speaks to Women*, Alice Mathews defines gender as "everything we associate with being masculine or feminine—the ways we think, feel, and behave that express femininity or masculinity in culturally accepted patterns."[4] To be specific, gender does not concern itself with biological traits that distinguish males from females, such as our chromosomal makeup or reproductive organs. Rather, gender is understood as masculine or feminine characteristics, socially constructed concepts that help humans distinguish differences between women and men beyond biological variances. As Mathews continues, "Gender differences do exist. The roots of those differences, however, lie in some combination of nature, nurture, and the environment in which the interaction occurs."[5] Larry Crabb concurs:

"There is an essential difference between men and women—a difference that is properly reflected in unique styles of relating both with their worlds and with one another."[6] Preaching with respect to gender cannot ignore these differences between men and women. We will identify some of these gender differences in a few moments.

How we typically handle gender differences, as we have witnessed in previous chapters, is to rely on stereotypes or employ reductionism. That is, we often generalize men and women into universal classifications (often polar opposites or extremes), such as assuming that all men are insensitive or that all women want to experience motherhood. Virginia Sapiro provides the following commonly held stereotypical differences between men and women: masculine traits include being aggressive, unemotional, logical, rough, blunt, direct, ambitious, active, independent, and sloppy; feminine traits are reduced to the polar opposites, being unaggressive, emotional, illogical, gentle, tactful, sneaky, unambitious, passive, dependent, and neat.[7]

Deborah Tannen observes, "Generalizations, while capturing similarities, obscure differences. . . . In innumerable ways, every person is utterly unlike anyone else—including anyone else from many of the same categories."[8] Tannen's words here provide some measure of relief for the preacher who is burdened with having to consider gender differences in preaching. That is, while one's biological sex is undeniable (we are either male *or* female), Tannen reminds us that the construct of gender is more pliable than we often recognize. As an example, it is common knowledge that crying is not categorically a feminine gender trait, nor is lifting weights reserved as a gender-specific activity for men. Samuel Shem and Janet Surrey acquiesce in their book *We Have to Talk: Healing Dialogues between Women and Men*, "When we write about 'men' and 'women,' we are describing group differences, those that are apparent in groups of men and groups of women. No individual man or woman will fit every single description. Sometimes a quality we say is more typically 'male' might turn out to be more characteristic of a particular woman."[9] Susan Nolen-Hoeksema further contends in an article in *Psychology Today*: "The majority of adult women these days define themselves not primarily as feminine or masculine, but as a comfortable mix of the two."[10] This ought to appease many preachers because rather than getting overwhelmed by having to generate exclusively gender-specific illustrations, examples, stories, applications, and more, the preacher can think more intentionally about sermonic relevance for uniquely women's needs, men's issues, and a host of characteristics that overlap between men and women (see fig. 7.1). This chapter will try to show us some practical ways toward a more gender-balanced sermon. Let's begin with hermeneutics and explore the three stages of the Homiletical Template.

Figure 7.1
The Gender Spectrum

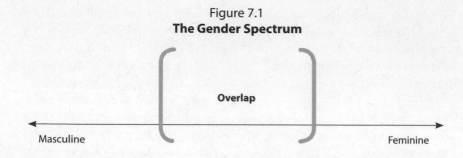

Stage 1: Follow Your HABIT

Scripture Text
Matthew 10:37–39

Historical, Grammatical, and Literary Context

Historical Context

As is common knowledge, Matthew's Gospel was primarily scribed for a Jewish readership, yet Gentiles remained fully in his sight lines.[11] The Gospel of Matthew, Michael Wilkins says, "serves as an evangelistic tool to Jews, contending that they should turn to Jesus as their long-awaited Messiah."[12] Although the family unit was invaluable in Jewish culture, Jesus's statement about the family in this text seems to diminish its importance in relation to the "conditions of discipleship."[13] Jesus puts it in no uncertain terms "that to love members of one's own family more than God disqualifies a person for discipleship."[14] How would Jesus's Jewish listeners have received his teachings about the family and discipleship? It would have resonated with them completely. Early followers of Jesus experienced what he commanded "because there were times when they were disowned by their families for following Christ."[15] Should our contemporary culture understand Jesus's prerequisite for discipleship literally or illustratively? By now, you would agree that how we interpret the text will depend not only on this histori- cally Jewish context but also on who's listening to our message today and how these varied congregants view the gravitas of the family unit or the lack thereof.

Grammatical Issues

The grammar of this short passage is rather straightforward. According to Grant Osborne, the grammatical structure of the text is as follows:

37a	Assertion	Anyone who loves a father or mother more than me is not worthy of me,
37b	Parallel 37a	and anyone who loves a son or daughter more than me is not worthy of me.
38	Expansion of 37	And whoever does not take up their cross and follow after me is not worthy of me.
39a	Basis	Whoever finds their life will lose it,
39b		and whoever loses their life for my sake will find it.

Grant R. Osborne, *Matthew*, Exegetical Commentary on the New Testament (Grand Rapids: Zondervan, 2010), 401.

Select word studies would be beneficial to unpack what Jesus is communicating about the characteristics of what distinguishes a legitimate disciple from a counterfeit. First, as you have already noticed, one common refrain is "not worthy of me." What does Jesus mean by "worthy," also translated as "deserving"?[16] With respect to gender, we want to be sensitive and explicitly communicate the meaning of "worthy" or "deserving" in their proper context. That is, Jesus is not flippantly using the word "worthy" as referring to one's own worth or self-esteem, since all human beings are unworthy or undeserving of him. Rather, he simply makes a strong comparison of one's devotion to him as seen in his use of "more than me" language. In contrast to how much we love Jesus, our love for family members should pale in comparison. Therefore, Jesus does not by any means jettison the family unit as altogether unimportant.[17] However, Jesus is more "worthy" and "deserving" of our entire lives, which includes even our own family. Craig Blomberg elucidates further: "'Worthy' here carries more the traditional sense of *deserving* and refers in context to those whom Jesus will accept."[18] This statement needs to be teased out in various parts of the sermon (such as our examples, illustrations, and applications), because both men and women, particularly from certain family-oriented cultures, can have strong ties to their families, thus making Jesus's words very difficult to hear.

A second major concept in this text to examine would be the meaning of "take up their cross and follow me" in verse 38 and similarly "loses their life for my sake will find it" in verse 39. As preachers, we know that Jesus is employing a familiar image for the disciples in reference "to the Roman custom of forcing a condemned man to carry his own cross to his crucifixion (cf. Matt. 27:32)."[19] Robert Mounce explains, "To 'take up the cross' means to consider oneself already sentenced and on the way to execution. It is complete self-denial."[20] Craig Keener also puts it in stark terms: "If we want to be followers of Jesus, we must be ready to *die*. If I value my life in this world more than I value Jesus and the life of the next world, I cannot be his disciple."[21] While "take up the cross" and "lose one's life" are commonplace jargon in the church today, they still remain amorphous for how they play out in real life.

We want to spend some quality time in our sermon preparation to locate parallel images of daily life for women and men regarding the specific shape and form that our crosses take today. For instance, stay-at-home parents may inherently feel that they have already sacrificed their lives in seeking to raise their children in a godly manner. In their minds, self-denial is a foregone conclusion. What else could Jesus possibly ask of them? They are utterly worn out as it is. As preachers, we want to extrapolate on the implications of what taking up our cross means for women and men who are spent and have very little energy left to give to Christ and the church.

Literary Study

This passage, along with its counterpart in Luke 14:25–33, is commonly referred to as the "conditions of discipleship."[22] What are we willing to give up in response and obedience to following the call of Christ? As C. S. Lewis is attributed as saying, "We don't need to suffer without purpose. When Jesus said, 'He must deny himself,' he was asking for something very specific.'" Further, the entire context of our passage (Matt. 10:37–39) represents a small segment of Jesus's "Mission Mandate,"[23] or "Mission Discourse,"[24] where he provides concrete instructions to the twelve disciples (or apostles) who are about to embark on their preaching ministry to "the lost sheep of Israel," the Jewish people (v. 6). His tone is quite serious as he encourages his disciples to demonstrate shrewdness (v. 16) and courage (v. 28) as they preach to an ambivalent culture that may or may not receive his message that "the kingdom of heaven has come near" (v. 7). Immediately before these verses, in 10:34–36, Jesus uses the language of war concerning the conflict that may ensue even within nuclear families who will be divided about the same gospel message. Specifically, Jesus says in verse 34, "Do not suppose that I have come to bring peace to the earth. I did not come to bring peace, but a sword." D. A. Carson observes, "Jesus does not mean he came to start wars but that, by the very fact that some in certain families would follow him whereas others would not, there would be interpersonal hostility ('a sword,' v. 34)."[25] We want to begin with an adequate period of studying the historical, grammatical, and literary contexts. From there, we progress to the author's world and cultural experience.

Author's Cultural Context

Especially in this early part of the movement of Christianity, Jesus needed to lay a firm groundwork for what it means to be a disciple. Following Jesus requires an all-or-nothing type of commitment, especially in light of the challenging cultural environment in which the disciples would preach their salvific message. Michael Wilkins explains, "Against the backdrop of a world increasingly hostile to Christianity, the author solidifies his church's identity as the true people of God, who transcend ethnic, economic, and religious barriers to find oneness in their adherence to Jesus Messiah. His Gospel becomes a manual on discipleship, as Jew and Gentile are made disciples of Jesus Messiah and learn to obey all that he commanded his original disciples."[26] Although we do not possess a complete manuscript of all that Jesus taught his disciples, the Gospels present more than sufficient description of what a disciple looks like and what a follower is to reproduce in making other disciples (Matt. 28:18–20). At this juncture it will be helpful to investigate more thoroughly the nature of discipleship in Matthew's context to better understand how modern notions of Christian discipleship have gone astray.[27]

As we know from reading Matthew and the other Gospel writers, Jesus literally required his disciples to leave their families and their nets (occupations) to follow him (e.g., Matt. 4:20, 22). In Jewish culture, the family unit was paramount in daily life. We observe the magnitude of the family in God's eyes in incorporating one's display of honor to parents as the primary human relationship in the fifth of the Ten Commandments. Craig Keener informs us that in Matthew 10:35, "Jesus selects these specific examples of in-laws (mother-in-law and daughter-in-law) because young couples generally lived with the man's family."[28] In many ways, Jesus's teaching here contradicts the social and family norms of Jewish culture, where "many viewed honoring one's parents as the highest social obligation."[29] For this reason, a natural connection point between the author's cultural context and our own would be to emphasize the importance of the family in the ancient Jewish world and our modern culture. Since family relationships were so valuable in Jesus's eyes, in Matthew 10 he strategically places the family as perhaps the ultimate hurdle for disciples to separate themselves from to substantiate one's wholehearted commitment to his mission.

Big Idea of the Text

Text: Matthew 10:37–39

Subject: Who does Jesus say can be his disciple?

Complement: The people who love Jesus more than family and are willing to deny themselves in obedience to him.

Exegetical Idea: Jesus says that the people who can be his disciples are the people who love Jesus more than family and are willing to deny themselves in obedience to him.

Homiletical Idea: Disciples love Jesus most and surrender everything to him.

Interpret in Your Context

Assumptions

Having now read over this passage several times, take a moment to consider the assumptions of our hearers. Oftentimes the immediate response of primarily men and perhaps some women when they read verses 38–39 is to assume that Jesus wants them to jettison their current occupation and enter some form of full-time vocational ministry. This may be true of a few select believers but not the case for the majority of our listeners. I once spoke at a men's retreat where I preached on a similar text from Luke 9:23 regarding Jesus's instructions on discipleship. Immediately after the session, a middle-aged man got up in my face and asked acerbically, "Are you preaching to high school kids? You are asking us to do the impossible. We can't give up our careers now. We can't give up our jobs and pick up and move to another country. We are too involved now to give up everything." Interestingly, I had never mentioned any of the things that this man was censuring me for saying. Rather, these statements were a reflection of the cultural assumptions that he made about the text. The women in our congregations will have their own sets of assumptions about what Jesus means to love him more than our own families and to give up our lives to follow him. We want to anticipate the assumptions and clarify what we mean and don't mean with respect to Jesus's words.

Conflicts

A possible area of conflict for men and perhaps women more poignantly will be what it looks like for us to love Jesus more than our family. While pastoring a church composed of mostly young families, I faced a regular challenge to encourage the mothers to focus on their spiritual lives as a greater priority amid the tiring task of raising children. Motherhood is all-encompassing. Fathers cannot completely comprehend a mother's heart and sacrifice. Here is an example, albeit an extreme case. My wife and I once had dinner with a couple in our home. For this particular couple, the husband had the stronger faith of the two. The wife was skeptical about Christianity. She expressed how she loved her two boys more than anything in this world. As the conversation progressed about what it means to be Jesus's disciple, she said something that I will never forget: "I don't love anything more than I love my two boys, and I don't care if I go to hell if I can ensure that my kids will be safe and have a successful life on this earth."

Although such staggering words may not be expressed ubiquitously, Jesus's words truly are confrontational in a culture where we prize and even idolize our offspring. In a culture that venerates academic accomplishment, winners over losers, and the leisure of recreation, parents will be forced to choose worshiping Jesus over pleasing their kids, teachers, and coaches. The concept of loving Jesus more than our own children will require intentional sermon time to be fleshed out, since this will be a clear tension point for many women *and* men in our churches. How does a parent carry out the discipleship mandate and raise a family at the same time? What does that entail in real life? Since raising a family can be all-consuming, parents will need concrete examples of how to raise children and simultaneously carry out their Christian service and grow in discipleship.

Questions

What questions might your male and female listeners have about this text? If we are honest with the state of the church at home and abroad, the discipleship that Jesus demands in Matthew 10 has not been lived out closely by those who call themselves disciples. In his book *Where Are All the Brothers?*, Eric Redmond shares many of the same raw questions and concerns that unbelieving skeptics and even churchgoers have about Christian disciples who can be so given over to hypocrisy:

I have seen such people, just as you have:

- They sing, shout, and wave their hands on Sunday but curse you out later that week.
- They exalt humility as a virtue but wear the finest clothes and drive the nicest cars as status symbols, and they look down on those who cannot.

- They are deacons, stewards, trustees, elders, and preachers who are supposed to set the example for the people but can be regularly seen leaving the corner store with a brown bag that is not concealing pork rinds.
- They say they love Jesus but abuse their children, cannot mend a relationship with an estranged family member, or are the worst workers in the office.
- They repeatedly tell you and everyone else that you need to be "saved" or "born again" and are judgmental of your every word or lifestyle, never seeing that their attitudes need to be "saved."[30]

Beyond questioning the behavior of other congregants in the church, our listeners will be wondering how the truth of this particular text will radically alter their lifestyles. The type of commitment that Jesus demands in this text will require for many a 180-degree transformation from how they presently live. Both male and female listeners will be challenged to consider the ways in which taking up their crosses and losing their lives to gain Christ will impact daily decisions, ethical behavior at work, and their dreams and possibilities. Verse 39 also calls into question what we are holding on to in this world in place of Christ. "The more we love this life's rewards (leisure, power, popularity, financial security), the more we will discover how empty they really are."[31] Take a moment to think about specific women and men in your congregation and jot down what questions they might have with respect to your sermon. What specific shackles of this life are preventing them from ultimate discipleship?

Theological Presuppositions

What theological presuppositions might our listeners hold when interpreting this text? A primary theological presupposition for both genders that we could highlight in this sermon may concern the concept of God's holy jealousy. Why does Jesus come across as being so extreme in his provisos for discipleship? The short answer is that those whose hearts are divided cannot devote themselves to serving God *and* be committed to his mission. Care for the family and self can become and often are life-consuming. Jesus and the work of expanding God's kingdom elicits undivided attention. Surely then, Jesus does not mean that we will leave our families behind like the twelve disciples to serve him, does he? In this particular sermon, leaving our listeners to their own skewed imaginations may prove detrimental. We want to raise theological concerns but also provide concrete examples of what Jesus means and what he does not mean by his instructions.

Stage 2: Build the BRIDGE

Beliefs

The beliefs we hold about ourselves and about the world concretize from an early age. Numerous societal influences shape girls' and boys' beliefs about themselves from teachers, television, coaches, peers, friends, social media, song lyrics, bullies, the church, and more. A woman whose parents shamed her at the formative age of seven, telling her she was overweight, unattractive, or unintelligent, will embrace this belief about herself perhaps for the rest of her life. A grown man whose father told him at the age of nine that he comes from a long family lineage of high school dropouts and drug addiction may believe that a different trajectory for his life is not possible. One of the foundational questions preachers can ask with respect to gender and beliefs is: What did this woman's and man's parents tell them about themselves from a young age that formed their beliefs about who they are today? Much of the topic of preaching and gender will naturally concern itself with the subject of psychology. In his book *The Listening Life*, Adam McHugh writes:

> When someone is passionate about something, there is almost always a personal reason behind it.
>
> - Why do you hold that belief?
> - Why is that important to you?
> - Why does that bother you?
> - Why did that hurt you?
> - Why do you feel that way?[32]

What do women and men believe to be true about themselves? Beliefs about the self, society, God, and the church largely influence the way they read and interpret a Scripture text and how they receive the sermon. Our cultural intelligence meter searches for opportunities to learn about our congregants and especially to name the experiential pain and suffering that linger long in their hearts and minds.

With respect to women's beliefs, Alice Mathews makes the following observations:

> Many women do not understand that they have other options. They have been taught that being passive is a proper female posture in life. Generally, women do not believe that they have the power, authority, or competency to act to

change the stressful situations in which they find themselves. Only men have that power or authority. Women's general disbelief in their ability to change their circumstances ought to be of deep concern to pastors. . . . Yet if women do not believe that as women they can act, they will not hear your message of empowerment in the same way that men might hear it.[33]

For preachers, as Mathews illuminates, the question is not how we can reinforce the plethora of harmful and belittling beliefs about women, but rather how we can help them foster positive beliefs about themselves and, more important, about God's ability to transform them into his likeness. What beliefs about women and men does this passage reinforce or put into question?

Rituals

Traditional gender roles before the 1960s intimated that men were the providers (i.e., the breadwinners) while women were the caregivers (i.e., the homemakers). For both genders, these rituals or traditions have been ingrained into many consciences. When a married couple deviated from these socially constructed gender roles, they were considered enigmatic. Today, however, traditional gender roles have been redefined. For a growing number of families, women are functioning in dual roles as provider and caregiver, while in some marriages husbands by virtue of choice or by making less income than their wives stay at home to raise the children. In Farnoosh Torabi's book *When She Makes More: 10 Rules for Breadwinning Women*, the author claims that one-quarter of all married women earn a higher salary than their husbands, which is approximately five million women in the United States. In comparison to 1960, four times the number of women make more money than their husband.[34] Times have certainly changed since television shows like *Leave It to Beaver*. At the same time, life outside the home has not diminished the expectation that the wife will still serve a primary nurturing quality within the home. What this means is that many women in our congregations are exhausted. They don't get a break. In society, women are expected to be sacrificial and to deny themselves, and this text, Matthew 10:37–39, reinforces an additional layer of burden. Brita L. Gill-Austern relates that women live "in a culture that substantially informs this sense of self by raising women to consider the needs of others, to take care of men, and to care for children."[35]

Additionally, many women, whose identities are wrapped up in others' well-being, struggle to possess a sense of self-identity. In their book *Women in Travail and Transition*, Maxine Glaz and Jeanne Stevenson Moessner share a story about a nurse named Ann who began attending a group therapy session. The following conversation ensued with the counselor:

> Ann: I take care of people. I'm a nurse. I'm a mother. I take care
> of my daughter; I am a daughter. I take care of my mother,
> who has Alzheimer's. She lives with us.
>
> Counselor: Tell us about yourself.
>
> Ann: I can't, I don't know who I am.[36]

While Ann's response is not universal for all women, many women frequently find their identity in their relationship to others, whereas men's identities are primarily defined by the individual and his achievements, position, and status. Societal rituals or traditions such as distinctive gender roles will be questioned in your sermon. Jesus's words sound harsh, unsympathetic, and even unloving. Many women and men in our congregations who have already adopted a selfless attitude in the home may struggle to come to terms with Jesus's statements in Matthew 10:37–39 concerning familial and self-sacrifice in comparison to one's devotion to Christ. Consider gender by providing moments in the sermon to acknowledge the internal melees of women and men who, after hearing Jesus's words, may be hit by yet another torrential wave of expectant self-denial. Explain how Jesus's teachings here are not intended to heap on sentiments of insignificance or worthlessness. Relate clearly how self-denial and sacrifice in the Christian sense guides us toward Christian maturity and discipleship and is different from the world's ways.

Idols

In these few verses (Matt. 10:37–39), Jesus challenges primarily two idols: the idol of family and the idol of self. In his sermon "The Family of God," John Charles Wynn uttered this explanation: "When he [Jesus] insisted that the requirements for discipleship transcend family loyalty, he was saying in effect that such discipleship is so important that it outweighs even the dearest and finest of earthly ties, even the family."[37] A vexing question, then, for certain listeners will concern Jesus's perspective on the family and on individual Christians. First, in our Scripture text at least a cursory reading suggests that Jesus diminishes the significance of family relations. Yet we know from reading other Gospel texts that Jesus placed a high value on the family unit by way of honoring one's parents (Mark 7:9–13), the gravity of marriage (Matt. 5:31–32; Mark 10:1–12; Luke 16:18), and even the value of children (Matt. 19:13–15), which in many ways postulated a necessary corrective to the misunderstandings of family relations among his Greco-Roman audience.[38] How do we reconcile Jesus's teaching in Matthew 10:37–39 with these other passages?

The boundary between caring for our family members and our own bodies and making them into idols is a very delicate line. When do our parents, spouse, children, grandchildren, siblings, and very selves become, as Timothy Keller puts it, "ultimate things"?[39] A tension firmly grips every person whereby giving attention to our family, self, or work becomes the very excuse barring us from loving God and people. Parents perhaps more than ever are pushing their children toward unhealthy expectations of success and achievement. Admissions rates at prestigious colleges are at an all-time low, reinforcing an even more competitive and cutthroat high school environment. Even in the early 2000s, when I served as a youth pastor, the number one reason why youth group members could not attend Bible study was because their parents wanted them to be studying at home. I can only imagine that this idolatry of academic achievement has exacerbated. After-school clubs, competitive sports, music lessons, art lessons, additional tutoring, community service, and other résumé-building activities are working our children to exhaustion. Amy Chua's book *Battle Hymn of the Tiger Mother* resonates with many ethnic minority and dominant culture parents who will give up everything to ensure success for their offspring, even to the extent of forfeiting their very souls.[40]

When a person reaches adulthood, work is very much part of the fabric of life. We are expected to work and to provide for ourselves and our families. Work was mandated by God to Adam and Eve in Genesis 1 and 2. The apostle Paul reminds Timothy, "Anyone who does not provide for their relatives, and especially for their own household, has denied the faith and is worse than an unbeliever" (1 Tim. 5:8). Paul also commanded the believers more generally at Thessalonica to work for their sustenance: "The one who is unwilling to work shall not eat" (2 Thess. 3:10). However, a growing number of men and women "live to work" rather than "work to live." Workaholic behaviors for self-aggrandizement or even for the sake of providing for our families is the new normal. When does work become an idol that hampers people's ability to live out Jesus's call in Matthew 10:38–39 to "take up their cross" and "lose . . . their life"? Preaching on faith and work is making some strides in certain populations of preachers. But many listeners today still fail to make the connection as to how their work during the week has anything to do with their Christian life. What is more, many Christians are experiencing workaholic tendencies, with little time or energy for anything else. In his book *Work Matters*, Tom Nelson explains, "If we are not careful, our work can become a black hole that eventually sucks the life out of us and hinders our relationship with God and others."[41] Idolatry reveals itself in how we use God's resources of money and time. In this important topic of gender, our responsibility as preachers is to prod our listeners to consider how their hyperactivity toward family and work life may be jeopardizing their commitment to the Lord. While idolatrous forms of family and the self are by no means novel to preachers, I encourage you to be more intentional in helping your listeners find greater satisfaction in losing their lives to find more of Christ.

Dreams

We all begin life with dreams, hopes, and expectations. It doesn't take long, however, to realize that life is full of disappointments. The ideology, at least in America, is that anything is possible for us if we are willing to work for it. But the reality is that many of our possible selves get swallowed up, so that living with disappointment and being a disappointment sets in. Hard work alone does not cut it, and suffering tastes all too familiarly like a bitter slice of humble pie. Over time, the scenery, colors, and images of our listeners' lives can morph drearily with each passing life stage, becoming darker and less auspicious (see, e.g., Thomas Cole's Voyage of Life series of paintings).

Consider the example of Dale from Mark Sayers' book *The Vertical Self*. Dale hates his job as an office supply store manager. He doesn't feel fulfilled while serving the youth group anymore. He compartmentalizes his life into different Dales: Christian Dale, Party Dale, Depressed Dale, Charming Dale, and Insecure Dale. Alone in his bedroom, he finds himself in volatile states. He's begun lifting weights in hopes that looking physically fit will improve his self-esteem. For Dale, life hasn't met his expectations.[42] Put differently, John Ortberg pens, "Somebody has a deeper hunger for a strong, rich, life-affirming marriage. Somebody hopes to have an education and pursue wonderful knowledge, but they grow up in poverty and never have the opportunity. Somebody hopes to be reconciled with an impossible parent. Somebody hopes that their child won't die. Then comes disappointment. . . . Disappointment is where dreams go to die."[43]

Women similarly experience varying degrees of disappointment in life. Dreams of having it all quickly shatter under the crushing weight of one's reality. Sometimes, as preachers, we play an unintentional role in smashing the dreams of Christian women. As Carolyn Custis James writes in *Half the Church*, "I grieve over the opportunities and blessings I have wasted because I didn't know about God's vision for his daughters—I didn't realize God expected so much of me. . . . I grieve that far too many women and girls are living with small visions of themselves and of their purpose."[44] The question faces us as preachers: What dreams are we advocating in our preaching and teaching? Perhaps we are guilty of encouraging dreams that our listeners are not meant to have. For example, Denise George records the following disappointments of Christian women concerning their pastors' sermons, particularly regarding the topic of singleness: one single woman writes, "My pastor just assumes that every single woman in his church is desperate to get married! . . . It always comes through in his sermons!" Another female respondent in George's study from Alabama shared this perspective:

> As a single woman, I wish pastors would learn how to preach more messages that speak to the hearts and needs of singles. I am burned out on topics like, "Being Single and Satisfied," "Lonely But Not Alone," and "How to Choose the Right Mate." I wish pastors would spend time talking with us who are single to find out what our needs are. . . . We each have different goals in life.[45]

In Matthew 10:37–39 and throughout the Gospels, Jesus presents a new dream for his listeners. Jesus challenges even the indirect disappointment of unfulfilled dreams in this chapter, such as infertility, whereby a woman being incapable of "leaving her family" is replaced with a new dream of fulfilling the will of God at all costs. The hope is that our preaching will shed light on this dream of becoming disciples who are dead to themselves so that they might live more purposefully for God. Develop relationships with your listeners so that you can contextualize Jesus's dreams for them as women and men.

God

All human beings try to understand how God employs our very finite ability. Brennan Manning observes, "Still, there is a chronic temptation to reduce God to human dimensions, to express Him in manageable ideas. . . . But God is God. . . . He is Unique, Uncreated, Infinite, Totally Other than we are. He surpasses and transcends all human concepts, considerations, and expectations. He is beyond anything we can intellectualize or imagine."[46] Do men and women view God in different ways? Whether intentionally or not, human nature ascribes feminine and masculine attributes to God, and these characteristics influence how our listeners hear a sermon. For example, since God is our Father in heaven and takes on a male pronoun in Scripture, many people naturally emphasize God's "masculine" characteristics, such as power, authority, judgment, and so on. However, using primarily masculine descriptors for God can stymie women and men's ability to imagine God holistically. Denise George learned the following from one of her female respondents: "'The biggest problem church women face today is an improper view of God,' says a California woman. 'We have been wounded in our pasts (many of us), and we view God the way we see men, our fathers, husbands, etc. We don't realize and understand God's infinite love for us.'"[47] Similarly, as Floyd McClung Jr. writes in *The Father Heart of God*,

> Our world is plagued by an epidemic of pain. With divorce rampant and child abuse screaming from the national headlines, it is not surprising that for many people the concept of a *Father* God evokes responses of anger, resentment, and rejection. Because they have not known of a kind, caring earthly father, they have a distorted view of the heavenly Father's love. In many cases these hurting individuals choose to simply deny or ignore His existence.[48]

To speak effectively to both genders, finding a greater balance between male and female attributes of God may resonate more clearly, whether consciously or not, with those who have encountered less than ideal fathers and male authority figures who have abused them. Feminine attributes of God are less often named in evangelical circles. Perhaps identifying more nurturing or "motherly" characteristics of God, when appropriate, would provide the necessary equilibrium for all listeners to appreciate the fullness of God.

Experiences

As preachers, our proclivity in every sermon is to focus on action items and to-do lists. Spiritual stagnancy is never an option. We tell ourselves and our churches that a trajectory of numeric and sanctifying growth is the only way forward. With similar widespread attitudes traversing among today's clergy, preachers forget to view their congregants as real people with real pain. Men and women in your congregation bring to the worship service each Sunday an assortment of pain. They are broken and hurting. Some wear the pain on their countenances while others try to mask it. Oftentimes in pastoral ministry and especially in preaching, preachers either disregard their listeners' pain or seek to mollify it as quickly as possible. If we are honest, we do not like it when our listeners are unhappy or in agony. "Unfortunately, lament is often missing from the narrative of the American church," Soong-Chan Rah writes.[49] To make oneself feel better, the preacher quickly darts toward biblical verses that seek to resolve our listeners' issues, or the preacher trivializes their pain by failing to acknowledge their suffering. The reality is that our congregants are bandaging lingering scabs and even raw sores in various facets of their lives.

Consider the following examples of the struggles women internalize from Bev Hislop's book *Shepherding Women in Pain*:

- Sheryl, in the face of infertility, experiences the repeated agony of grieving the loss of a child every month and seeks to isolate herself, suffering silently.
- Beth is worn down emotionally by the silent, restless "impacted grief" of a past abortion, yet has no understanding of her own seemingly irrational behaviors indicative of post-abortion stress.
- Cassie anxiously hurries out the church door the minute an event is over, fearing her husband will inflict further emotional or physical abuse on her or the children if she is even one minute late coming home.
- Monique's disproportionate focus on dieting, exercising, and body image has drawn her into unhealthy obsessions.
- Feelings of betrayal from her recent divorce are sabotaging Shannon's ability to generate healthy friendships.[50]

How do we address our listeners' experiences and pains? Hislop helpfully articulates that men and women have different ways of addressing their pain. Men, for instance, often want a short list of action items to expedite the healing process. Women, on the other hand, find solace in talking about their feelings and reliving their experiences. "This is often the reason many women feel a lack of healing after hearing a male church leader's advice to read the Bible more, or pray more, or 'try harder to love him.' The most important step for women has been bypassed."[51] One of the ways we can reach men and women in the congregation who receive healing through verbalizing feelings and experiences is to share more openly from the pulpit about our experiences and feelings and thus to be discerningly vulnerable.

Here in this specific text, the preacher will aid a number of listeners by simply naming the hardships involved in Jesus's call for discipleship. How can we possibly love Jesus more than our family, especially more than our children? What does greater obedience look like for those who are already enduring various pains in life? In my preaching ministry as a senior pastor, I regret that I often expressed the ideals of Jesus's teachings in an insensitive manner, without acknowledging the present realities of my hearers by asking questions like these: "Why can't we obey Jesus more?" or "What is holding us back from living as Jesus's disciples?" All the while my listeners are silently griping from the pews, "Matt, you don't understand my life!"

Identifying with our listeners' pain, circumstances, and experiences will encourage many to develop in their spiritual maturity. How? It will allow them to experience their pain without the preacher providing a three-step program to escape or remedy their hardships. Acknowledge how difficult it is to work more than one job, raise children as a single parent, care for an aging parent, battle various illnesses, and other life challenges. Yes indeed, Jesus is the solution for every human problem, but listeners don't want to hear from preachers that their present hurdles will be a quick fix. Provide your listeners contextual empathy and show them how they can move forward in discipleship in spite of their earthly struggles.

Stage 3: Speak Their DIALECT

Delivery

The tone of the preacher is often a neglected ingredient in one's sermon. Specifically, the tone of the text should match the tone of the sermon, and the tone of the sermon should be contextualized for the listeners in the pews.[52] In *Rewiring Your Preaching*, Richard Cox states, "Perception is a combination of *fact* and *feeling*. What does this have to do with preaching? Everything. Productive preaching requires both *fact* and *feeling*."[53] Like a trial lawyer, most preachers focus on delivering the facts: accurate historical details, correct biblical exegesis, verifiable illustrations, and the like. This is not where preachers usually go awry. Rather, our sermons plow disconnected pathways due to our tone. "Tone" can be defined as "a quality, feeling, or attitude expressed by the words that someone uses in speaking or writing."[54] In *The Story Factor*, Annette Simmons suggests, "When you speak, words are less than 15 percent of what listeners 'hear.'"[55] Patricia Batten fills in some of the remaining 85 percent of these nonverbal elements: "Listeners judge us by far more than the words we say. They receive information from our facial expressions, our posture, our gestures, our clothes, our eye movement, our tone and a variety of other non-verbal forms of communication."[56]

In many ways, fundamentally speaking, men and women communicate differently and with different intentions. "Women use conversation to seek confirmation, to make connections, and to reinforce intimacy; men, on the other hand, use conversation primarily to protect their independence and to negotiate status."[57] In *Gender, Power, and Persuasion*, Mignon Jacobs observes

similar inclinations among men in the workplace: "The male may expect to
be complimented or nurtured by his female colleagues and to be praised for
all his efforts—whether or not these efforts are praiseworthy. Likewise, the
male may expect to be treated as the superior in terms of ability—whether or
not he is more skilled or intelligent than his female counterpart."[58]

Imagine placing yourself in the shoes of the opposite gender. What does
communication look like from the perspective of the other gender? Differences
abound. Therefore, gender-consciousness in communication does matter,
and these gender differences manifest themselves in preaching as well. Since
relationships are important for many women, preaching relationally and with
a relational tone goes far in helping men preach effectively to women. As
Daniel Overdorf suggests, "Ladies connect best, therefore, with preachers
who speak relationally—in a conversational manner, and with a warm tone
and body language. They appreciate speakers who let their guards down,
laugh at themselves, and share their own stories."[59]

The tone of our voice matters. We can say the exact same sentence with
myriad tones. Try saying aloud, "Jesus wants us to love him more than we
love our family." This sentence, based on our Scripture text, contains twelve
words. We can say the same sentence twelve times in a row by emphasizing
one different word in the sentence during each reading. For instance, "*Jesus*
wants us to love him more than we love our family," or "Jesus *wants* us to
love him more than we love our family," or "Jesus wants *us* to love him more
than we love our family," and so on. Words that we choose to emphasize
and the tone attributed to that word will determine how listeners hear the
sentence. As Cox highlighted earlier, fact and feeling go together. The question is which tone we use to get the message across. Watch the tone of your
sermon so that your words will receive a proper hearing. Listen to the tone of
your sermons. Are they appropriately joyful? Are they unnecessarily harsh?
How might the men and women in your congregation hear your tone, even
if your word choice is spot on?

Illustrations

Illustrations influence the overall efficacy of the sermon more than we realize.
The primary function of an illustration is to clarify or explain something.[60]
That means, by their very nature, that illustrations should not be included
capriciously—for example, to be humorous or simply because the preacher
feels compelled to cram it into this particular message. Illustrations are
like anything in life that fits the "choice" or "select" categories, such as

succulent meat from the menu of a fine-dining establishment, mouthwatering
milk chocolate from Switzerland, or a sharply designed dress or suit from
a high-end clothing retailer. Simply put, illustrations are not intended to be
one-size-fits-all features. Here are two reminders when considering gender
and illustrations.

The first is more obvious: limit stereotypes in your use of illustrations. Erin
Wheeler writes, "We are all women, but we are not all the same. Practicing
the art of good listening will help you see variation, and it will help you better respond to the diverse kinds of women in your pastoral care, *especially* in
your preaching."[61] Distancing oneself from the practice of gender stereotypes
involves ruminating and marinating. Try not to insert the first or even second illustration that comes to the surface. Denise George explains: "Just as
all men don't like fly-fishing or baseball or aren't all mechanically inclined,
women aren't the same either. For example, while some women love to cook,
other women hate to cook. Some women like to shop; other women hate to
shop. Some single women want to get married; other single women want to
stay single. Some women want to become mothers; other women don't want
children. You get the idea."[62] While it is impossible to avoid gender stereotypes altogether and select gender stereotypes are occasionally warranted,
the culturally intelligent preacher finds opportunities to balance stereotypical
illustrations of men and women with nonstereotypical ones.

Second, consider switching the pronoun of the persons or protagonists in
your illustration. In most male preachers' use of narratives, the hero, leader,
or protagonist is usually, if not always, a man. However, what if your main
character in the story or example is a female? Several years ago, I witnessed
an illustration on a PowerPoint slide showcasing four of the world's most
powerful people. All four images—powerful figures in the worlds of politics,
entertainment, education, and finance—were the countenances of men. Not
a single woman made it onto this preacher's radar of influential persons,
even though women hold the highest office in a number of countries. To
reach more than half the church, a simple adjustment would be all it took to
acknowledge, encourage, and even empower the women in his congregation.
Remember and include women!

As an example of gender inclusivity, I heard the following "puzzle" in a
preaching class with only male students enrolled. A father goes skiing with
his son. Making a sharp turn and losing his balance, the son hits his head
on the side of the mountain and needs immediate emergency care. When he
gets to the operating room, the surgeon appears distraught and says: "I can't
possibly perform the surgery. This is my son!" How can this be?[63] The group
of male students in the class looked blankly at one another. The answer is

that the surgeon is the boy's mother. I later asked this same riddle to my wife, who solved it immediately without flinching. Carolyn Custis James writes,

> Instead of addressing the wide range of questions and situations women are facing today, we focus mainly on marriage and motherhood, and that within a two-parent, single-income family. We overlook all the other seasons of a woman's life—which impacts every girl and adult woman and excludes entirely women whose lives follow a different path. Our message has taken on a negative, defensive tone and doesn't capitalize on the positive, life-affirming, kingdom nature of God's message for women.[64]

Decrease the use of stereotypical illustrations and be inclusive of both genders to speak effectively to the entire church. These slight adjustments will have a lasting impact on your preaching ministry with respect to illustrating well.

Application

Application may be, for many preachers, the single most difficult component in preparing any sermon. This applicational challenge is especially poignant when seeking to be effective with regard to both genders. Jay E. Adams defines application summarily as "truth related to the listener."[65] The struggle in many congregations is for the preacher to name tangible applications in view of the women in the church. In his book *enGendered*, Sam Andreades recounts a familiar Sunday scene for many women in the church today. After Andreades preached on gender roles in the church, a woman from the congregation approached him and said:

> "I have heard plenty of times what I cannot do. Okay. Even if I accept that, it doesn't move me an inch toward knowing what I should be doing." . . . With her two sentences, I saw my failure, and the church's failure in general, to give Rachel what she really needed. What did Rachel need? Something to embrace. Something to pursue. A positive vision for how she, specifically as a woman, furthered God's purposes, how she, as a woman, meant something to the kingdom of heaven. I could not give her that by just telling her what she shouldn't be doing. I was not giving her a reason to rejoice in the commands the Bible gives her.[66]

The women in our churches deserve contextualized applications. The challenge is that for most of Scripture, what preachers regard as application is not clearly nuanced in terms of gender differences. A lucid example of gender-specific application is Paul's exhortation to the Ephesian Christians in Ephesians 5:21–33 concerning the marriage relationship and a short list of concrete manifestations of love expressed between a husband and a wife. However, in most biblical texts we are not privy to such clearly defined applications. Therefore, the onus is on the preacher to determine how best to preach to someone like Andreades's listener, Rachel, and other women in our congregations.

Preparatory Stages of Application

Richard Cox argues that preachers have a tendency to jump too quickly into action for their listeners when it comes to application.[67] We assume that the Holy Spirit will grip their hearts and immediately lead them to repent and change their behavior, much like the Jewish listeners of Peter's sermon in Acts 2. We may not like to admit it, but transformation takes time and sometimes a lot of it. The process that Cox advocates for behavioral change—or in our case, application—is adapted from the work of James Prochaska, who envisions three prior steps before soliciting action: precontemplation, contemplation, and preparation.[68] These three previous steps may enable the preacher to help both genders apply God's Word more effectively.

First, precontemplation is the stage where listeners may be unfamiliar with the nature of preaching and various conditions, such as "family interference or support, occupational conflicts, educational biases and so on,"[69] that can hamper their ability to live out God's commands. The second stage, contemplation, considers listeners who might be sitting on the fence because of how the biblical principle being discussed may impact their lifestyle, but they still remain involved in church life in spite of their noncommitted state.[70] Third, in the preparation stage, "old beliefs are being reexamined, consequences of possible changes are being debated, plans are being made if anticipated changes don't work out, and overt experimentation with new thinking and action is taking place. . . . They are likely the most ready to receive the preached message."[71] These preparatory stages of application serve as helpful tools to gauge listeners' present disposition toward the application. Rushing our listeners into immediate action may stymie their potential to change. What would it look like for our sermon in Matthew 10:37–39 to include one, two, or all three preparatory stages in the application?

Include Relational Applications

In much preaching today in North America, sermon application is highly individualistic. We frequently challenge listeners to search inside for how this sermon applies to the individual self. However, as we know, biblical authors were often writing not to individuals but to entire nations, a diaspora, communities, and congregations. One way to foster gender-balanced application is to articulate relational/communal applications. Alice Mathews explains the importance of relationships for women in general: "Women tend to define themselves in terms of relationships, and they also evaluate themselves morally in terms of their ability to care. . . . Women, in general, appear to be much more oriented to interdependence than to what they see as masculine individualism."[72] Jacqueline Roese makes a similar observation: "Women are more sensitive to interpersonal relationships—those with God and each other, and the rippling effects of those relationships on the community."[73]

What this means is that our sermon applications might discuss the relational impact of responding to Christ. We want to acknowledge the sheer difficulty of Christ's command to love him more than we love our family. What are the implications of this decision with respect to our familial relationships? Will this require me to cut ties with my family members who may adhere to another world religion? Does Christ's call mean I must diminish tending to the needs of my mother, father, brother, sister, or children? Naming specific or perhaps hypothetical scenarios may quell some of the misunderstandings that our hearers might have about the application. In every sermon, the culturally intelligent preacher incorporates both individual and relational applications to speak with sensitivity to both men and women.

Language

Francis Schaeffer says, "If we wish to communicate, then we must take time and trouble to learn our hearers' use of language so that they understand what we intend to convey."[74] The point here is that men and women may speak the same language but employ a different dialect. What is heard by the other gender can often be worlds apart from its intended meaning. Adapting to "genderlects" may mitigate some of the miscommunication commonly experienced between women and men.[75] "Genderlects" is a term coined by Deborah Tannen, resembling the notion of dialects and designating that men and women simply communicate differently, which ultimately can lead to misunderstandings. Jeffrey D. Arthurs provides the following example of genderlects:

> In American culture, men tend to be more direct than women because they view communication as a means to accomplish a task. But for women, with their high

value of smooth interpersonal relationships, communication is a means of communing. They tend to avoid confrontation by leaving the other person options. A conversation might sound like this when Michelle says to Robin, "Do you want to eat somewhere?" Robin asks, "Are you getting hungry?" Michelle, "Yeah, a little." "Me too, do you think we should eat?" Michelle says, "Sure, sounds good to me. Where do you want to go?" A man might say, "I'm hungry. Let's eat." But that genderlect would feel brusque or even confrontational to a woman's ears.[76]

With respect to preaching, adapting to genderlects naturally lends itself to asking more questions in the sermon rather than stating truths or principles bluntly. For example, we might ask our listeners, "What does it mean for Christians to 'take up our cross and follow' Jesus?," rather than saying directly, "Stop living for yourself." We can ask more open-ended questions, which typically women are more adept at doing than men. Another outworking of genderlects is the tone in which we speak. We mentioned tone earlier in this chapter regarding our delivery. We can speak with authority and be direct without sounding agitated. This is something that especially male preachers might consider more intentionally.

A third example of genderlects is to share more details. Men's and women's communication styles are different, generally speaking, when it comes to discussing the details of our lives. For instance, when I talk to my brother Dennis on the phone once or twice per month, our conversations typically sound like "report talk,"[77] where we give short reports on slices of life: "Hi, Matt, how are you?" I respond, "Good, Dennis, how are you doing?" "Good," Dennis says. "How's the family?" Dennis asks. I respond, "Everyone is good. Sarah and the boys are doing well. How is work going, Dennis?" "Work is busy but it's going well." You get the picture. Men view communication as "report talk," divulging just the bare essentials. That's fine for both of us.

On the other hand, my sister-in-law and my wife talk on a daily basis. Their conversations are prime examples of "rapport talk,"[78] where they converse about specific details such as creative food ideas, recipes, baking techniques, shopping deals, medical remedies, interactions with coworkers, the current happenings at church, fun social activities with friends, engaging television shows, hobbies, the latest news feeds, what books they are reading, and the list goes on and on.[79] In contrast, since male preachers tend not to talk about the mundane moments in life, adapting to genderlects encourages the male preacher not to "neglect everyday experiences like childcare, tension at work, and walking for exercise."[80]

In addition to details, the language of women commonly includes colorful images through interjecting various adjectives and adverbs.[81] Our vocabulary or terminology also matters. Here are some terms that, according to Woodleigh Hope Volland, may or may not resonate with male listeners. Generally speaking, men do not view themselves as "lost" or having to be "saved." Men refrain from the language of "love" and identify more with admiration and respect. And men often view community and fellowship as a way toward being a "band of brothers" who advance the cause of Christ, not simply to share life and feelings with one another.[82] Language and word choice distinguish men and women in overt and subtle ways. Being somewhat bilingual or cross-cultural in our communication between genders will serve the church well from the pulpit and in every sphere of Christian community in general.

Embrace

What we find in much of the curriculum in seminary education today focuses on the pastor as preacher, teacher, leader, and communicator. Consequently, pastors forget that ministry is not always about offering one-way communication—that is, preachers speaking to the people. Rather, ministry is a delicate balance between speaking and listening, with a greater prominence given to listening. Dietrich Bonhoeffer writes, "Many people are looking for an ear that will listen. They do not find it among Christians, because Christians are talking when they should be listening."[83] Listening is not a highly touted skill in our society. We reward lions that roar and not mice that squeak. Whether it's in school, society, or in the church, good listeners do not receive positive reinforcement or accolades. Put differently, the art of good listening encompasses the peculiar knack for being uncomfortable. Adam McHugh writes, "Let's be honest: we often want others to be okay so we can feel okay. We want them to feel better and move on so our lives can return to normal. We try to control the conversation as a way of compensating for our anxiety."[84] However, embracing our listeners involves listening to their struggles, pains, suffering, lament, questions, concerns, doubts, worries, frustration, ambiguity, loss, misunderstandings, desperation, among so many other prickly topics.

Oftentimes male pastors preach for a quick remedy. In essence, we provide weekly scriptural prescriptions packaged in the attractive box of application— that is, two or three steps to allay the pain or to temporarily redirect the listeners' vision onto what Christ has accomplished so that we may postpone thinking about our captivity to sin. While we preach "Christ and him crucified" (1 Cor. 2:2), the preacher is also called to sit with the people where they are. That means giving our listeners freedom and permission to mourn, grieve, and feel. What do we do with congregants (men and women) who are experiencing clinical depression, addictive behaviors, loss and grief, trauma, anxiety, physical ailments, cancer treatment, infertility, and a litany of other human struggles and emotions?

To embrace our listeners means we are engaging in empathy, which "literally means 'to feel into'; when we act with empathy we seek to enter, as much as possible, into the world of another person," McHugh writes.[85] He illustrates: "A hurting person is in a storm. They are cold, wet, shivering and scared. Preaching, platitudes and advice will not get them out of the storm. Don't tell someone in a storm that it's a sunny day. There will likely come a day when the clouds part, but it is not today. It's not your job to pull them out of the storm. It's your job to get soaked with them."[86] As a pastor, there were so many moments in my preaching ministry where the nucleus of the sermon was directed toward spiritual maturity and obedience yet without acknowledging the current realities of my listeners. I felt this disconnect most acutely with female congregants. They weren't interested in seeing my banner of discipleship when their immediate hurts obscured their vision.

A second way to embrace our listeners, women in particular, is to diminish or even jettison the incessant emphasis on gender roles and distinctions in a ministry context. Instead, the women in our congregation, whether we hold to a complementarian or egalitarian position, want to hear about how they can serve God rather than being reminded about the manifold ways they are prohibited from serving in Christian ministry. Denise George heard one female church member say, "Many women, including myself, are struggling to find where we fit into the church in regard to how God wants us to use our spiritual gifts. I know who I am in Christ, and I know what God has called me—and gifted me—to do. However, I feel inhibited and underutilized."[87] The underlying or sometimes overt applications in our sermons are that women's work falls under one of four major realms: food ministry, music ministry, women's ministry, and children's ministry.[88]

The application of every Scripture text, however, cannot be neatly fulfilled by serving in one or more of these four "acceptable" ministry areas reserved for female Christians—whether that is our perspective on gender roles or not. It takes hard work to apply Scripture contextually. We don't want to be armchair preachers when it comes to preaching and gender. Ask real and meaningful questions, listen without interrupting, refrain from offering immediate solutions, develop focus groups with men and focus groups with women, and provide new visions and dreams for your female and male listeners in using their spiritual gifts for God's kingdom. While many aspects of embracing our listeners could be mentioned here, preaching and gender considerations demand that we reflect on a core element of human existence:

the women and men in our churches are suffering on many levels (economically, relationally, physically, and spiritually), and we are called as preachers to embrace them as we suffer with them and practically show them ways to apply God's truth to their lives.

Content

The culture in North America and the world has shifted with respect to gender issues, but the church is often playing catch-up. For many congregations, the only times that gender receives attention from the pulpit is on Mother's Day, Father's Day, or when preachers offer wisdom about parenting or how to live with purity as a single person in a sex-crazed culture. As culturally intelligent preachers, my hope is that pastors will be bold enough to address the key issues of our time in a winsome way.

When was the last time you preached or heard a sermon on one of the following issues: human trafficking; LGBTQ issues, gender dysphoria, and sexual sins such as assault, cohabitation, fornication, pornography, adultery, divorce and remarriage; workplace ethics; evangelism; abortion; euthanasia; suicide; aging; addictions of all kinds; issues of power and control; anger; worry; hedonism; physical beauty and body image; and other iterations of idolatry and sin? Our homiletical attention to gender transcends specific times like Valentine's Day and stereotypical categories like parenting or marriage tips. The goal is ultimately that women and men, girls and boys, are provided clear guidance from the pulpit on how to be and live as disciples of Jesus Christ in every sphere of life. As you plan your next preaching series, designate concrete ways to address the concerns of men and women in your congregation. Every single sermon requires intentionality in speaking to needs and applications for women and men in expository sermons, whether while working through an entire biblical book or via topical messages.

Trust

Last, in this discussion on delivery, we consider trust or the lack thereof between people of different genders and of the same gender. In particular, the issue of power and control is universal. Men and women are both prone to desire power and unhealthy manifestations of power. Mignon Jacobs explains the dynamics of power this way: "Like males, females will seek their own interests and wield their power to maintain their privilege. The fallacy of gender alliance is that women will support women simply because they are women. Rather, lines of loyalty are blurred when self-interest becomes a priority."[89] Power dynamics exist in every congregation. The abuse of power for clergy and parents has led to the disintegration of trust in our society, family, and congregations. For this reason, Rick Richardson says, "Trust issues are immense, and only people willing to recognize the evils of the past can build the trust to be heard."[90] We cannot expect unmerited trust from our listeners. The world in which we live demands that as preachers we earn the right to preach and speak God's Word into the lives of our hearers. As preachers, we can earn the trust of women and men in three primary ways.

First, trust is earned by our presence. Abandonment, whether physically or emotionally, is a real-life experience for many women and men in the church. Our credibility in the pulpit is often determined by whether we show up when people need us most: to visit them or a loved one in the hospital, when they need pastoral presence at the courthouse, when unexpected tragedy strikes, when cancer seizes an outwardly healthy life, when children inevitably disappoint, when adultery shatters a married couple, and also in moments of joyous celebrations in your listeners' lives such as piano recitals, soccer games, graduations, weddings, anniversaries, the birth of a child, award ceremonies, and the like.[91]

Second, trust is earned by our integrity. It seems to be all too common to hear about yet another moral failure in pastoral ministry. How we relate to the opposite sex matters. The directness of my words here is as self-reflective as it is communal. Is our moral compass so disoriented that we place ourselves in compromising situations with members of the opposite sex? Do we use our influence and position to flirt with temptation? Do we treat our congregants in speech and actions with respect and dignity at all times? Do we guard our eyes and how we look at a person of the opposite gender who is not our spouse? Our position as preachers places us in a precarious situation of great influence and significance. Trust is earned through being preachers who live with integrity.

Third, trust is earned by asking for forgiveness. Why would I ask for forgiveness when I did nothing wrong? Parishioners rarely tell their pastor that the pastor has offended them or hurt them in some way. The inaudible by-product of our perceived or actual blunder is never seeing them again at church and only hearing murmurings in the church narthex afterward by a third-party church member. Our congregants, both males and females, are bruised and battered. In *Worship Words*, Debra and Ron Rienstra present the unpleasant reality that "the world is full of people who wish not only to make women yield but [also] to violate them."[92] The statistics are clear that abuse and violations are rampant in our society for men and more acutely for women: "At least

1 in 4 women and 1 in 6 men are or will be victims of sexual assault in their lifetime. Most victims (approximately 80%) are assaulted by an acquaintance (relative, friend, dating partner, spouse, pastor, teacher, boss, coach, therapist, doctor, etc.)."[93] Even if we have not been direct perpetrators of violence and abuse, preachers can operate out of a posture of requesting forgiveness for humanity's sins. We live in a world marred by systemic sin. We can ask our listeners for forgiveness and do our best by God's grace never to hurt these individuals. We may never know who in our church has been victimized by a pastor, friend, family, or those in positions of authority. Perhaps more than any other category in DIALECT, we want to earn and preserve the trust of our hearers. This trust may take time and may even need to be earned by those we never expected.

Conclusion

Preaching regarding gender is a consideration worth exploring on a regular basis. While we may not be able to include all eighteen steps of the homiletical sequence each week in our preparation, find proactive ways to be sensitive to women and men in the church, recognizing that there are real similarities and differences in how men and women communicate and interpret that communication. We will continue to make mistakes, but that should not deter us from learning about and speaking with greater cultural intelligence to men and women in our congregation.

8

Preaching and Locations

Location, location, location—*the* buzzword in real estate. The location of your property determines its value. In a similar way, location influences the mind-set of the people and informs the way you minister and preach to your local congregation. Imagine yourself transitioning into a new pastoral context. In previous churches you served in sprawling urban metropolises like New York City or Los Angeles. However, for your new pastorate God has commissioned you to a rural village on the outskirts of Omaha, with a population of 1,500. You are now sixty days into your new ministry, settling into this foreign terrain: you're in *rural* America. The culture shock has still not worn off. Beware that the inability to adapt and embrace your new surroundings may accidentally terminate your pastorate prematurely. In his book *Ten Commandments for Pastors New to a Congregation*, Lawrence Farris shares this all-too-common pastoral experience: "Well, Reverend Farris, it's like this. I never saw Reverend Flint but what he had on a three-piece suit—tie, vest, wingtips, everything. Heck, in this town, even the bankers and undertakers don't wear three-piece suits! Reverend Flint just didn't get it. He never, ever took the time to get to know who we are and how we live. And that's why he's gone!"[1]

It is crucial to understand the dynamics of the location in which we reside and minister, especially when transitioning to an unfamiliar context. In this chapter we will begin to explore the dynamics of preaching and location for urban, suburban, and rural listeners. In many ways the location of our congregations will dictate how we prepare and deliver sermons. In this chapter, I will try something different and start with a brief description of some imaginary listeners who you could envision sitting in your sanctuary on Sunday morning.[2] In using these posed persons as illustrations, some stereotyping will be involved, and not every listener will fit each bill. Rural, suburban, and urban congregations are not monolithic: they are inherently diverse.[3] Over the course of ministry, you will continue to find opportunities to hear the stories of your own congregants, who will deepen your cultural intelligence concerning your location. However, the initial goal here is that you will have a more concrete image of the type of people in your own congregation for whom you can apply these concepts and communicate God's Word with greater cultural intelligence. We will occasionally refer back to these characters for practical consideration throughout this chapter.

Urban Listener: Chad

Chad, age twenty-eight, is a single African American male living in New York City. A graduate of Dartmouth College with a major in economics, he works as a venture capitalist for a small investment firm in Midtown. His social network consists of friends from a plurality of races and religious expressions who hold more liberal beliefs and values than most of your church members. He lives in an affluent neighborhood in Manhattan that has become increasingly gentrified. Chad is heavily motivated in life by upward mobility, materialism, power, and popularity. His identity and self-worth are primarily wrapped up in professional advancement and padding his bank account. He is steadily growing in his faith and commitment to Christ, but he clearly still has a foot in both worlds: the pressures of materialism in NYC as distinct from the friendly pleasantries found with people in his church small group. Chad compartmentalizes his faith because he does not see the connection between work and his spiritual life. His theological presupposition is that God possesses unconditional love for him regardless of his life choices. Chad enjoys running and frequenting local coffee shops and fine steak restaurants.

Suburban Listener: Judy

Judy, age forty-seven, is a Caucasian female, married, and a mother of three teenagers in the suburbs of Minneapolis. She graduated from the University of Minnesota with a major in nursing and works as a nurse at the university hospital. Her primary joy in life is raising her son and two daughters. Her husband, John, is a defense attorney who is nominal in his faith. They live in Edina, an affluent suburb near the Twin Cities. Judy has been a Christian since accepting Christ in her junior year of college. As a young mother, her faith became stagnant due to her many responsibilities as a mother, wife, and nurse. She has conservative Christian values but has become increasingly apathetic in her faith and service to the church. Over time, her default theological position has become one of comfort in viewing God primarily through the lens of Jehovah-Jireh, the God who provides. Her friends consist primarily of other middle-aged mothers who were her college friends. Some of these college friends are Christians, but a few of them have left the faith. Judy feels stuck in her spiritual life and does not know how to regain her spiritual excitement. She enjoys yoga, spending time with her children, shopping, and vacationing in Europe.

Rural Listener: George

George, age sixty-eight, is a retired dairy farmer and the father of three adult children and grandfather of eight. His wife, Marie, passed away a few years ago from cancer. George served in the Vietnam War. His family came from a long tradition of dairy farmers near Sacramento. He is a fully invested member of the church and has often served in leadership capacities. George never went to college, but he possesses high business acumen. He is heavily introverted and does not work all that cooperatively with others in the congregation. In fact, he enjoys leadership positions and making decisions on behalf of the church. By his own self-estimation, he is one of the wise ones in the congregation. Having been raised in the church from birth, George is well versed in the Bible. He often takes a literal reading and interpretation of the Bible and has not matured spiritually very much since his early days as a believer. George finds joy in woodworking, spending time with his grandchildren, and enjoying a morning cup of coffee at the local restaurant with the same small group of friends.

Keep these three individuals in mind as we move forward in our Homiletical Template for preaching culturally intelligent sermons. Our first stage is to follow our HABIT in interpreting the Scripture text.

Stage 1: Follow Your HABIT

Scripture Text
Jeremiah 29:4–9

Historical, Grammatical, and Literary Context

Historical Context

The biblical passage for our consideration in terms of preaching and location is Jeremiah 29:4–9. In this familiar text, Jeremiah, the Lord's prophet, receives instructions from God about how this initial batch of migrant Israelites is to live as a community of faith in their newfound exilic location of Babylon.[4] By means of a letter, Jeremiah relays the Lord's message to the exilic people, now living in Babylon, to encourage them not only to survive but also to make the most of their situation as they subject themselves to the reign of King Nebuchadnezzar. As God's chosen people, they are to put down roots among their pagan neighbors and "seek the peace and prosperity of the city."[5]

When contemplating issues of location, the crux of this passage regards the historic situation of the Jewish people living as exilic people in Babylon (about fifty miles south of modern-day Baghdad, Iraq).[6] We cannot understate the importance of this specific *exilic* moment in Israel's history (known as the Babylonian exile/captivity). God is not commanding the Jews to promote the peace and welfare of the city of Babylon under normal conditions. Rather, the Jewish people are commanded to lead purposeful and hopeful lives in a country not their own and under the rule of Nebuchadnezzar. The cultural and religious tension for the exiles was keen: "Not only was the possession of the Land an article of faith (Deut. 26.5–10), but a foreign land was unclean."[7] While an imperfect comparison, we might think of political refugees making a new home for themselves in other countries even though it was not their choice to leave their homelands. Regardless, God calls this exilic people not only to survive but also to settle down and even flourish in spite of hopeless circumstances. Even at this early stage of exegesis, jot down areas of your congregants' lives where they may be undergoing similar "exilic" circumstances. More on this topic later on.

The locational cultural intelligence that we require pertains to the city of Babylon. What cultural information concerning Babylon will help us to explain our historical setting to our urban, suburban, and rural listeners? In much contemporary preaching, the preacher might mention the city of Babylon as the destination of the exilic people, but the description of what actually living in Babylon looked like, with its varied pagan and cultural practices, would go largely unnamed. The culturally intelligent preacher seeks to paint even a momentary portrait of what Babylon looked like at the time of the exile in order to add color and touch points to the sermon for city, suburban, or rural listeners.

As the capital of Babylonia, Babylon had become a powerful city during the time of Nebuchadnezzar and "one of the most impressive cities in the ancient Near East."[8] Babylon is described as a city "built on the banks of the Euphrates River with a large, imposing bridge connecting the two banks. Huge public buildings, places, and temples lined the banks of the river. The city was enclosed by two walls."[9] Other major features of Babylon were "its city gates [named after each of the eight Babylonian deities], the city streets, palaces, the ziggurat, the temple of Marduk, and the bridge."[10] Its proximity to the Euphrates River made it a natural trade route.[11] Culturally, the city was enamored with idol worship, as depicted in Jeremiah 50–51, and became a major religious center.[12] For the Jewish people, Babylonia represented the "literary symbol epitomizing all of Israel's enemies"[13] on account of their destruction of Jerusalem. However, in time they learned to adapt to their new surroundings and made the Babylonian culture part of their own. For instance, scholars note:

> As the minority culture Jews were always affected by the majority culture. However, they were able to absorb it in such a way as to make it Jewish. That process began in Babylon. For example, in the Five Books of Moses and until the Babylonian exile the months were called by a Hebrew number: for example, the "First Month," the "Second Month," etc. However, the names in use now like Tishrei, Kislev, Tammuz, etc. are all Babylonian. Even more strangely, Tammuz, which takes place in the heat of the summer, was the Babylonian god of fire, whom they burned children to. It is even mentioned in the Bible as the name of one of their gods. Yet, it became a part of Jewish life.[14]

Further, during the exile, as Alfred Hoerth comments, the deported Jews experienced "freedom of worship" and were even "allowed a form of local government."[15] What comparisons could be made with other cities or places that might help our listeners situate Babylon in their minds? What modern cities would facilitate mental images for our listeners to relate to? Providing your hearers with the historical setting of Babylon (its architecture, location, and cultural context) will add dimensions of cultural intelligence to the sermon, thus linking our *authorial-cultural* hermeneutic with the cultural knowledge and experience of our listeners in their context. Connect the dots for them so that the faraway and long ago elements enter the living rooms of their minds.

Grammatical Issues

Our grammatical study should further enrich our understanding of the cultural dynamics in our passage: what it meant for the Jews to live as exiles in Babylon. The struggle for the exiles at the end of Jeremiah 29:8 was that they were hearing false teaching from deceivers who spoke contradictory words purportedly from the Lord. Specifically, "the people were given conflicting advice, for there were prophets in exile who gave exactly the advice they wanted to hear,"[16] that they would shortly return to Jerusalem. Perhaps for this reason Jeremiah uses repetition and restatement in verses 8–9 in quoting God: "'Do not let the prophets and diviners among you deceive you. Do not listen to the dreams you encourage them to have. They are prophesying lies to you in my name. I have not sent them,' declares the LORD." The prophet is driving home his point that the exiles are not to listen to the deceptive teaching of false teachers but to heed the Word of God. In a similar way, perhaps in our preaching, one tool to reinforce our cultural warnings is to include repetition and restatement.

Our sermon may also include word studies to help our listeners explore what God means by "seek[ing] the peace and prosperity of the city." As Timothy Keller puts it, "In Jeremiah 29:7, God calls the Jews not just to live in the city but to love it and work for its shalom—its economic, social and spiritual flourishing."[17] We want to unpack the word "peace," or "shalom" (also translated as "prosperity, well-being, health, completeness, safety"),[18] in this biblical time period and find modern parallel concepts for today and what this looks like in urban, suburban, and rural contexts. Here we are told that "Jeremiah's audience is invited to abandon hope in a 'holy revolt' against Babylon, which had been inspired by the false prophets' promises that God would bring the exiles back in a short time, and to place their hope instead in the LORD and a new way of life."[19]

Literary Study

Genre is the primary focus with respect to literary considerations. In prophetical books like Jeremiah, prophets were called by God to serve as moral agents and religious leaders of their day.[20] Thus they served as the prophetic voice that spoke God's truth into the culture. That prophetic voice often took the form of "urgency and grimness" as they faced invasions from other countries.[21] Our particular text for consideration, Jeremiah 29:4–9, is a letter from God to the exiles. God delivers a big blow to their spirits in letting the exiles know that this banishment to Babylon will last an extended period of time. As Tremper Longman states, "These commands [to settle down in Babylon] imply that their exile will be multigenerational."[22] While stern in tone, God's letter to the exiles offers glimpses of hope. God wants the exiles to flourish, and as they prosper, the Babylonians will prosper too.[23] Once we explore the historical, grammatical, and literary contexts, we delve further into the cultural context of the biblical author and his world.

Author's Cultural Context

What do we know about Jeremiah's cultural context? Nicknamed "a prophet of doom" or "the weeping prophet," Jeremiah, a seventh-century prophet (ca. 627–585 BC), empathized greatly with the spiritual malaise and idolatry of the people of Jerusalem.[24] He served as God's prophet during the reigns of Kings Josiah, Jehoiakim, and Zedekiah (Jer. 1:2–3). The feelings of helplessness and depression, particularly due to the destruction of Solomon's temple and exile to Babylon, loomed large over the people. To understand Jeremiah's context, although it may be difficult, we must imagine ourselves as a people being uprooted unwillingly, taken into a hostile foreign land as a form of discipline on account of our sins against the Lord, and needing to establish new homes in this alien land while living among the enemies who have just taken us into captivity. The overarching message from God through the prophet Jeremiah is clear: "submit to Babylon's rule and live a 'normal' life in Babylon."[25] Jeremiah 29:4–9 provides specific instructions to the exiles on how they are to live "normally" among the Babylonians.

Two major cultural practices are emphasized in this prophetical book. First, Jeremiah's cultural context was steeped in idol worship. Throughout the book, God reminds Judah and Israel of their idolatrous and unfaithful ways. God says in Jeremiah 2:11, "But my people have exchanged their glorious God for worthless idols." Another primary rebuke of the culture concerns their penchant to forget the Lord and that they lack fear and reverence for him. For example, in Jeremiah 5:22, the Lord asks, "'Should you not fear me?' declares the LORD. 'Should you not tremble in my presence?'" God's chosen people had forsaken him for idols and forgotten their sense of awe before God and his mighty deeds. As they were prone to wander in their minds from the Lord and his instructions, God reminds them in our text, Jeremiah 29:8–9, that they are not to listen to the voice of false teachers because God did not send them. When we are able to locate the dominant cultural practices of the biblical peoples in our text, we can then compare and contrast these practices with the listeners in our specific locations.

Big Idea of the Text

Subject: How does God instruct the Israelites to live as exilic people in Babylon?

Complement: To settle down among the Babylonians, to seek the peace and prosperity of the city, and to guard themselves against false prophets.

Exegetical Idea: God instructs the Israelites to live as exilic people in Babylon, to settle down among the Babylonians, to seek the peace and prosperity of the city, and to guard themselves against false prophets.

Homiletical Idea: God calls us to live faithful lives wherever he leads us and to be agents of peace.

Interpret in Your Context

The location of our congregation influences how the Scriptures are interpreted. While we recognize the importance of understanding Scripture in its biblical and historical context, we do not interpret Scripture in a vacuum. For instance, if we preach in an urban context, according to Harvie Conn, "*A more balanced urban hermeneutic is needed. What is the proper mix between the urban horizon of the biblical text and the contemporary urban horizons of Minneapolis and Mexico City? How can the academic disciplines of urban sociology and urban anthropology aid our search of Scripture, and vice-versa, as we develop a functional theology for urban mission?*"[26] The challenges for interpreting the Scripture text in hand for our specific location will require greater sensitivity to the cultural milieu and location of our people. In this fourth stage, our hermeneutical task is to acknowledge the assumptions, conflicts, and questions that stand out for our listeners when *they* read the text.

Assumptions

Our interpretation in context invites an opportunity for us, as preachers, to hypothetically step into the craniums of our listeners. First, what assumptions are made by our listeners as they read Jeremiah 29:4–9? For example, members of rural communities, especially agricultural suppliers, may link the image of prosperity with fertility of the ground as they cultivate the soil for the country's food production. Urban dwellers may naturally gravitate toward the necessity of peaceful living while amid a climate of religious pluralism, racial hostility, and gratuitous crime. Suburbanites may interpret the passage literally by placing primary emphasis on building custom homes and making for themselves the perfect dwelling place. Let's take the example of Chad, our urban listener. What assumptions might he make about this text?

Conflicts

Regardless of their rural, suburban, and urban location, affluenza is a social and spiritual condition that affects all people, where "we all find a certain degree of satisfaction in many things we own and consume."[27] The American Dream is a dominant lens through which many people in the United States and abroad naturally read and interpret Scripture. What does God denote by "prosperity" in this text, and how do we explain this concept to our listeners? A major conversation piece in our sermon may deal with the meaning of "prosperity" in its context as discussed in verse 7. God does not promote individual prosperity alone, but rather he commands them to "seek the peace and prosperity of *the city* to which I have carried you into exile" (Jer. 29:7, emphasis added). Here is where the conflict can lie as we debunk individual prosperity theology so that we might envision a broader scope of community and communal well-being. Consider Judy, our suburban listener. What conflicts might she raise about our passage?

Questions

What questions does this text stimulate for my hearers? For instance, when my listener hears the word "prosperity," what does she immediately think of while living in a small farming community outside of Des Moines? When my listener hears the word "peace," what does his mind naturally gravitate toward as a citizen of the inner-city of Detroit? How do my suburban listeners on the outskirts of Denver guard against false teachers in their communities? Every Scripture text raises questions in the minds of our listeners, and we want to do our due diligence in this hermeneutical process to anticipate the questions our hearers will ask. In your study notes, take some time to write down the questions your listeners will have as rural, suburban, and urban people regarding this specific passage. If it helps, select a few congregants and take note of the questions they might raise. Think about what questions someone like George might have as a rural listener.

Theological Presuppositions

In this fifth and final hermeneutical stage, we ask ourselves, "What do I and my listeners believe about God as I/they read this text?" Mark Gornik writes, "Effective preaching is gospel reflection on reality, theology done in context."[28] All parts of the Scripture are theological in that they speak truth about the character, actions, and will of God. This specific text forces us to consider our view and our listeners' view of a God who permits suffering in the form of the exile. Why does God allow the Babylonians "to carry" the Israelites into captivity and exile?

In verse 4, God is the primary agent who allows the people of Jerusalem "to be carried away" by the Babylonians. Matthew Henry comments, "All the force of the king of Babylon could not have done it if God had not ordered it; nor could he have any power against them but what was given him from above."[29] In each location, whether in urban, suburban, or rural contexts, our listeners are processing what it means to worship a God who permits the exile.

The exile, in contemporary terms, represents different things to different people. A growing problem in many cities around the globe and in the United States is human trafficking and slavery. Our listeners wonder why God would allow such heinous crimes to be prolonged for so many women and children. For others, perhaps in rural settings, the exile represents the incredible shortage of water in states like California, experiencing drought that affects farmers and their ability to grow crops.[30] Suburbanites may, unbeknownst to them, find exilic streams in their own captivity to material goods as well as other "inner fears, illusions, and guilts" that they have difficulty escaping.[31] Theological presuppositions must be named in the sermon, to acknowledge on behalf of our listeners that we are also wrestling with their struggles and questions about the nature and character of God. These theological perspectives often become stumbling blocks for our hearers and sometimes even excuses for their disbelief or disappointment in God.

In following our HABIT, stay close to the ancient world of the biblical author and his cultural context. In this case, we have explored Babylon and a few of the complexities of the Jewish people living at a new location, the city of Babylon. As we become more familiar with the author's cultural context, we are simultaneously trying to see how the author's culture intersects with our specific urban, suburban, or rural cultural context. In the second stage, we will build the bridge and enter our listeners' worlds.

Stage 2: Build the BRIDGE

Beliefs

Urbanites: Achievement

A primary belief or value for urban people is a high regard for achievement. Regardless of one's profession, the urban mind-set places extraordinary weight on results and checking off goals.[32] Urban listeners will expect tangible ways to grow spiritually and relationally, for example. The preacher in an urban context would benefit from providing periodic visions and goals for the congregation to pursue and concrete metrics to verify the progress the congregation makes toward achieving these spiritual aspirations. The urban preacher will want to regularly refer back to the church's beliefs, vision, and values to see if tweaks or even major overhauls need to be made, and then in their preaching clearly communicate the defined and redefined goals and visions to the church. With reference to the author's context, where might achievement find a place in the sermon for cultural contact? In what concrete ways will your listeners appreciate the various forms of human or spiritual achievements as the exilic people make a new home for themselves in Babylon?

Suburbanites: Privacy

Privacy is an unspoken but dominant belief or value among suburban Christians. Having pastored a unique church of suburbanites who commuted into the city for worship on Sundays, I can attest to the strong predilection toward privacy. While congregants enjoyed coming over for dinner at the parsonage, they seldom invited us into their homes. My wife and I stepped into the residences of less than 20 percent of the congregation over a six-year period. While in some contexts this may be an overstatement, suburbanites simply want to be left alone. Even living in our suburban neighborhood on the North Shore of Boston, I have seen the furnishings of only one home in our cul-de-sac of eleven houses, and that was for a child's birthday party.

Suburban Christians enjoy their physical privacy, which congruently impacts their craving for spiritual privacy and inward focus. Though gifted in many ways, suburbanites are often overworked and overextended, which creates a myopic perspective on the Christian life. They tend to be insular and focus their lives primarily on their immediate family and perhaps their immediate church family. A culturally intelligent suburban preacher will locate moments in the sermon to endorse communal and global needs and thereby help suburban listeners get out of the individualistic mind-set that breeds "havens for self-pitying, complaining people."[33] Suburban preachers with growing cultural intelligence will increase their effectiveness by revealing the brokenness of our world and the material and spiritual needs of those in our "Jerusalem, Judea, and Samaria" and the wider culture. As Arthur DeKruyter and Quentin Schultze remind us, "The heart of every true church, including those in comfortable suburbs, must beat for the redemption of the world."[34] How might your suburban listeners interpret our Scripture text in light of their propensity toward comfort and privacy? What cultural examples may find similarities and differences between the author's context of Babylon and your suburban hearers?

Ruralites: Uncertainty

Rural Americans are affected by uncertainty, especially economic uncertainty. More rural Americans than urbanites now live in a state of poverty.[35] In particular, farming communities experience the cruel fickleness of nature in providing or withholding requisite and consistent rain to produce crops. For agrarian people, daily life is "extremely unpredictable" where their "livelihood is consistently subject to factors beyond their control."[36] The instability of life causes "significant pressure in the lives of rural people."[37] Again, we search for cultural congruence with the author's culture in our text. In what ways were the exiles feeling uncertainty in their lives? For example, provide your listeners with clear connection points between the author's world and your listeners' lives, which in this case could mean abiding by the laws of a new local government in Babylon (v. 4), engaging in agriculture and farming (v. 5), or perhaps dealing with the uncertainty caused by false teachers (vv. 8–9).

Martin Giese presents a list of characteristic differences between rural and urban people, which may guide us in developing cultural intelligence.

Table 8.1 Rural Mind-Set versus Urban Mind-Set

Rural Mind-Set	Urban Mind-Set
Few people	Many people
Small institutions of all types	Large institutions of all types
Independence	Cooperation
General practitioner	Specialist orientation
Low verbal communication	High verbal communication
Cooperation for survival	Cooperation for achievement
Single-tier management	Multilevel management
Preservation	Innovation
Provincial	Cosmopolitan
Experiential	Experimental
Incidental relationships	Intentional relationships
Cautious	Assertive

From Martin Giese, "Understanding Your Ministry Context," RHMA Small Town Pastors' Conference, April 18–20, 2016, unpublished notes. Used by permission.

Not only do we want to build the bridge for the dominant beliefs of our listeners; we also want to appreciate their rituals.

Rituals

Every congregation in America holds to different rituals, customs, traditions, observances, and mores. Become familiar with the rituals of your congregation. Andrew Miles and Rae Jean Proeschold-Bell underscore the importance of rural ministry exploration: "Despite the fact that nearly one-third of churches in the United States are located in predominately rural areas, researchers have paid little attention to rural churches and experiences of their clergy."[38] Here are some observations that Fred Edie shares concerning the usual rituals or traditions of rural churches: "Most rural congregations are characterized by relatively small memberships of between 50 and 150 persons. They are often family centered—in fact, a congregation may be almost entirely constituted by one or two extended families. They tend to be traditional because they have usually been around for a while and because of their historic connections to family matriarchs and patriarchs."[39]

While all rural churches vary, find out what holidays, observances, traditions, and customs are significant in the life of your church, particularly early in your pastorate. Rituals may also include worship styles, preferences for how Communion is celebrated, traditions for new-member induction or baptismal services, whether national holidays like Veterans Day or Memorial Day are remembered and observed on a Sunday morning, missing the Sunday worship service to watch the games of local sports teams (e.g., football), and the list goes on and on. The rituals of your church were instituted at some point before your arrival, by earlier pastors or laypersons, and they are now deeply embedded in the hearts of your congregants. Depending on your church context, seeking to modify, add, or delete worship services such as Christmas Eve or New Year's celebrations may be frowned on or even hotly contested. Listen, observe, ask questions, and find out what makes your church tick. For example, in the church where I pastored in Denver, Mother's Day and Father's Day were major days of celebration. Congregants wanted to hear sermons specifically addressing familial/parental matters and strengthening and honoring the parents in our church. Your congregation may highlight Veterans Day or Martin Luther King Jr.'s birthday. Rituals will differ in various urban, suburban, and rural sectors. Appreciate and value the traditions and customs of your church as long as they don't compete with God's values.

Idols

In his book *Preaching to Suburban Captives*, Alvin Porteous observes, "Because of their relative power and wealth and their more expansive opportunities for self-expression, suburban captives may be more potently tempted by the sin of idolatry. They are easily tempted into regarding their own culture, values, and life-style as normative for all people."[40] However, idolatry captures the affections of listeners across urban, suburban, and rural contexts just as they attracted the Israelites throughout their history. There is a reason why God lists idolatry as the first and second commandments in the Ten Commandments. Idolatry is powerful. It plagued Israel's history, and it wages war in the souls of modern Christians as well. More than any other section of the BRIDGE, studying the cultural idols in our location may be the most crucial.

In every city, suburb, and rural village, cultural idols exist and are expressed differently. The apostle Paul in Acts 17, when he entered Athens, took a stroll around the city to observe what idols the local people worshiped. He found many. While Paul witnessed physical idols hanging or standing on the streets, the cultural idols of today are not always external but rather internal. Nor do people see their idolatry as comparable to biblical forms of idolatry. For instance, Lee Eclov writes, "If the truth be told, most of our people cannot conceive that even their gross indulgences, their over-doings ('Too much TV, I know') are anything like biblical idolatry."[41] Each region of the country and even each city, suburb, or rural village will worship one, two, or more dominant idols. Our responsibility will be to discern which idols grip the hearts of our people. In *Why Cities Matter*, the authors list cultural idols across cities in the United States, including these examples: Boston: knowledge; Silicon Valley: success; Washington, DC: power; San Francisco: equality; Oklahoma City: family; Las Vegas: pleasure; Austin: independence; Boulder: adventure; Los Angeles: image; Detroit: hope; and New York: success.[42] What is the primary cultural idol in your city, suburb, or rural town? Try to name it in a single word.

Idolatry can be centered on anyone or anything: beauty, self-image, education, family, success, social media, power, sex, control, money, relationships, and so forth. Two universal idols that we face constantly in churches today in all locations regard wealth and work. The author of Ecclesiastes had it right when he says in 5:10, "Whoever loves money never has enough; whoever loves wealth is never satisfied with their income." The struggle is that the term "whoever" refers to most, if not all, people in our congregations. Work is another idol that merits further exposure in our preaching. For most congregants, work consumes most of their daily waking hours. Some individuals work to live, but many live to work. Yet oftentimes our church members have difficulty articulating how their work relates to their Christian life, and sadly we have not preached in such a way as to help them understand this relationship. Wealth and work are also germane topics in Jeremiah 29:4–9. How can we better address the cultural idols that seize our listeners in their specific settings? Try to write down four or five major idols in the lives of your people.

Dreams

We can learn so much by asking people what they dream about. In the Bible, God takes human dreams and visions seriously. We know all too well that Proverbs 29:18 is true: "Where there is no vision [or dream], the people perish" (KJV). In some shape or form, dreaming occurs for our listeners on a regular basis. They are dreaming about their present reality and their future, their children's future, their grandchildren's future, their business, their church, and hopefully their spiritual lives.

At some point in the sermon, one of our goals should be to help our congregants dream about what our churches could look like and what positive impact our churches can make for our town, suburb, or city. In the movie *Rudy*, suburbanite Daniel Ruettiger (Rudy) dreams of playing football at the University of Notre Dame. Having less than average athletic prowess or intellectual gifts, Ruettiger's teachers and even his family members in Joliet, Illinois, mock his aspiration. Yet Rudy pursues his dream and eventually achieves it. *Rudy* energizes me every time I watch the film. Its story inspires me to trust Jesus when he says, "With God all things are possible" (Matt. 19:26), even when we feel utterly discouraged by what is happening or not happening in our churches and communities.

Dreams are culturally conditioned. Perhaps in some inner-city neighborhoods in Chicago or Detroit or for communities of struggling farmers in Oklahoma, the dream is simply daily survival. Eric Russ writes, "The issue of opportunity is what separates urban from inner city. . . . For example, the key residual effect from the inner city is that the people will often struggle with a sense of dignity. They find it hard to not consider themselves second tier because of the hardship they have experienced as an inner city native."[43] For many suburban folks, the cultural dream of families is to achieve educational and professional success. Beyond cultural dreams, individual dreams can also be named. Our congregants dream about getting married, owning a home, having children, advancing in their careers, leaving a legacy for their children and grandchildren, and more spiritual dreams like sharing the love of Christ with their neighbors. By providing sermonic space for our listeners to dream together and individually, our congregations will make breakthroughs as they begin to see how God can use their gifts, time, and resources for "seeking the peace and prosperity" even where they live. Take a few moments to reflect on what dreams your people have for your location and consider how you could introduce "dreaming sessions" in your upcoming sermon series.

God

While the topic of God is very broad, over the years we have all witnessed the variety of ways in which people view God. A person or culture's view of God significantly expands or contracts the ability to grow in spiritual maturity and Christlikeness. As humans, we try our best to make sense, using our own limited reasoning to understand who God is. If we are honest, our narrow understanding of God forces us to rely on our own experiences of what God has or has not done for us or what he allows or disallows. Depending on our experiences in the city, suburbs, or rural towns, our view of God takes on either positive or negative characteristics.

Amid rampant poverty, addiction, suffering, pain, and brokenness, urban Christians tend to have an awestruck view of God. That is, urbanites have witnessed miraculous transformation of broken people living on the streets. They tend to see a God who is at work, who is active in the lives of his people. Urbanites also view God as a God of diversity. Nowhere do we see the range of diversity of peoples, whether ethnically, religiously, or socioeconomically, as in urban cities. Rural American Christians will view God differently from urbanites. Rural Christians, by living closer to nature, tend to notice the beauty of God in creation. Rolling hills, endless rows of grain, and the majestic sunsets overlooking ponds and lakes daily reinforce the God of nature. Meanwhile suburban Christians may focus on God's attributes, such as whether he is generous or miserly, whether God is extremely critical or loving, or whether God blesses or curses. In each location, our listeners have formed opinions about who they believe God is. This proper (or improper) understanding of God and his character profoundly influences how they receive our communication about God. Another significant way to grow in cultural intelligence on this topic is to probe our listeners on who they think God is and why they believe what they do about God.

Experiences

Last, there is nothing that reaches the heart of our listeners more than connecting with their own life experiences. Memorable experiences, whether encouraging or harmful, will cloud our listeners' thinking. That is, no one will forget the horrific events of 9/11, especially those who were impacted most directly by it in New York City; Washington, DC; and rural Pennsylvania.

Throughout the sermon, make contact with the real experiences of our people in urban, suburban, or rural contexts. The closer we make contact to real-life experiences, the stronger our sermon will be. How we approach the topic of experience is open-ended and perhaps too amorphous for some preachers. However, it will take some investigative legwork to learn about our listeners and their experiences in their areas of residence and in their workplaces. Let's exert due diligence to find out why our listeners have chosen to relocate and move into our city, suburb, or town. Perhaps they have never left. Listen to their past fears, pains, challenges, and joys of living in your location. For example, Ray Bakke felt the call of God in 1965 to move his family into inner-city Chicago and minister to urban people. He recounts:

> Could it be, I asked in 1965, that God was asking me to seek the *shalom* of Chicago, this dirty, ugly, flat, corrupt city? Could I believe that if I truly did so, God would bless my own family with true *shalom*? . . . This text rearranged my priorities. . . . In retrospect, we can see that God was using the Babylonian exile [and his own relocation to inner-city Chicago] to teach Israel [the church] profound truths with enormous mission significance.[44]

How do your listeners feel about living in your context? What do they wish they could change? In what ways might these past experiences color their hearing of the Word? How can you relate their experiences to what the people in your biblical story experienced? In our particular text, find connection points by encouraging your listeners to recall feelings of displacement or life scenes in which they encountered the shalom of God from an unlikely source. Making connections with our listeners' experiences will energize them as they become firsthand witnesses of how God works in and through the lives of biblical people and people just like themselves. Taking what we have learned from crossing over the bridge, let's move into the final stage, on delivery and how to preach culturally intelligent messages for our people.

Stage 3: Speak Their DIALECT

Delivery

Sermon Structure

In reality, our delivery carries the same communicational weight as our content. A preacher may have extraordinary sermonic content, but the sermon flops because of not giving enough attention to delivery. No doubt "delivery" means different things to different preachers. Here, with respect to location, I want us to primarily consider the issues of sermon structure and tone.

What sermon structure works best in urban contexts? What about in the suburbs or in small towns? Well, obviously it depends on the literary genre and the flow of the passage. However, our natural preaching tendency is to structure according to our style and preference, whether that is deductive (big idea up-front), inductive (big idea at the end), or semi-inductive (big idea in the middle), and to do so regardless of who is listening or the location of our listeners. How does the location of our church affect our sermon structure? People mentally engage with the sermon differently. Keith Willhite explains, "When faced with a sermon's claim, a listener may choose to accept the claim, or reject, ignore, or challenge it."[45] One rural pastor observes, "A sermon structure attuned to the text and to the people to whom you preach may help them hear the gospel in a familiar voice, aiding them in conforming their life to the gospel we are called to preach."[46] Therefore, knowledge of our listeners and how to convey the gospel truth to them will enable them to participate in the gospel and develop in discipleship.

As we grow in cultural intelligence, our homiletical radars will be able to detect which sermon structure may be most effective for our urban, suburban, and rural listeners. Let's take the example of our text. If we are preaching in a rural context, what route should I take with regard to sermon structure: deductive, inductive, or semi-inductive? Let's say that the central truth that I want to communicate (big idea) in this sermon is that *God calls us to live faithful lives wherever he leads us and to be his agents of peace.* What objections might my rural listeners have to this homiletical idea? For a moment consider again our imaginary listener, George. Are there any commands in God's letter to the exiles that George and other rural listeners would disagree with or object to? If the answer is yes, then our strategy might be to preach an inductive or semi-inductive message where we could state the main idea toward the end of the sermon and apply the central truth of the message in their context. The key is to know our rural (or urban or suburban) listeners well enough that we can structure the sermon effectively to facilitate their belief.

Tone

A second delivery element relates to our tone. Our delivery tone (mood and voice) should match the tone of the biblical text. Here in Jeremiah 29:4–9 we gather the impression that there are primarily two tones, lament and hope. First, we must acknowledge that many evangelical Western preachers have an aversion to lament. We want jovial congregants who live productive and carefree lives. We don't want people in the church who lament. But depending on our church's location and the kinds of events taking place in our cities, suburbs, and towns, many people are hurting and seek opportunities to lament to us, to one another, and to the Lord. At this current moment in American history, our country is reeling in lament over the numerous hate crimes committed against African Americans. Cities like New York City and Baltimore and suburbs like Ferguson, Missouri, are bewildered by the atrocities against African American citizens. Just as the exiles lamented about their banishment to Babylon, we too can lament with and for our people in the ways that they are brokenhearted from the effects of sin.

At the same time, our passage leaves the readers/listeners with hope. While God takes sin seriously and disciplines the exiles for their disobedience, God has clearly not abandoned the people of Judah to the devices of the Babylonians. The tone of the text is optimistic. God encourages the people to live life in Babylon just as they would in Jerusalem. He wants them to settle down and to flourish in their new surroundings for generations to come. He wants them to find opportunities to promote peace and well-being.

The tone of our sermons requires cultural sensitivity, flexibility, and faithfulness to resemble the tone of the passage. By growing in our cultural intelligence, we will be able to adapt our tone to communicate in the ways our people will hear from God. You will find moments in the sermon, as Paul encourages Timothy in 2 Timothy 3:16, to use Scripture for teaching, rebuking, correcting, and training in righteousness, and to foster hope in God while taking into consideration the tone of the text. Depending on our location, the tone of our sermon will take nuancing but employ our cultural knowledge to address listeners where they are.

Illustrations

Do your illustrations resonate with the people in your location? Illustrations are tricky because our inclination is to believe that everyone echoes our interests and humor. In her book *Preaching as Local Theology and Folk Art*, Leonora Tubbs Tisdale shares this realization of a young pastoral couple:

> Tim and Beth, a clergy couple, moved from their post as associate pastors in a highly educated and politically active urban congregation, to become co-pastors of a blue-collar congregation in a small town. "What we miss the most," said Beth, "are people like us that we can talk to about literature or politics or the challenges of juggling professional careers and family." . . . "As for preaching,"

Beth continues, "you know how much I love poetry, and love to craft sermons that use a lot of poetic imagery and subtlety. I'm wondering if I can get away with that here. I'm wondering if people will even understand what I'm trying to say if I don't say it more simply and directly."[47]

One pastor of a rural congregation noted that he "uses images more than illustrations," much as Jesus did in the Gospels. The pastor explained further, "I try to communicate the text and images that are familiar to my congregation. The side of a road on the way to Jerusalem becomes the country road leading into town. The path Jesus walks becomes the canals and waterways around our farms."[48] Images are clearly a beneficial way to meet listeners where they are and to elucidate our points. Jennifer Lord contends, "Imagery is not optional for preaching. It is not an additive to conceptual or theoretical writing. It is how our minds work to make sense of life."[49]

Establishing surface-level rapport with our listeners through illustration is important but can become stale quickly. When my brother was in law school, at the beginning of every sermon his pastor would invariably talk about the most recent victory or loss of the basketball team at his university campus that week. Initially helpful, this tactic rapidly wore off its luster. Broadening our illustrations even beyond our normal illustrative types will lengthen our reach in the sermon. Our tendency is to draw illustrations from a small subset of hobbyhorses such as sports, movies, or the headliner on the front page. A skill to develop in our communication is to diversify our portfolio of illustrations as we get to know our listeners and their interests.

At my former church in Colorado, it was commonplace for church members to ask me to leave my study and venture out with them into recreational activities in the outdoors. Growing up in Chicago, I had seldom experienced nature and wildlife as I experienced in the majestic foothills outside Denver. To connect with my listeners, my illustrations needed to become less about me and my interests and more about what my listeners appreciated and enjoyed. I began to learn about how to tie a fly to effectively fly-fish. I found a new appreciation for wakeboarding, snowboarding, and mountain biking. I searched the internet for resources that pushed me to explore connection points with my listeners. Our initial cultural intelligence permits us to access the surface-level cultural contact points. My hope is that we will find more significant access points that truly reach our listeners' hearts.

Let's consider George, our rural listener, and think about his life circumstances. What illustrations work most effectively for people living in rural towns? Refer back to the BRIDGE and the cultural intelligence gained from this exercise. Are there beliefs, rituals, idols, dreams, notions of God, or experiences that we can help clarify for our listeners and connect their world to the biblical story? Perhaps in one of your illustrations you could focus in on dreams. What were the new dreams of the exiles in our text now that they find themselves in Babylon? What dreams do your listeners have for their rural context? Dreams are the most comprehensive component to the BRIDGE, because in many ways our dreams are a summative representation of our beliefs, rituals, idols, view of God, and experiences. Endorsing or shunning dreams can either embolden or dismantle the spirits of any person beyond measure. Our dreams matter because they provide purpose and meaning to life. A rural pastor shared with me how in his rural church his congregants had the following dreams:

> I find that the older generation, very clearly and in no uncertain terms, wants to leave something for the church in the coming generations. In my community this often translates into building facilities and renovating old facilities. This is a project that is measurable, that engages in work, that they can work on personally, that they now have the money to accomplish, and that leaves something tangible. This has huge benefits for the church, in terms of amazing facilities and space for God's kingdom to grow.[50]

We can find natural connection points between our congregants' dreams for our church and the possible dreams of the exiles in our text. God calls the exiles to settle down and "seek the peace and prosperity" of Babylon for generations to come. By illustrating through personal and communal dreams, our listeners will find cultural connection points with the biblical story in view, and hopefully this will increase their faith in God and in his Word.

Since we cannot illustrate perfectly for each listener every single Sunday, target a few different types of listeners in the congregation, find opportunities to illustrate the Scriptures for them, and then move on to a few other listeners the following week. Take a moment now to think about three different types of listeners in your urban, suburban, or rural church context. As you think about Jeremiah 29:4–9, what kinds of illustrations would be most effective in relating to people like Chad, Judy, or George? It will amaze our people when we explore the terrains of their lives and offer illustrations that speak to them and not just to our own lives. Our cultural intelligence equips us to illustrate with tangible, custom-fitted illustrations rather than rely on cookie-cutter generalities.

Application

For many preachers, application is the most challenging element to sermon writing. It has always been so for me too. The purpose of application is not simply to modify sinful behaviors. As Jeffrey D. Arthurs and others declare, the point of application is to move the listener's heart and thereby change people holistically and not merely behaviorally.[51] Murray Capill observes, "In Hebraic thought, the heart is the core of our entire being. It is the center and soul of who we are, comprising the seat of all our thoughts, feelings, and actions. The heart is the real us. So when you shoot at the heart, you are shooting at the whole person, including their thinking and their feeling."[52] What would be some contextual, heart-centered applications for our rural, suburban, and urban listeners from Jeremiah 29?

Building our Homiletical Bridge, are any themes emerging from our Scripture text that naturally lend themselves toward sermonic application? What heart issues arise from these verses that we could apply to our listeners? Perhaps one application from this text for our suburban congregants is to name the beliefs and idols in our people's lives and to show them that as believers in Christ we are to seek shalom and peace and prosperity not only for our immediate families but also for entire communities. What would it look like for our listeners to seek the prosperity and welfare of Lowell, Massachusetts, or Anchorage, Alaska? The application forces us to look into the mirror of our hearts and come to terms with our suburban inclinations toward privacy, comfort, and individual prosperity.

Another application could include praying for our enemies, which is what God commands his people to do in praying for the Babylonians. In our specific church's location, who are the enemies in our midst? Strongly encourage your people to write down the names of specific "enemies" and specific prayer requests. Not only can we pray for our enemies but we can also pray for our local government. Seldom in today's churches do we call on God to bring wisdom to our local government officials and name central issues dividing our citizens. At the end of the service, set aside time for prayer to bolster active participation as a form of application.

A third application might involve raising to our listeners' consciousness some of the false teachings that they have been internalizing and that conflict with God's instructions. What lies have they believed in? Specific false teachings will come to mind depending on your church's location. Perhaps in small-group discussions later that week, your congregation could center on identifying and praying for specific false teachings circulating in the body of Christ, particularly as they relate to the local concerns. If you are cognizant of local heresies being spread in your town, you can publicize them openly in the sermon and instruct the congregation on why such false doctrines are erroneous.

In general, find ways to promote balance in your sermon applications where the sermon's challenges to be and to do are individual and corporate. How does this particular sermon text inform, test, question our beliefs, rituals, idols, dreams, view of God, and experiences? In your sermon preparation, stop each week to consider the text and the tangible ways that this passage connects to the heart of people like Chad, Judy, and George in your congregation.[53]

Language

Depending on where one grows up, different words are used to identify the same object. For example, growing up in Chicago in the Midwest, the word for Coca-Cola or any kind of carbonated beverage was "pop." "Can I have a pop?" is the way Chicagoans ask for a can of soda. If you ask for a "pop" from someone on the fast-paced streets of New York City, you might get a right hook on your cheekbone or hear the other person ask if you've lost your father. Words mean different things in different places. It takes time to become familiar with local words. The types of words we use will vary markedly if we are located in inner-city Chicago; Simi Valley, California; or Birmingham, Alabama. In general, the English language has become increasingly less formal and more truncated. More conjunctions are being used whenever possible, and advertisements and the culture at large try to shorten the number of syllables, such as "aight" for "alright" and even spelling "nite" for "night." Depending on where we are ministering and preaching, our listeners will appreciate our adaptation to the local dialect and the use of familiar words.

Although we are referring to the English language, our words and their meanings vary vastly depending on where we are located. In cities, the tendency is toward the use of more slang and local vernacular, which we may not be accustomed to using. In highly educated congregations, especially near university settings, preachers may employ more formal language. Depending on the major industry in your location, we may need to become familiar with the technical language and words commonly used in conversation among your listeners. For instance, in San Jose you may want to sit down with your listeners to get a feel for language and terms commonplace in the IT world, or in genres of music if you live near Nashville. Find out about local cuisines and specialty foods in your area.

What are crawdads, hot browns, or po' boys? Become familiar with the ethnic sections of your town or community like Little Warsaw or Koreatown. Sit down in a local coffee shop and listen to the communication going on around you. What dialect are they speaking? If you are especially new to a town, you can visit with some church members to hear the range of words and terms being thrown out as you ask questions and learn about their environment.

Are any words unfamiliar for you? Our language matters, and especially in preaching we want to ensure that our listeners hear language and words and phrases that they will naturally comprehend.

Embrace

Rarely in preaching books do we read about embracing or loving our listeners. Overcoming our cultural prejudices finds itself even in the realm of location. By our nature we take what is normative for us and apply it to all situations and places. We postulate, speculate, and come to conclusions about what city folk, townies, or suburbanites are like, and those preconceptions can be quite difficult to unlearn. Most of our stereotyping revolves around the negative images that we possess about a certain group of people, based on their location. A necessary but challenging undertaking in our communication is to learn to embrace the differences that we have with listeners in our locational context.

Kenneth Lorne Bender writes, "The pastor must above all else have a respect for the rural way of life. Those that see the rural dweller as uneducated, unsophisticated, and out of touch with the real world cannot expect to have any significant ministry in a rural setting."[54] What I am advocating is not a blind, simplistic tolerance of sinful behaviors or beliefs but rather the ability to embrace cultural differences with listeners who may act, think, and live in community differently than we do, depending on what is normative in their location: urban, suburban, or rural modes of thought and ways of life. Sometimes our minds cannot see past the fact that people eat certain types of foods, read certain types of magazines or literature, watch certain types of news programs, celebrate certain holidays, drive certain kinds of vehicles, live in certain neighborhoods, work in certain professions, smell a certain way, participate in certain community events—and the list goes on and on. We must be able to overcome such locational cultural barriers with our listeners and not think that somehow we must change them into our own image and to appreciate our preferences.

In the task of preaching, how do we embrace our listeners based on their location? First, do we know what our facial expressions look like when we communicate and preach to people who come from different locations? Do you smile with sincerity, smirk pejoratively, or unconsciously scowl? Do we embrace them with our words of welcome, celebration, hand gestures, body language, tone, eye contact? One test of our embracing is whether we are able to include ourselves among our congregants and identify with them by using the pronoun "we" rather than "you." Do you truly consider yourself one of them? The truth is that all people know and feel the difference between genuine love and insincere sufferance. When we lack the ability to embrace our listeners from a certain location, we remember to pause and pray for the Spirit's enablement to overcome our human prejudices, so that our proclamation might be heard and felt by our listeners in lasting ways.

Content

Whether we live in urban, suburban, or rural contexts, an overarching question looms over every preacher: "What am I going to preach about this Sunday?" Yes, our hope is always that the Word of God in its context will be faithfully expounded to contemporary people. Yet, beyond that, what sermonic content is included and excluded will depend on the specific groups of listeners in our zip codes. Since all preaching is contextual, the content of our sermon will be impacted by what is taking place in our world, country, state, city, suburb, and town.

Consider the content of urban sermons. Roger Greenway asserts, "Messages preached in a city pulpit must boldly address the complexities of urban life, and to reflect the wide variety of interests and experiences in the average city congregation. . . . City people are bombarded by a host of ideas, issues, problems, and events, and this breadth of interest must be matched in the sermons they hear on Sunday."[55] For this reason, urban preachers will naturally gravitate toward sermon topics on justice, mercy, compassion, grace, forgiveness, acceptance, reconciliation, and more hot topics of the day like human sexuality, LGBTQ issues, human trafficking, abortion, politics, international crises, and others.[56] Erwin Lutzer explains how many of his sermons over the years have focused on the brokenness of people living in the city, "broken families, sexuality, problems in terms of where people are at"; speaking into the lives of the business community regarding ethics and integrity; and the need for reconciliation.[57] Ronald J. Allen shares his experience of living in an urban context in Indianapolis. He encourages us to build stronger bridges with urban dwellers by familiarizing ourselves with and asking questions about daily realities such as injustices, brutalities, fear, depression, anger, and hopelessness.[58]

So what do our people need to hear? As Lutzer and Allen convey it, our preaching ministry is highly contextual and also highly sensitive to the pressing and immediate concerns of the people in our local context. Cultural intelligence in preaching demands commitment to gain knowledge about our surroundings and think more deeply about how the Scriptures intersect with the challenges and complexities of urban, suburban, and rural life.

Trust

Finally, preaching with cultural intelligence involves trust. Pastors, by our nature, are agents of change. We do not appreciate the status quo. We are looking for ways to transform culture and to change the culture of our congregations. To mobilize a congregation requires high levels of trust. For more experienced preachers, you know that trust is not automatically given by congregants but rather is earned. How do we earn the trust of our listeners in our varied locations?

Ed Rowell writes, "Love does cover a multitude of pastoral sins. If my flock recognizes my voice as that of a loving undershepherd, they will listen with ears of trust and faith. They'll know instinctively I have their best interests at heart."[59] The love we show our listeners is expressed differently in each context. For instance, in rural areas the preacher earns trust by going into the fields with them and doing "real work," which usually means manual labor. Peter Rhea Jones Sr. shares this story:

> Several farmers in the church were organized informally, mostly by family, to do planting and harvesting together. When they were baling hay, I showed up in blue jeans and tossed bales on the truck. . . . Now the people and I had a relationship, and they heard my sermons in a new way. I had not realized how much the persona of the pastor, how he or she is seen, plays into the reception of the gospel.[60]

Since hard work is such a dominant belief among rural parishioners (and hard work equals physical labor and not working in an air-conditioned office), trust can be officially gained when we find opportunities to labor together and experience firsthand what the people's lives are like on a daily basis.

In urban congregations, especially with long church histories, trust may be earned when the preacher respects tradition. Adhering to the church calendar, following the church's order of worship, and advocating the church's programs and other traditions (without immediately seeking to modify them) are ways that we can earn trust from our listeners in cities. And in the suburban church context, I have found that upper-class and middle-class listeners want the preacher to spend quality time with them by partaking in their hobbies and leisure activities. Amazingly, hearts warm up to the pastor when we take a day to ski, wakeboard, fly-fish, cycle around town, golf, and the list goes on. In every context, we become like chameleons and adapt in the ways we express care and love to our people. By leaving our comfort zones, we are communicating to our listeners that they are important and that what matters to them is important to us. Without trust, our preaching will not receive a hearing in these varied ecclesial contexts.

Conclusion

The location of our church shapes the way we communicate to our listeners. Although we have barely touched the surface with respect to urban, suburban, and rural listeners, the opportunity ahead for each of us is to gather cultural intelligence along the way that we can incorporate into our preaching ministry and preaching style. We ask ourselves a central question: How does the culture of the text intersect with the culture of my local church context? My hope is that each week we can attempt to implement another aspect of cultural intelligence into our sermon and build our Homiletical Bridge by speaking our listeners' urban, suburban, and rural dialects.

9

Preaching and Religions

Winfried Corduan, in his book *Neighboring Faiths*, defines religion as "a system of beliefs and practices that provides values to give life meaning and coherence by directing a person toward transcendence."[1] This search for transcendence has led to the plurality of religions in the world today. From the earliest times in human history, people have worshiped "other gods." The Bible records innumerable occasions where the nation of Israel bowed down to "foreign gods" (Deut. 31:16) like Molech (Lev. 20:2–5) and Chemosh (2 Kings 23:13), and how God made clear his abhorrence of his chosen people's idolatrous practices. In seeking to understand other influential religious faiths today, we want to become better acquainted with other faiths, from "Islam, Buddhism, Hinduism, and Confucianism to 'new' religions or sects [such] as Mormonism, Jehovah's Witnesses, and any number of New Age movements."[2] World religions are categorized into two primary groups: Western religions and Eastern religions. Western religions include Judaism, Islam, and Christianity, whereas major Eastern religions comprise Hinduism, Buddhism, Jainism, Confucianism, Doaism, Shinto, and Sikhism.[3] Of course, there are a host of other religious expressions such as African tribal religions, animism, Wicca, Zoroastrianism, and select others that may require our exploration, depending on our cultural context and the people in our spheres of influence. In this final chapter, we will explore the intersection of preaching and religions.

The subtle and overt impact of world religions on our society and churches presses into us. Seekers attending our worship service may belong to a different religious faith; others may have recently converted to Christianity and cannot shake themselves free from tenets or practices from their religious past. Opportunities may arise to preach on a university campus to a mixed audience who embrace various world religions. For others, our congregants interact daily with their family members, coworkers, neighbors, friends, and other networks who belong to other religious faiths. Some church members are enthusiastically engaged in yoga and other forms of Eastern meditation without considering the theological implications and consequences of their seemingly innocent forms of exercise.

But ultimately, understanding world religions matters because the eternal destination of *all* people is at stake. Soberly, all Christians will stand before the Lord and be held accountable for sharing or withholding the gospel from Muslims and other religious followers. Timothy Tennent says, "It is quite astonishing that theological students in the West will spend countless hours learning about the writings of a few well-known, now deceased, German theologians whose global devotees are actually quite small and yet completely ignore over one billion living, breathing Muslims who represent one of the most formidable challenges to the Christian gospel today."[4]

How does one preach with cultural intelligence to those who profess beliefs that diverge from evangelical Christianity? What cultural intelligence is required to become conversant with followers of other religions? At the outset, I regret that each of the twelve major world religions cannot be discussed in this chapter. The terrain is much too expansive. To provide a sense of continuity, however, the religion of Islam[5] will serve as our primary conversation partner and will provide a rubric for understanding other world religions. However, when appropriate, references will be made to other religions as well.

Religious Affiliation Abroad and at Home

While Christianity remains the religion most people in the world today profess, we are still far from the majority. In *The Future of World Religions* study, Christians represented only 31.4 percent of the world's population in 2010. Projections into 2050 reveal no change for Christianity's growth. The religion gaining most traction in the world is Islam. Muslims constituted 23.2 percent of the global population in 2010, but in 2050 the prediction is that they will represent a 29.7 percent share of the world's major religions. Religiously unaffiliated persons are on the rise, comprising the third largest category of "major religious groups" at 16.4 percent, followed by Hindus (15 percent), Buddhists (7.1 percent), folk religions (5.9 percent), other religions (0.8 percent), and Jews (0.2 percent).[6]

In the United States, the projections for 2050 reveal attrition among the Christian population and an increase in the number of unaffiliated persons (also known as "The Nones"), Buddhists, Muslims, Hindus, folk religions, and other religious traditions.[7] What this means for evangelical churches is that preachers can no longer afford to be ignorant of other world religions and the nonreligious. Formulating opinions and perpetuating stereotypes about all Muslims (as being terrorists and extremists) and people of other religions based on what we hear on the news has undercut truly understanding the actual religion of Islam and other faiths.

Rather, the responsibility and joy as preachers of the Word is to learn about the beliefs, cultures, and practices of other world religions. Every day, people of other religious faiths living in the United States remain ignorant about the gospel of Jesus Christ. They are perishing without the good news. The apostle Paul passionately invokes the Roman Christians in Romans 10:14, "How, then, can they call on the one they have not believed in? And how can they believe in the one of whom they have not heard? And how can they hear without someone preaching to them?" Paul would throw down the gauntlet to evangelical preachers and ask the same crucial questions of us. The time for preaching with cultural intelligence to those perishing in their pursuit of other world religions is now. How will we respond to the challenge?

Let's begin by exploring the Homiletical Template and working our way through each of the three stages.

Stage 1: Follow Your HABIT

Scripture Text
1 Kings 18:16–46

Historical, Grammatical, and Literary Context

Historical Context

The books of 1 and 2 Kings represent the historical narratives of the events taking place in Israel's history, beginning with the transfer of leadership from David to Solomon and concluding with King Jehoiachin's release from prison.[8] In the first eleven chapters of 1 Kings, Israel remains an undivided kingdom, but in chapters 12–22 the narrative shifts to the episodes of a monarchy divided between the northern kingdom of Israel and the southern kingdom of Judah. In 1 Kings 18:16–46, our specific text, King Ahab, an evil and detestable king, takes over the kingship of Israel and rules for twenty-two years, beginning in 874 BC (see 1 Kings 16:29). He marries Jezebel, the daughter of the Sidonian king Ethbaal, and together Ahab and Jezebel lead the Jewish people astray by worshiping and serving the gods of Baal and Asherah. During this rebellious time in Israel, God raises up the prophet Elijah to challenge King Ahab and Jezebel's idolatry, to minister to the people, and to lead them back to God. The historical setting is one also marked by a severe three-year drought and famine in Samaria, which impairs the social and economic conditions of Israel. Elijah puts Ahab to the test and requests the prophets of Baal and Asherah to meet him at Mount Carmel for a clash between Elijah's God and the idols, to expose their identity as false gods and false prophets.

Grammatical Issues

For this particular sermon, two grammatical issues stand out that could add texture to our sermon while relating to idolatry and world religions. First, investigate the word *yepassekhu*, which, according to Lissa M. Wray Beal, shares the same root (*pasakh*) as in the *dance* of the prophets of Baal (v. 26) and the *wavering* of the people's faith (v. 21).[9] The imagery here is fascinating, because it reveals the vacillating or wavering posture that people have about who the real God is in their lives. The false prophets' dance is a response to the inactivity of their god Baal as they vigorously try to gain his attention. In contrast, Elijah stays still while YHWH is moving and stirring behind the scenes to manifest his power by eventually engulfing the water-saturated altar in flames. In what ways do listeners from other religions "dance" and "waver" in their faith? How are they wrestling with indecision about placing their faith in our God? Spend a few moments pondering how this significant wordplay could be highlighted in the message.

Second, an interesting grammatical exploration would be to study Elijah's taunting of the prophets of Baal in 1 Kings 18:27. Elijah's tone is one of sarcastic mockery.[10] Beal explains Elijah's goad:

Perhaps, Elijah taunts, Baal is "musing" or "turned aside" (probably a euphemistic taunt that Baal is busy in the bathroom; Rendsburg 1988). . . . The taunt about the journey or Baal's slumber snidely uses the myth of Baal's yearly descent to the underworld of Mot where he is held powerless until the growing season begins (W. Herrmann 1999). Elijah mocks that Baal's inability to return or answer from his underworld imprisonment shows he is no god at all.[11]

Oftentimes a Bible character's unabashed confidence in the Lord pokes fun at the adversaries, such as the anointed David's ridicule of Goliath in 1 Samuel 17:26, 36 in referring insultingly to him as an "uncircumcised Philistine." In the next section, the discussion on literary genre will help to determine which route or tone this sermon will take in communicating the narrative to listeners of other religious faiths—that is, employing a disposition of mockery or of respect.

Literary Study

The literary genre of this text is historical narrative. As such, the tension always exists as to which elements of the story are *prescriptive* and which parts *descriptive*. The temptation for all preachers is to make descriptive elements in the biblical narrative prescriptive by encouraging listeners to practice literally what they learn from its characters, even though the biblical author intended it to be descriptive only. In this historical passage, the prophet Elijah's emboldened approach of mocking the false prophets to intensify the impending futility of their god, Baal, is a character quality that can be seen as a platform to convince listeners from other religions that Christianity is the only way to God. As Thomas Long observes from the mainline tradition, "When we identify with a character in a story, whatever happens to that character happens to us at the level of imagination. . . . A variation on this theme of identification with character involves those stories which present a certain character as a model or ideal. These stories say or imply at the end, 'Now go and do likewise.' While we may not initially identify with the character, the function of the story is to create the desire in us to be like the person."[12]

Reading this story, who would not want to be like the prophet Elijah? Particularly, as preachers, a subtle desire may be to infuse into listeners who are already professing Christians a comparable dose of the Lord's confidence as they evangelize and debunk the beliefs held by other religions. However, the point of the story is not the greatness of Elijah's faith and buoyancy, but on who Yahweh is. Iain Provan writes, "The book of Kings is not only a narrative about the past. It is also a narrative that seeks to teach its readers a number of things about God and his ways."[13] In this specific narrative, Provan reminds the reader of its primary function that only the God of the Bible is truly God, and he alone controls nature.[14] In being faithful to the literary genre of historical narrative and respectful of diverse listeners, the preacher can underscore the greatness of God in contrast to demonizing the impotence and nonexistence of idols and deities that are worshiped in other religions of the world.

Author's Cultural Context

The authorship of 1 and 2 Kings is inconclusive.[15] Keeping this in view, this segment on the author's cultural context will hone in on the cultural issues of the prophet Elijah's day, issues regarding Canaanite religion and, in particular, the worship of Baal and Asherah. First, Baal was the most prominent god of the Canaanites. Alfred Hoerth explains, "The Canaanites were polytheists like the rest of the Near Eastern cultures. Canaanite deities were rather fluid in personality and function."[16] Taking the physical form of a bull, the idols of Baal were worshiped for their "strength and fertility."[17] Ahab disobeyed the Lord by constructing an altar and temple for Baal worship in the capital city, Samaria.[18] Specifically, Baal served as "the god of vegetation and rain,"[19] and "his voice was thunder."[20] His "powers" were directly put to the test in light of the ongoing famine. Prayers were frequently offered to Baal and other Canaanite gods to get their attention. In the case of Elijah's display of religious cultural intelligence in 1 Kings 18:27, it meant summoning a god who may be "deep in thought, busy, or traveling" or "sleeping."[21] A further glimpse into the Canaanite cultural context is referenced where "Canaanites were primarily interested in ritualistic outward acts that would make their gods treat them more favorably."[22] Examples of such "outward acts" in Baal worship can be found in 18:26, where the prophets of Baal "danced around the altar," and in 18:28, where they "shouted louder and slashed themselves with swords and spears, as was their custom, until their blood flowed." Depending on the listeners and their specific world religions, determine what commonalities and differences they share with the Canaanite followers of Baal.

Second, the goddess Asherah, also known as Ashtoreth or Asherim (plural), was "the Canaanite mother goddess" and the wife of the god El.[23] Locals worshiped her for her powers as a goddess of fertility. Intriguingly, Baal was the most powerful among the children of El and Asherah.[24] Asherah's name is mentioned forty times in the Old Testament, often in conjunction with poles.[25] Asherah poles were trees or actual wooden poles carved and erected to resemble Asherah and represent a visible symbol of Canaanite worship.[26] You will recall that in 2 Kings 23:14 King Josiah chopped down the Asherah poles in his mission to obliterate idolatry in Jerusalem. As we consider the author's cultural context, consider what comparisons can be made in the sermon, whether directly or indirectly, to demonstrate the falsehood of their idols and other gods with Baal and Asherah. In what ways do listeners look to false deities like Baal and Asherah in their worship of gods in other religions, whether physical idols, nonmaterial deities, or other spirits?

Big Idea of the Text

Subject: What does Elijah's contest with the prophets of Baal and Asherah reveal about God?

Complement: Only the God of Elijah controls nature and is the one and only true and living God.

Exegetical Idea: Elijah's contest with the prophets of Baal and Asherah reveals that only the God of Elijah is the God who controls nature and is the one and only true and living God.

Homiletical Idea: There is only one God, and he controls nature and everything in it.

Interpret in Your Context

Assumptions

Listeners who are already professing Christians will hear this particular sermon in a completely different way from those of other religious faiths. Christians will certainly hear this Old Testament story and assume that the events in this story actually happened and that the outcome points to the fact that our God defeated the idols of Baal and Asherah several thousand years ago on Mount Carmel. Through these events, God firmly established his position as the one and only true deity. However, those of other world religions may not be so easily convinced. One of the major stumbling blocks that Christians face when preaching to followers of other faiths is that every religionist believes that theirs is the one true religion. Lee Strobel writes, "Now let's consider the following two truth claims: Christianity is the one true religion. Islam is the one true religion. The New Testament of the Bible and Islam's holy book, the Qur'an, make these claims. Both cannot be true. Either both are false (that is, God does not exist or another religion, such as Hinduism, is true) or one or the other is true."[27]

The historical narrative in 1 Kings 18 concludes with Yahweh's triumphant victory over Baal and Asherah, but the Muslim or Buddhist or Hindu will not necessarily identify with the same conclusion. For Christian preachers, we must assume that the narrative we present in sermon form, even in its historical accuracy, is insufficient evidence to persuade members of other religious traditions. The hermeneutical challenge is to read the passage from the religious perspective of a Muslim or Buddhist, recognizing their assumption that Christianity is a false religion and that even what we consider to be historical events may simply be errant stories that have somehow been corrupted.[28] Assume that your listeners will hear your sermon with suspicion and will no doubt challenge the historicity of your message. Some may find agreement with your proposition that Baal and Asherah are false gods, but this does not automatically discredit the existence and hegemony of the gods of their own religions.

Conflicts

Next, what conflicts might our listeners who practice other world religions have with this particular story from 1 Kings 18? In preaching this text, the preacher confronts a very real and practical dilemma regarding how to refer to Baal, Asherah, Buddha, or Allah. Should the preacher use the language of these gods as being "real gods" or as being mere idols? Derek Cooper suggests that there are two ways to understand various Old Testament references to "gods": they are either "real beings" or simply unreal "images or idols."[29] Christians dismiss the very existence of other gods and idols because we believe in the Bible's truth claim in the Decalogue that there is only one God and that God is the God of the Bible. However, to be respectful of other religions, would it be in the best interest of the preacher to equate those religions' deity as being on the same playing field as that of the Christian God or acknowledge the existence of their so-called god?

Imagine that a Muslim, Buddhist, Hindu, and/or Jehovah's Witness are/is sitting in your congregation. How would they feel if their religion or expression of *god* in whom they have placed their entire faith was completely dismissed and relegated to the status of an idol, deemed nonexistent, or simply a figment of the imagination? Would they continue to listen to your message? For the sake of the listeners, we may want to suspend the language, at least on one's first hearing of a Christian sermon, that their god does not exist or that their religion is not a viable religion. Other conflicts that arise from this text will depend on the particular listeners in your congregation and the objections they may hold.

Questions

Last, we want to consider the questions that our listeners from other religions may have about the Scripture passage. For Christians and nonbelievers alike, a number of questions may be asked by our readers, especially for those who remain skeptical toward the Christian faith. One of the initial questions that a Muslim or those religious traditions that believe in prophets will have can be found in King Ahab's greeting of Elijah in verse 17. For Muslims, prophets are known for their character and virtue, but here in verse 17 Ahab refers to Elijah as the "troubler of Israel." This dubious and demeaning title ascribed to Elijah will presumably perplex readers of other world religions. The preacher may want to anticipate their question and explain what King Ahab means by "troubler of Israel."[30]

A second context-specific question that we may wonder about in studying this text is why Elijah summons Ahab to bring 450 prophets of Baal to him on Mount Carmel but only 400 prophets of Asherah in verse 19. What is the significance of this numeric discrepancy? Third, for Hindus and other Eastern religions, cows and bulls are commonly considered sacred animals, but in verse 23 Elijah commands the false prophets to prepare two bulls to be used for sacrifice. This is a question that the culturally intelligent preacher must answer on behalf of the listeners from world religions that hold such beliefs about sacred animals. Fourth, some religious persons may wonder why Elijah puts God to the test when, according to their religions, this testing of God would be ill-founded and inappropriate. Last, in light of the history of bloodshed between Muslims and Christians, many Muslims and others would find it deeply problematic that Elijah slaughters the prophets of Baal in verse 40. Why does the Christian God seem to allow the perpetuation of violence against those who reject him? Anticipating your listeners' questions will enable you to gain a hearing from listeners whose voices may be physically muzzled due to the nature of preaching, but whose minds are active in trekking with the preacher on various levels.

Theological Presuppositions

Each religion holds theological presuppositions about the Christian God and their god(s). These theological or doctrinal presuppositions are handed down from generation to generation. Most religions in the world are polytheistic, and therefore their adherents hold the theological presuppositions that many gods exist simultaneously and serve different purposes. What the Christian preacher wants to know is what these religions believe about Jesus Christ, his dual nature as being fully God and fully human, his sacrificial life, crucifixion, burial, resurrection, and ascension, which are the distinguishing features of Christianity.

In this narrative, the initial theological presupposition that the preacher seeks to elucidate for members of other world religions is that the God of the Bible is the only and most powerful deity. This is obviously the central point of the story. Elijah makes the point clear when he asks the crowd in verse 21, "How long will you waver between two opinions? If the LORD is God, follow him; but if Baal is God, follow him." The events of the story reveal the truth that Yahweh is Lord over nature. He not only controls when it rains but also controls the entire universe. Wrestle with the reasons why other religions see Christianity as deficient or inferior to their religion or their idol. While King Ahab commands the prophets of Baal and Asherah to engage in this epic test between their god and the prophet Elijah's God, it seems that the false prophets' initial compliance with Elijah's commands still reveals a confidence that Baal and Asherah will come through for them. However, as the day unfolds, the prophets of Baal become increasingly uncertain, and in verse 29 they are frantically seeking a response from their gods, but to no avail.

In the sermon, the preacher can raise questions to the listeners from other religions to assess their confidence level in their gods: How certain are you that if Allah or Buddha or other idols were the other deities being tested in this story that your god would triumph over the God of Israel? What examples can you give in your life that manifest miraculous evidence of your god's existence and might? At the same time, acknowledge that Christians too struggle at times to feel God's presence in their lives. Philip Yancey points out that "the prophets of Israel gave voice to the feeling of disappointment with God. Why do godless nations flourish? they asked. Why is there such poverty and depravity in the world? Why so few miracles? Where are you, God? 'Why do you always forget us? Why do you forsake us so long?' Show yourself; break your silence."[31] Both Christians and listeners from other religions long for the preacher to respond to these and similar types of questions. Elijah's experience on Mount Carmel is obviously not the normal method by which God manifests his deity and omnipotence to the world. Remind your listeners that God is present at all times even though he is seemingly absent at times. Theological presuppositions are a central consideration for the preacher when seeking to understand the listeners' beliefs about who God is and in particular how they view Jesus.

Stage 2: Build the BRIDGE

Beliefs

As evangelical Christians, we hold *the* truth about who God is and his plan to redeem the world only through the person and work of Jesus Christ. If only every person shared our religious commitments! Obfuscating this truth about Jesus are the followers of other world religions who assert identical claims that they too possess the one true path to God. Harold Netland comments, "The Christian appeals to the Bible as the supreme authority; the Muslim rejects the Bible in favor of the Qur'an; the Zen Buddhist claims to have direct access to ultimate reality through the experience of enlightenment or *satori*; the Advaita Vedantin Hindu appeals to the authority of the Upanishads and the experience of *samadhi*; and so on."[32] Beliefs are unique to every religion, and the preacher's homework is to become familiar with the religious belief systems of our listeners.

Each religion in the world embraces a set of core beliefs or doctrines. Many of these religions are complicated and complex for Christians to understand. It involves becoming acquainted with new languages, terminologies, peculiar names, images, idols, concepts, and systems that do not naturally draw direct parallels with Christianity. There are also various branches, sects, or schools of religions much like our denominations (e.g., Sunni Muslims and Shiite Muslims, Theravada Buddhism and Mahayana Buddhism) to comprehend, which further confounds the process of gathering cultural intelligence.

The starting point to understanding any religious faith is taking it one step at a time. Pick up a basic introductory primer on world religions. I recommend several helpful resources: (1) *Christianity and World Religions: An Introduction to the World's Major Faiths*; (2) *Christianity at the Religious Roundtable: Evangelicalism in Conversation with Hinduism, Buddhism, and Islam*; and (3) *World Religions: A Guide to the Essentials*.[33] These and other resources will give you an important foundation with regard to the dominant beliefs of the major world religions. Another way to learn about the beliefs of religions is to audit a seminary course on Islam, Buddhism, Hinduism, or other religions. A third approach is to read English translations of their sacred texts, such as the Qur'an and Hadith (Islam); the Pali Canon or Tripitaka (Theravada Buddhism); various *sutras* such as the Lankavatra Sutra (Mahayana Buddhism); the Five Classics and the Four Books (Confucianism); the four Vedas (Hinduism); the Book of Mormon (Mormonism); and others. Last, put it in your schedule to take congregants out for coffee or a meal to learn more about their religious tradition and ask questions.

David Platt shares one common feature: "In every religion, a teacher (or a series of teachers) prescribes certain paths to follow in order to honor God (or different gods) and experience salvation (however that is described)."[34] What is the thrust of each religion's major beliefs? Begin the process by learning about the religion's main doctrinal emphasis. We cannot learn everything about a world religion instantaneously. Try to see the process of cultivating knowledge of other religions from the perspective of learning to play a musical piece. Having played the violin and piano, I learned the arduous way that students of music require the discipline and patience to play each note one measure at a time. After mastering the first measure, the student then progresses to the second measure, and so forth until he can play the entire piece.

Below is a table regarding three of the major world religions—their primary beliefs, rituals, idols, and view of God—which can serve as an initial launching pad to further discovery. As mentioned earlier, find a primer on world religions and get acclimated to the religions' foundational beliefs. Understanding the belief is not the end but rather a means to the end. As we learn about the central tenets of other religions, we can determine the theological or doctrinal issues that prevent adherents from a particular religion from believing in Christianity. The end is that they will come to faith in Jesus Christ, but in our proclamation and evangelism this will require our prior knowledge of their religious beliefs. Grasping other religions' core beliefs is an important foundation to build toward cultural intelligence. We also want to learn about their rituals.

Table 9.1 Religions and CQ Knowledge

Religion	Beliefs	Rituals	Founder/Idol	God
Islam	Belief in one God	The Five Pillars of Islam; Hadith	Muhammad/no physical idols	Allah, a merciful but impersonal god
Hinduism	High regard for the Vedas; belief in karma and reincarnation	Caste system; Yoga	Founder unknown/many idols	One supreme god but also polytheistic
Buddhism	The Four Noble Truths	Eightfold Path to Enlightenment	Siddhārtha Gautama, known as Buddha	Denial of a personal god

Rituals

Food

Food is a necessary and natural ritual to understand when it comes to world religions, and its significance should be taken seriously. No matter what country or province the food comes from, it is steeped in a particular culture, but it can have religious connections as well (e.g., Peter's dietary restrictions in Acts 11). Awkwardness strikes when we are uninformed about what kinds of food other cultures enjoy or avoid. We want to be sensitive to those of other religious faiths and what they find culturally acceptable for consumption and even discussion.

Years ago, the congregation that I served in Denver hosted a large group of Muslim refugees from Myanmar at our annual Christmas worship service and luncheon. After the worship service, we invited our guests to the fellowship hall to share a meal together. We served them by bringing plates of food to their tables. On completion of the meal, they thanked us and left the building. When we began to clean up and picked up their plates, we saw that they had barely eaten anything. It later came to our attention that ham was the primary protein for the meal. That was the problem. Muslims do not eat meat from pigs. Anything that touched the slice of ham became ritually unclean. They ate only the corn and salad that didn't make contact with the ham. Thomas Robinson and Hillary Rodrigues explain, "The basic [Muslim food] prohibitions somewhat follow the food taboos of the Hebrew Bible: pork, blood, meat offered to idols, birds of prey, and improperly killed animals are prohibited, although Muslims have a wider range of acceptable animals."[35]

On a different occasion, I made a slipup in my sermon when I described my love for succulent steak. I did not realize that one of our leaders had invited a Hindu couple from his workplace to the worship service. It didn't cross my mind to be culturally and religiously sensitive to these visitors as I spoke extensively about how I wanted my meat to be seasoned and prepared. By sharing these details in the message, I later received a generous gift card to a choice steak house in Denver from a gracious church member, but concurrently offended cherished Hindu visitors. Religious cultures are different. Food is important in terms of world religions and is involved both when we are eating together and when we speak from the pulpit regarding certain types of food that other religions may consider impure.

Religious Practices

Every world religion expresses its religiosity by engaging in religious practices as a form of ritual. In other religions, rituals are seen as "a series of repeated actions that are performed in order to bring about a desired result."[36] Take as an example Muslims who integrate their religious beliefs and practices into every sphere of life, even stopping work to observe their religious rituals. Derek Cooper shares a story of his experiences in Palestine, where "the muezzin (a person standing atop the minaret in a nearby mosque) called for prayer. The owner of the restaurant obediently pulled out his prayer mat and began praying in the middle of the restaurant. This man's piety underscores the importance of prayer in the Muslim world."[37]

Islam demands the practice of The Five Pillars of Islam, or rituals, that include reciting the creed, times of prayer, giving of alms, fasting, and pilgrimage.[38] These pillars of the Islamic faith represent the heartbeat of all Muslims, but the question begging to be answered is, Why? Why is it that these five specific rituals are considered the pillars of Islam and not five others? In her book *Islam in America*, Jane Smith writes, "Muslims believe what they do, and practice as they do, because of the example of Prophet Muhammad."[39] Could it be that the five pillars of Islamic faith are heavily steeped in the prophet Muhammad's personal experiences—for example, in finding spirituality through the exercises of prayer and fasting, that almsgiving resulted from his experience of poverty in being orphaned at a young age, and that the final two pillars serve as a reminder to return to Mecca, the place of his birth? While Muslims do not have answers to all of these questions and obey in sheer faith, the evidence seems to indicate that much of Islamic thought and practice filter through the life, teachings, and experiences of Muhammad. Therefore, further exploration into Muhammad's life would be worthwhile for any preacher. In the next few months, take some time for religious cultural exegesis. Learn more about the rituals of your congregants who come from the background of other world religions and the source from which these rituals are derived.

Idols

Try to acquire a proper understanding of a religion's idols or images. What separated ancient Judaism from pagan religions in the Greco-Roman world was that Jews did not make for themselves a physical image or representation of God.[40] This was God's original intent for the Jews as he articulated in the first two of the Ten Commandments and throughout the Old Testament. However, the Jews' abstention from idol worship did not last for very long. As Paul comments in Romans 1:22–23, "Although they claimed to be wise, they became fools and exchanged the glory of the immortal God for images made to look like a mortal human being and birds and animals and reptiles." The Israelites went on to abandon God in favor of worshiping a golden calf in Exodus 32 and various idols of neighboring lands, such as Baal, Asherah, and Molech. What are the idols that persons of other religions in your congregation worship today?

We can consider the theme of idols in three distinct ways. First, some world religions believe in actual deities other than the Christian God. That is,

names like Allah (Islam); Brahma, Vishnu, and Shiva (Hinduism); or Ahura
Mazda (Zoroastrianism) are worshiped as "real" gods and not simply idols
or images. These gods are obviously distinct from the Christian God and
are known for the specific powers that they hold, such as Brahma, who is
the creator god; Vishnu, the preserver god; and Shiva, called the destroyer.
Ahura Mazda is known in Zoroastrianism (an Iranian religion) as "the
creator and preserver of the natural order."[41] In the exploration of these
different gods, become familiar with who they are and what they represent
to the people. Vishnu, for instance, writes Corduan, "is most concerned
with maintaining the *dharma*, the true ways of the gods. Thus, whenever
it appears that the world is particularly out of sync, he lets himself be
born in the world, either as a heroic animal or as a human hero in order to
straighten things out. He lives a complete life and eventually dies, but he is
always ready to come again if needed."[42] Further discussion on the subject
of gods will be taken up shortly.

Second, certain religions do not worship deities but rather physical idols
or images. In evangelical circles, idols exist in our hearts but may not take
a physical form. Idols can represent anything or any person that we deem
more significant than God, such as money, power, family, education, success,
beauty, and so forth. In other world religions, the worship of or meditation
on physical idols or images is still a common practice. Depending on which
religion your listeners belong to, engaging in dialogue regarding the worship of idols and images will enable the preacher to understand the idol and
what occurs when the idol is worshiped. The ritual of idol worship warrants
further examination from the Christian preacher. In other words, consider
what powers these idols possess according to their religion.

Third, in some cases getting to know the founder of the religion is in many
ways comparable in importance to knowing about their god. For example,
Hans Küng explains the importance of understanding the founder of a world
religion as in the case of Muhammad for Islam: "Muhammad is . . . an ultimately irreducible figure, who cannot be simply derived from what preceded
him, but stands radically apart from it as he, with the Qur'an, establishes
permanent new standards. . . . Without Muhammad as a source, there would
be no stream; without this sprig, there would be no tree."[43] Similarly, in *Ask
Your Muslim Friend*, Andreas Maurer writes, "In Islam, Muhammad is the
final and greatest prophet of all, and of much nobler character than any other
prophet, including Jesus."[44] Read about the founders of other religions like
Siddhārtha Gautama (Buddhism), Joseph Smith (Mormonism), Confucius
(Confucianism), Guru Nanak Dev (Sikhism), Charles Taze Russell (Jehovah's

Witnesses), and so many others to gain a deeper understanding of the origins of these religions.

Dreams

Our neighbors belonging to other religions live in American society as "normal" humans, just as we do. They face the same struggles and pressures and aspire toward semblances of the so-called American Dream.[45] Robert Wuthnow, in *America and the Challenges of Religious Diversity*, writes, "Most are middle-class, college-educated professionals who live in the same kinds of neighborhoods as other Americans, send their children to the same schools, vote in the same elections, shop at the same stores, and watch the same programs on television."[46]

And yet they co-opt a quite different dream when it comes to their religious faith. A dominant but elusive dream for many adherents of other religious faiths, a doctrine that evangelical Christians take for granted, is the assurance of salvation. Many who practice other world religions live in constant fear or shame and zealously practice their faith because of the uncertainty of their religious standing before their god(s). For instance, oftentimes Jehovah's Witnesses live in fear because they do not know if their earthly actions will qualify them to become one of 144,000 to enter heaven. Jehovah's Witnesses take a literal interpretation of Revelation 7:4–8. As I spoke with a Jehovah's Witness, he explained that his motivation for speaking to me about his god Jehovah was selfishly motivated: it was one additional way to appease God in hopes of earning a coveted seat in eternity. His countenance reflected a man who enjoyed no measure of assurance as to whether he would be one of the 144,000 to live with God forever.

Muslims also share an ominous uncertainty about their eternal security. Thus, Keith Stump writes, "Muslims have no definite assurance of salvation until they reach that final day. They can never rest in the certainty of eternal salvation. To many, it is a painfully unsatisfying, unfulfilling and precarious state of existence."[47] For this reason, "in popular Islam there are constant efforts to gain assurance of forgiveness."[48] What we offer the world in the gospel of Jesus Christ is a message of certainty that those who place their exclusive faith in the death, burial, and resurrection of Jesus Christ will inherit eternal life and have salvation secured for all time. As we preach on the assurance of salvation, on a regular basis, we will etch into the minds of other religious adherents that Christianity provides eternal certainty and hope, which other religions simply cannot replicate in their religious traditions. We can provide our listeners with a new dream, which can then lead them to a new reality.

God

How do other religions view God (if they believe in an actual deity)? Religions have varying opinions about God, God's character, and how humans can relate to this God. The more we explore other gods, the more we assist listeners in seeing how different the Christian God really is. In Islam, ninety-nine "Excellent Names" are employed to denote the characteristics of God.[49] Although Muslims commonly refer to God as "the Merciful, the Compassionate,"[50] the focus of Islam is not on the relationship between Allah and his people but rather on the people awaiting Allah's judgment.

Another major point of divergence with Islam and Christianity concerns the Trinity. Miroslav Volf explains:

> The oneness of God (*tawhid*) is the principle at the very heart of Islam. That is the central issue for Muslims disputing Christian claims about God. The reason is simple: if the Father, Son, and Holy Spirit cannot be understood as one, according to Muslim interpretations of God's unity, then Muslims and Christians do not worship the same God. . . . Christians would be worshiping three gods or, at best, one true God and two idols in addition to God. This would be what Muslims call *shirk*, the unforgivable, blasphemous sin of associating other beings with God.[51]

Jews also question the validity of Christianity being a monotheistic religion. How might the Christian preacher provide a coherent and winsome apology for the trinitarian God? For religions that deny the Trinity, Volf articulates two angles to explain "this intimate connection between the divine Three who are indivisibly one."[52] First, Volf encourages the view that "*God's acts* are *undivided, inseparable*. Every act of one 'Person' is always caused by all three."[53] Second, Volf espouses a clear explanation of "how the divine 'Persons' are tied together is their *mutual indwelling* or, in technical terminology, *perichoresis*."[54] What has been your approach to defend the concept of the Trinity to skeptics from other religions?

On the opposite spectrum, Hindus believe in an estimated 330 million different gods.[55] Corduan states, "Just saying all of their names at the rate of five seconds a name would take fifty-two years."[56] A common view of God in the Hindu tradition can be understood in this way, Cooper writes: "There is one supreme God that cannot be fully known or understood. The gods we talk about on earth and give devotion to are simply manifestations of that one supreme God."[57] In other words, "Although each person seems to be worshiping a different god, the person is really worshiping only the one true God, who is manifest through Shiva or Kali or whomever."[58] A Hindu priest once explained the Hindu's practice of choosing which god to consult and pray to: "People worship this god or that god based on their need of the moment. Are you about to go on a business trip? Then ask for guidance from Ganesha, the god of venture and journey. Are you in need of money? Then ask Lakshmi!"[59] In Hinduism and other religions, gods and deities are distinct, with highly specialized purposes, as seen in these examples from Hindu religion.

What differentiates the Christian God from all other gods? The God of the Bible is the Creator who is also personal, relational, involved in humans' lives, sacrificial, loving, listening, forgiving, merciful, compassionate, holy, righteous, just, and so much more.[60] How Christian preachers present the Christian God to other religious faiths will require cultural intelligence about how others view God, his nature, and characteristics. In your study, find points of connection and points of divergence to approach the various perspectives on God in a way that your listeners will understand.

Experiences

Religiocultural Empathy

The final section of the bridge involves learning about the life experiences of those from other religions. Preachers can practice what Fred Craddock calls *empathetic imagination*: "the capacity to achieve a large measure of understanding of another person without having had that person's experiences."[61] He provides a simple exercise to initiate the process. Begin by writing the following question at the top of the page: "What's It Like to Be a _____?"[62] For preaching purposes, we might fill in the blank with a person from a specific religious faith such as a Muslim, a Buddhist, a Jew, or a Mormon, and so on. Craddock explains, "For the next fifteen minutes scribble on the page every thought, recollection, feeling, experience, name, place, sound, smell, or taste that comes to mind."[63] After you write down your observations and reflections, read through the sermon's text again to think about how a person from this particular world religion would read and interpret this text in light of their life experiences as a member of this religious tradition. If we lack specific knowledge about a particular religious group represented in our church, this process of empathetic imagination will uncover our cultural ignorance to show us that we need to learn more about it.

In considering life experiences, aim directly at the person's needs and their religious experience. For example, as a marginalized person in society, in what ways would a Muslim female identify with the Samaritan woman at the well, with whom Jesus speaks in John 4? What are the similarities and what are the differences between their experiences? How would a Muslim female internalize the shame she may feel in being a member of a patriarchal society, where women do not hold the same rights as men? Or take the example of blind Bartimaeus in Mark 10:46–52 and how a Buddhist might interpret this story. Consider how a Buddhist would seek to eliminate suffering, to make sense of karma (the law of cause and effect), and to ascertain what element in karma may have caused Bartimaeus's blindness. In exploring our specific text, 1 Kings 18, how might those who worship idols hear and respond to the story of Elijah on Mount Carmel, where the gods Baal and Asherah remain silent and Israel's God shows up and delivers in verse 38, burning up the drenched altar? What other evidence might convince idol worshipers of the historical accuracy of this narrative, which from the argument of Baal's silence dismisses the validity of their gods?

Other Religions Permeate All of Life

North American Christians often compartmentalize religious practice from their sense of self: we often equate going to church as just something that we do. However, many other religions strongly attest that their religion permeates all of life and is their entire raison d'être.[64] They cannot imagine separating their religion from their nationality, identity, or personhood. For instance, Gerald McDermott explains,

> Muslims also tend to view the West, particularly the United States, as irreligious and godless because of the practice of separation of church and state. If God is sovereign over the cosmos, Muslims argue, then every aspect of life—including the state—ought to come under the rule of his laws. Islamic law (*Shari'ah*) should therefore serve as a set of fundamental principles informing the laws of every nation on earth.[65]

The separation of church and state is only one example. As we have witnessed from previous examples, the religions of Islam, Buddhism, and Hinduism and others are in many ways all-consuming. Since Jesus intended for his followers to exhibit the same spiritual commitment and tenacity, members of other religions deserve respect for their religious zeal. The message we present cannot simply dabble in the realm of the cognitive. We must deliver the Christian message from as many life angles as possible, since their religion permeates their entire lives. In this third stage, we will try to formulate strategies on how best to communicate God's truth to followers of other religions.

Stage 3: Speak Their DIALECT

Delivery

Our tone matters especially when preaching to those from other religions. Nantachai Mejudhon believes that the attitude of meekness may be the desirable characteristic for working among other religious communities like the Thai people and being able to present the gospel to them. He writes, "I believe that the Christian church in Thailand is viewed as having violated the cultural and religious values of reciprocity and harmony by its use of aggressive methods and is now deprived of the opportunity to initiate dialogue about the gospel."[66] A spirit of meekness creates space for the gospel's power to take root in hearers and will go a long way in reaching those of other religions. Read your sermon manuscript out loud and listen to the mood of your sermonic voice. Is it positive or pejorative toward the Other? Is your tone in any manner shaming your listeners or belittling them for their beliefs and practices? Do you mock or make fun of their idols and deities? If you can answer yes to any of these questions, you may want to modify your tone to elicit a more favorable response to the Christian message.

Illustrations

Illustrations are the primary vehicles that preachers employ to make real connections with listeners. For members of other world religions, Christians have a reputation of being intolerant and even unwilling to listen to the perspectives of other religious faiths. We are known for the positions we stand against rather than what we affirm. Try to temper your victorious illustrations and seek to expose your greatest fears, doubts, shame, disappointment, guilt, severed relationships, anger, injustice, boredom, expectations, and other related topics. Moreover, in such a dramatic and miraculous text as ours in 1 Kings 18, another general recommendation would be to utilize "normal, ordinary" illustrations rather than the supernatural. That is, how does God reveal himself in the daily hardships of life? While this may seem counterintuitive, a display of humility and a disclosure of our humanity may enable the preacher to connect on a broader level.

Take a Defensive Posture

Typically, in gathering sermon illustrations for Elijah's contest in 1 Kings 18 our natural inclination may be to take an offensive posture and find conquest stories or alarming facts in hopes of persuading listeners to denounce their gods and affirm the superiority of Yahweh. However, is it possible that people would listen more intently if we took a more defensive posture and asked more questions of our own religion, rather than heaping illustrative evidence to prove our convictions? Mark Cahill, in his book *One Thing You Can't Do in Heaven*, provides this illustration: "How would you answer if someone asked you if you were wrong and this whole Jesus thing wasn't true? Have you ever thought about that? You see that everyone cannot be right here. For example, Muslims do not believe that Jesus died on the cross, let alone rose from the dead, whereas Christ's death and resurrection are the whole basis for Christianity. We cannot all be right. What if *we* are wrong?"[67]

Though we know the truth, illustrating for members of other world religions might find greater traction when we expose our own hidden fears, doubts, and worries. The primary rationale for this approach is that our listeners are hearing the sermon from a similar mood of uncertainty, where some are asking the same questions about their religion. If we can take them on a journey of how we have come to saving faith in Jesus Christ and name our greatest questions and fears along the way, followers of other religious traditions may give us a second hearing and perhaps even multiple hearings.

Limit Western Illustrations

Living in the West, illustrations often bolster consumerism, individualism, materialism, comfort, narcissism, democracy, and other Western concepts that are familiar to us. For many listeners coming from non-Western cultures, illustrations from topics like the ones just mentioned are not the foremost thoughts on their minds. Our goal is to find out what types of illustrations make sense to our hearers. The Bible comes to life for many individuals from non-Western religions when we can offer illustrations that recount biblical narratives regarding warring factions and nations and crises taking place around the globe. Illustrations that deal with suffering, disease, poverty, injustice, human trafficking, abuse, hierarchy, socialism, power, and conflict, among other topics, are more apt to speak to the experiences of adherents from non-Christian backgrounds than are progress, prosperity, and affluence. By illustrating broadly from a number of different points of view, we will be able to connect with listeners where they are.

Application

Allow Them to Reach Their Own Conclusions

When we search for sermon applications, we often think of concrete exercises that the listeners can immediately put into practice in response to the truth of the sermon. At the end of the sermon, preachers sometimes hand out a checklist of action items for the listeners to apply in the following week. Andreas Maurer shares how the shape of application may differ in Islamic contexts: "Asking Muslims good questions challenges them to find the truth for themselves! . . . Think and pray of new ways and methods of engaging with Muslims."[68] This is particularly true when we try to respond to the sermon by proposing an application when we do not even know the questions being asked. Earl Palmer writes, "We preachers have a tendency—some innate drive—to offer answers to our listeners before they've even heard the questions. We want to help, but sometimes we forget the process required."[69] Allowing the listeners of other world religions to make their own applications could be a helpful technique in the beginning, because we may not know how the application fits with their unique setting. Eventually, as we familiarize ourselves with their religious beliefs and rituals, our applications can be more direct and personal.

Think Collectively about Applications

In many world religions, life is not merely about one's individual journey but often seen in communal fashion. Just as many of the New Testament letters were written to churches and Christians within a geographic region, our applications could focus on the whole community rather than just individuals. Notice that even in our Scripture text in 1 Kings 18, Elijah is not seeking a response from any individual. Rather, he wants the entire crowd watching on Mount Carmel to render a decision about which God they will serve. Since many world religions find comfort in relationships and communal gatherings, we would be wise to apply the message in such a way that the entire family or community can get involved.

How does collectivism play out in the sermon's application? Usually, in North American churches, forgiveness is limited to a singular process where individuals are encouraged to forgive the wrongdoings of an individual perpetrator. In collectivist cultures, however, forgiveness is seen on a macro level, where one considers how the entire family, community, state, religion, or ethnic group has sinned against Others. It explores how we as a community need to request forgiveness for our sins against Others. In addition, if my personal sin has engendered hurt against an individual, my application would be to seek forgiveness from both the individual and the Other's entire family.

Conversion and the Cost of Discipleship

A growing problem for new Christians, especially from Muslim backgrounds, stems from Christian preachers' inability to convey clearly how difficult these new converts' lives will be for them and their families after conversion to the Christian faith. Many Muslim converts lose their faith in Christ because they are ill-prepared for the fallout they will inevitably experience with their family members and communities after renouncing Islam. As William Wagner explains, "In witnessing to a Muslim you must be aware that the person you are working with, if they accept Christ, will probably be persecuted and could even be killed. Many Americans simply do not realize how serious a change in religion can be in a Muslim context."[70] A similar example is provided in *Effective Discipling in Muslim Communities*, where Don Little shares about his colleague Cheri, who evangelized young Muslim converts only in conjunction with preparing them for the possible backlash: "Cheri would not lead them in prayers of repentance and faith in Christ until she was fully assured that they knew, understood and were willing to embrace all that conversion to Christ might entail for them, including possibly severe persecution, being divorced by their husbands, losing their jobs, and so on."[71]

The crucial application of 1 Kings 18 for nonbelieving listeners is to put their faith in our Triune God: Father, Son, and Holy Spirit. Yet from the outset we need to elucidate the point for our listeners that conversion comes at a cost. Listeners from other world religions will make their profession of faith in Christ at a great sacrifice in renouncing their idols and gods. Explain how they may lose precious relationships and social standing with family members, friends, and people in their religious communities. In our application, emphasize that they will not be alone in this journey. We will partner with them to do life together in Christian community and to grow together in discipleship. Our homiletical task is not simply to convert them but also to nurture them in the faith so that they become fully mature disciples of Jesus.

Language

Eugene Nida coined the concept "dynamic equivalence" for the purpose of translation and contextualization. He tried to help missionaries locate words in the host language with which there would be some form of equivalent term in English. Dynamic equivalence represents the "quality of a translation in which the message of the original text has been so transported into the receptor language that the *response* of the *receptor* is essentially like that of the original receptors."[72] That is, one of our aims as preachers is to sift through the sea of words available to us (in our case English) and find the exact word or concept that will connect us with our hearers. James Nieman puts it this way: "By employing widely available forms like conversation, stories, and sayings, language helps people to bond together, interpret a common setting, express shared values, and plan for their mutual efforts."[73]

Richards and O'Brien explain, "When we cross a culture, as when we read the Bible, we often assume that what goes without being said in our culture and language also goes without being said in the other cultures and languages. This can lead to profound misunderstanding."[74] I once heard a story about a missionary who sought to explain the concept of Communion, the Lord's Supper, with the members of his local village. He lifted the elements of bread and wine off the table and explained that the bread represents Jesus's body and that the wine represents his blood shed on the cross. And he immediately noticed a stumbling block with the members of his community. For this particular context, they did not eat bread as part of their culture's diet. Instead, rice was their staple. The missionary took a bowl of rice and passed it around his community, finding common ground and a common food that they would understand.

In many ways, we are constantly on the search for a dynamic equivalent—a tangible word or concept our listeners can wrap their heads around. This may not always be an easy feat, especially in certain religions and cultures. When a dynamic equivalent is difficult to locate, find someone in the community to facilitate the "translation" process. Timothy Tennent observes that "Muslims, Buddhists, and Hindus are now our coworkers, our schoolmates, and our neighbors."[75] Therefore, locate religious concepts that resonate with them such as *dukkha*, karma, Allah, bodhisattva, feng shui, Ramadan, *jen*, filial piety, and others. This can happen only when we commit to actively engage in learning about other world religions. Such learning includes the ability to speak their religious language. The hope is that those listening in the pews on Sunday morning will summon us to rise to the challenge and begin speaking the language of different world religions.

Embrace

What does it mean to embrace members of other religions? Of course, embracement is not a call to endorse religious pluralism or syncretism. Timothy

George writes, "To affirm the sole sufficiency of Jesus Christ as the only way of salvation for all persons everywhere . . . is not to deny that there is also truth in other religions for we affirm general revelation and common grace. But it is to oppose theologies of uncritical pluralism and syncretism."[76] However, for many evangelicals the tendency is that their religion monopolizes or clouds our thinking to the extent that all we see in this individual is their errant religion. In essence, they become one-dimensional human beings, with their religion taking center stage. In speaking of adherents to other religions, Kenneth Thomas states, "As fellow citizens and human beings we obviously share many of the same concerns: the provision of sufficient food, and maintenance of health, the need for education, the opportunity for employment, the establishment of just and equitable government institutions, and many others."[77] As preachers, we frequently lose sight of the fact that they are first and foremost real people.

Embracing adherents of other religions first means showing respect. In 1 Peter 3:15–16, the apostle Peter has this to say to leaders in the church: "Always be prepared to give an answer to everyone who asks you to give the reason for the hope that you have. But do this with gentleness and respect, keeping a clear conscience, so that those who speak maliciously against your good behavior in Christ may be ashamed of their slander." Peter presents a real-life scenario for relating to people of other religious faiths. What if a Buddhist or Wiccan asked you about the source of hope in your life? The ensuing conversation ought not to commence by your blasting their religious views. Rather, the culturally intelligent preacher employs the Word of God (in this case, 1 Pet. 3:15) as a double-edged sword while recognizing the bluntness of one side of the blade. The posture we take is not one of judgment alone, but is also marked by respect. On many levels, our religious counterparts display grand and admirable fervency for their religion. Oftentimes we must remember that their religion and culture are inseparable. Their religion is their culture, and their culture is their religion. In our proclamation, we can respect the Other by commending their sincere devotion to their god. We can avoid language that attacks or criticizes their god or demeans their scriptures. Instead, we can praise their devoutness to practice their religious rituals on a consistent basis. And we can appreciate their unyielding zeal to proselytize and share their faith with others.[78]

Content

What distinguishes Christianity from all other world religions? Jesus Christ, of course! For Christians, the person and work of Jesus Christ define Christianity.

We believe that Jesus is fully God and fully man and that he lived a perfect life, endured earthly suffering, was crucified on the cross, was buried in the tomb, and was resurrected from the dead, thereby conquering Satan in restoring humanity's severed relationship with God. As Luke declares triumphantly in Acts 4:12 concerning Jesus, "Salvation is found in no one else, for there is no other name under heaven given to [hu]mankind by which we must be saved." The obstacle for all major world religions is that they find one or more christological doctrines problematic. For instance, "Muslims are fiercely monotheistic," Keith Stump notes. "The central dogma of Islam is the absolute unity of God (Allah). To Muslims, the biblical teaching of the deity of Jesus Christ is thus polytheistic and blasphemous. It is the major problem confronting Christians who endeavor to reach Muslims with the gospel of Jesus Christ."[79] Likewise, M. S. Vasanthakumar explains that in Buddhist circles "it is not an easy task to convince the people about the absolute deity of Jesus Christ and his unique role in offering salvation to [hu]mankind. All our defenses concerning Jesus Christ will appear to the Buddhists as futile and they think of Jesus Christ similar to that of Buddha prior to his enlightenment or like one of the Hindu gods. . . . Consequently, in the Buddhist mind Jesus Christ occupies the lowest position."[80] Therefore, pounding home christological truths in our sermons may not get us very far, especially with Muslims, Buddhists, and others.

Instead, the sermonic spotlight could shine on making Jesus attractive to them. Jesus is already an attractive person for a number of cultural groups. Vinoth Ramachandra observes:

> Jesus of Nazareth continues to fascinate men and women of all cultures. Many are attracted by the power of his teaching, others by the way he ruthlessly exposed the barrenness and hypocrisy of the religious establishment. His witty aphorisms and devastating parables are continuing sources of delight and admiration to professional communicators and literary critics. Many women see in him a man who was liberated from the pervasive chauvinism of his society, at ease in the company of women. Many social reformers and political revolutionaries have found in Jesus an aspiring model in the struggle for social justice. He was not reluctant to trample upon oppressive social conventions and taboos.[81]

For followers of world religions, we can emphasize a defining characteristic of Jesus in the Gospels in relational quality. In most religions other than Christianity, God is unknowable. Jesus Christ differentiates himself from all other gods through his incarnation and the face-to-face relationships he established with his disciples and others. The Gospel writers also highlight

Jesus's great compassion and love for his people. In particular, Luke's Gospel account offers hope to those on the margins of society, and we can help those from other religious faiths become attracted to Jesus by narrating the stories of Jesus embracing those whom society had rejected. The four Gospels record how Jesus befriended tax collectors like Matthew (Matt. 9:9–13) and Zacchaeus (Luke 19:1–10), unclean lepers (Luke 5:12; 17:11–19), a prostitute (Luke 7:36–50), demon-possessed persons (Mark 5:2–20), a bleeding woman (Luke 8:43–48), a Samaritan woman (John 4:1–26), the blind (Mark 10:46–52), the paralyzed (John 5:1–15), the mute (Matt. 9:33), and many others who were dehumanized or demonized in society.

This same Jesus desires a relationship with those who follow other gods. With respect to Islam, "It is therefore not surprising that when Muslims learn of Jesus' life of love and forgiveness, and come to know him as a living, personal savior, he is irresistible," Stump writes.[82] In regard to Buddhism, Derek Morris writes, "To know and love Jesus personally and supremely is essential. Buddhists have good moral teachings but lack a personal relationship with a living, loving Savior."[83] The more we mention the ways Jesus clearly differentiates himself from other "gods," the more we will be able to point others to his relationality and ultimately to his divinity. Therefore, whenever possible, the content of our messages for the world's religions is Jesus himself, so point them to him.

Trust

Last, build healthy relationships with your listeners outside the pulpit. Although God uses the itinerant preaching of his Word to evangelize, convict, mature, and transform listeners, preaching consistently in the local church as a pastor fosters an added depth to our sermons because we know the people well. Ian Pitt-Watson observes, "Preaching divorced from pastoral concern is blind. It neither knows what it is talking about nor to whom it is talking."[84] In Acts 17, Paul preaches the gospel and teaches the Scriptures in the city of Athens. But before Paul communicated biblical truth with the local philosophers and skeptics, Luke records in verse 16 that Paul took time to get to know the spiritual condition of the city. Then verse 17 reports, "He reasoned in the synagogue with both Jews and God-fearing Greeks, as well as in the marketplace day by day with those who happened to be there." In other words, Paul didn't simply preach Christ and his resurrection without building relationships with the people, but he did so in conjunction with spending time with them and interacting with their questions and concerns.

In *Connecting Christ: How to Discuss Jesus in a World of Diverse Paths*, Paul Louis Metzger writes, "People are not simply wired to assent to truths; they must live them in relation to this God who is the living truth. As Christ's people, we must continually seek to engage people relationally—case by case, and not in some fixed, packaged manner."[85] He emphasizes, "But no matter how good the argument or how contextual, winsome, and striking the message, nothing replaces sacrificial love for others; this is how trust is built."[86] While preaching with words will be effective for some, words coupled with actions will increase our gospel influence, especially to those of other religious traditions.

We are called not simply to preach to them on Sunday mornings but also to build trust, even by inviting them into our homes and offering them hospitality. In *The Gospel for Muslims*, Thabiti Anyabwile says, "Maybe the best way for us Christians to build relationships with Muslim neighbors the Lord has brought to our doorsteps is to host them in our homes. We may reach the world for Christ by simply reaching across our picket fences or crossing the street and then inviting them into our dining and family rooms."[87] Through hospitality, we provide a safe atmosphere toward mutual engagement, learning about one another's entire lives and not just disseminating religious beliefs. Just as in any other human relationship, developing trust takes time, intentionality, and face-to-face interaction. Form trusting relationships with those of other religions beyond Sunday morning's worship service. Seek out those of other religious affiliations, and pursue relational evangelism in conjunction with your faithful proclamation.

Conclusion

In his book *One Thing You Can't Do in Heaven*, Mark Cahill writes, "Three-hundred-million years from now, the only thing that will matter is who is in heaven and who is in hell. And if that is the only thing that will matter then, that should be one of our greatest concerns now."[88] He challenges readers: "One thing you cannot do in Heaven is share your faith with a non-believer. Why? Because everyone in Heaven is a believer. Do you realize that when you take your last breath, you will never again be able to talk with a lost person? Since that is true, shouldn't it be a priority of your life to reach out to all the lost people on earth while you can?"[89] The apostle Paul reminds the church in Ephesus: "For our struggle is not against flesh and blood, but against the rulers, against the authorities, against the powers of this dark world and against the spiritual forces of evil in the heavenly realms" (Eph. 6:12).

We are naive to think that the evil one will accommodate our wishes to bring those of other faiths into a saving relationship with Jesus Christ. The groundwork for all preaching, including to those from other religious faiths, begins with prayer. While prayer is critical for every moment in the pulpit, we dare not enter the pulpit without bathing the sermon in prayer, especially when communicating with those from other religions. Preaching to adherents of other religions is not without its challenges, but the rewards are immeasurable: heaven rejoices with each new believer who renounces their gods and idols in favor of the one true and living God—Father, Son, and Holy Spirit. May that bring preachers much joy as well!

Conclusion

One of my favorite passages in all of Scripture is Jesus's parable of the good Samaritan. You know the story. Jesus challenges the Jews' pejorative perceptions of who these half-blooded Samaritan people are. Remember, it is not the religious leader or pious person but rather a Samaritan man who goes above and beyond customary expectations to love and care for a person truly in need. In this book I have tried to replicate Jesus's vision in this parable—reminding us of the incredible significance and value of every single person regardless of their culture, denomination, ethnicity, gender, location, religious tradition, and more.

My hope is that as preachers living in the twenty-first century, we will adopt the same Samaritan heart as in Jesus's parable and be willing to care even sacrificially for those who do not share our cultural backgrounds and even require immediate hermeneutical, cultural, and homiletical attention. We may have pastoral and homiletical moments when our hearts resemble the hearts of the religious leaders who walked right by the broken and destitute. However, God's economy of who and what is valuable thankfully diverges from normal human reasoning. The simple answer is that the one person who listens to our sermons on the margins, the so-called Other, matters to God and matters to the kingdom of God. In the words of Gabriel Salguero, "People must feel more than tolerated; they must feel welcomed and loved."[1]

Walter Brueggemann issues this declaration about the status quo regarding American society: "The world that is being reshaped and relinquished among us is that of a homogenous, white, male-dominated, straight society. The world that is emerging before us is a world peopled by others who do not fit that neat, reassuring arrangement."[2] For preachers in the evangelical world, this book may in actuality be several decades too late in the writing. Culture

215

has already morphed so drastically that we are behind the times. And yet, simultaneously, this book is well-positioned "for such a time as this" (Esther 4:4), as evangelical preachers lead congregations that require greater cultural intelligence on so many different levels.

As I was writing this book, my precious younger brother, Timothy David Kim (November 3, 1979–November 7, 2015), who was living and working in Manila, Philippines, for over three years as an operations manager for an international marketing company, was brutally murdered. This tragic news jolted our family and also comes as a shock to you. Allow me to briefly acquaint you with Tim. He was the epitome of the Renaissance man. God blessed Tim with a brilliant mind. Tim occasionally reminded me that he was a member of Mensa, an elite society reserved for individuals with the highest IQs in the world. Not only did Tim possess an incredible intellect; he also embodied cultural intelligence, enabling him to navigate various cultures for over a decade as he worked in a few different Asian countries before his death. Tim was simultaneously a gifted athlete in basketball, football, volleyball, and baseball. His sense of humor was unrivaled. But what is most important, Tim adorned the heart of Christ and gave sacrificially to others, resembling the selfless and altruistic person in Jesus's parable of the good Samaritan. Ultimately the very people with whom Tim shared his life and cared for on a daily basis, the Filipino people, ended up being the same ethnic group who terminated his life prematurely. In the weeks immediately following Tim's passing, our mother made a comment that will be imprinted on my heart for the rest of my days on this earth: "I wonder if God will send your dad and me one day to the Philippines as missionaries." With this alarming and sobering statement, our mom was conveying a simple yet deep message: "Even they [the people who murdered your brother and Filipinos] need to hear the gospel of Jesus Christ." In the midst of such heartrending pain, devastation, and loss, our godly mother's ultimate concern similarly reflected the heart of the good Samaritan.

Preaching with cultural intelligence involves such a heart and approach to life. Cultural intelligence in preaching is another way to demonstrate our love for God and for people. However, we acknowledge fully that it is never easy, nor was it ever meant to be easy. Anything worth doing, especially in the pastorate, involves regular doses of humility and exercises in labors of love. It will require varying degrees of self-sacrifice and the commitment to stretch ourselves beyond our limits of comfort and willingness even to make cultural faux pas on account of our ignorance. Preaching with cultural intelligence means altering not simply our conventional methods for sermon preparation, but also, even greater, our habits of life. It involves spending quantity and quality time with people who think differently, eat differently, learn differently, dress differently, praise differently, work differently, spend differently, behave differently, play differently, pray differently, smell differently, and do life altogether differently. But most important, it will compel us to have the heart and mind of our Lord and Savior Jesus Christ, whose love knows no bounds and who knows no cultural distinctions.

This book serves as a conversation starter; by no means has it answered all of your questions about navigating cultural differences. If anything, the contents here have hopefully, in some tangible way, piqued your interest and encouraged you to love your neighbor as yourself—from the casual visitor at your church to the opposite extreme of someone who has stolen someone precious to you. As we take proactive steps toward cultural intelligence in our preaching, be assured that every "elephant" in the room has taken one palpable stride closer to the Savior. Those same "elephants" will one day embrace us for our efforts, and our reward is that they will worship the Lord alongside of us, shoulder to shoulder, for the rest of eternity. Preaching with cultural intelligence *is* worth it. Wouldn't you agree?

The Homiletical Template

Scripture Text: _____

Stage 1: Follow Your HABIT

Try to make it a HABIT to incorporate all five steps in your sermon preparation each week.

Historical, Grammatical, and Literary Context
    Historical Context:
    Grammatical Issues:
    Literary Study:

Author's Cultural Context
Write down one or two cultural practices under each column below.

Cultural Practices in the Bible	Cultural Practices Today
1.	1.
2.	2.

Big Idea of the Text
Subject: What is the author talking about?

Complement: What is the author saying about what he's talking about?

Exegetical Idea: Take off the interrogative and combine the subject and complement to get the exegetical idea.

Homiletical Idea: Find a clear, concise, catchy, and contemporary way to state the basic thrust of the exegetical idea to your listeners. (Are there idioms that your listeners may not understand?)

Interpret in Your Context
   Assumptions—
   Conflicts—
   Questions—

Theological Presuppositions

Stage 2: Build the BRIDGE

Try to include at least one section of the BRIDGE (Beliefs, Rituals, Idols, Dreams, God, Experiences) per week for your cultural context. For assistance on gathering information for your listeners' BRIDGE, see appendix 2.

Stage 3: Speak Their DIALECT

Try to include at least one or two elements of DIALECT per week for your cultural context.

Delivery
How does your delivery require modification to accommodate other listeners?

   Tone—
   Gestures—
   Body Language—
   Word Choice—
   Humor—

Illustrations
   Can I find culturally specific illustrations that will be a better fit with some
      listeners?

Can I include illustrations where the Other is a protagonist, hero, positive example, or a nonstereotypical example?

Am I using illustrations that marginalize Others or demonize them in any way?

Application

How can my applications reach the specific life situations of nonmajority-culture listeners?

How can I broaden my applications to both individuals and the entire community?

Are my applications limited to doing actions, or is the text also asking them to grow in their being or becoming?

Language

Do I use vocabulary and terms that everyone will understand?

Can I use words from non-English speakers' languages to help them better understand the sermon?

Have I found the best dynamic equivalents possible?

Embrace

In what ways can I embrace my listeners more?

Are there ways that my sermons alienate or ostracize my hearers?

Have I told my listeners lately that I love them?

Content

What topics do my listeners need to hear about from the pulpit?

Are there books of the Bible, biblical genres, or topics in life that I tend to avoid?

Does the content of my sermon reflect the actual message of the text?

Trust

Is my lifestyle consistent with what I'm preaching?

How can I cultivate greater trust from the pulpit for the Others?

Have I spent time this week with someone from another cultural group?

APPENDIX 2

Worksheet for Understanding Culture

Whenever possible, as you go through this worksheet begin by trying to answer the same questions for the author's cultural context.

1. Culture as a Way of Living

For each of the categories below, try to answer these three questions:

A. What types of food, clothing, language, music, celebrations, and view of time do the Others in your congregation eat, wear, speak, hear, celebrate, and hold?

B. How do you feel about their culture's food, clothing, language, music, celebrations, and view of time?

C. In what ways do their food, clothing, language, music, celebrations, and view of time differ or conflict with your own culture?

Food

A. _____

_____

_____

_____

B. _____

_____

_____

_____

C. _____

_____

_____

_____

Clothing

A. _____

_____

_____

_____

B. _____

_____

_____

_____

C. _____

_____

_____

_____

Language

A. _____

_____

_____

_____

B. _____

_____

_____

_____

C. _____

_____

_____

_____

Music

A. _____

_____

_____

_____

B. _____

_____

_____

_____

C. _____

_____

_____

_____

Celebrations

A. _____

_____

_____

_____

B. _____

_____

_____

_____

C. _____

_____

_____

_____

Time

A. _____

_____

_____

_____

B. _____

_____

_____

_____

C. _____

_____

_____

_____

2. Culture as a Way of Thinking (Build the BRIDGE)

(Each week as you prepare your sermon, try to answer these questions as you build the BRIDGE into your listeners' lives.)

Beliefs

What *confessional beliefs* does this Scripture text support or challenge for your listeners?

What *convictional beliefs* does this Scripture text nurture or refute for your listeners?

What *cultural beliefs* do your listeners embrace that conflict with Scripture?

Rituals

Write down three to five rituals or traditions that are most important to your congregants.

Write below one or two rituals/traditions for each of these categories that promote or conflict with your Scripture text this week:

Individual	
Family	
Ethnic/Cultural	
Church	

Idols

Write down the idols of your listeners that they will struggle to hand over to God in this week's sermon.

Individual	

Family	
Ethnic/Cultural	
Church	

Dreams

What is God's dream for your listeners in this week's sermon?

What dreams or possible selves are most prominent for your listeners with respect to this week's Scripture text?

Individual	
Family	
Ethnic/Cultural	
Physical	
Emotional	
Relational	

Spiritual	

In what ways do your listeners' dreams align with or diverge from God's dreams for them in this Scripture text?

God

Which characteristics of God would your listeners most identify with in this week's sermon? Try to address these attributes of God in your sermon this week.

Are there characteristics of God in this text that Others would more aptly relate to than my dominant context?

Experiences

What life experiences are most influential for your listeners as they either positively or negatively receive this week's sermon? Place them in two rows.

Positive	
Negative	

3. Culture as a Way of Behaving

For each category of behavior below, try to learn about the Others in your congregation and how they might answer these questions with respect to your text.

Ethics

What is right?

What is wrong?

What are the gray areas?

What cultural differences exist with respect to ethics?

Decisions

Who ultimately makes the decision?

Is decision making based on age, gender, title, position, and so forth?

Are decisions made in light of what's best for the individual, family, church, cultural group, or organization?

Mores

What is considered acceptable behavior?

Do you agree or disagree with Others' cultural mores? Why or why not?

How does your sermon condone or combat differences in cultural mores?

Love

Which expressions of love are culturally appropriate?

Do expressions of love differ in your context? If so, how?

Am I learning about how Others receive love?

Fairness

What is just or unjust?

On what basis is fairness determined?

What power dynamics influence fairness?

Actions

How do those in Other cultures behave and act specifically with regard to your Scripture text?

How can those actions and behaviors be affirmed according to Scripture?

How can those actions and behaviors be challenged according to Scripture?

APPENDIX 3

Sample Sermon

Revere God by Remembering Others

Scripture Text: Nehemiah 5

Subject: What do Nehemiah's actions show about how he viewed the lowest persons in society in difficult economic times?

Complement: He valued them as God's people and cared generously for their needs.

Exegetical Idea: Nehemiah's actions showed that he valued the lowest persons in society in difficult economic times as God's people and cared generously for their needs.

Homiletical Idea: *Out of reverence for God, care for others, and God will remember you.*

Listeners: Primarily affluent Asian Americans in Denver, Colorado

Introduction

[Content] The sermon focuses on God's and Nehemiah's justice in spite of human injustices.

[Delivery] The tone of the message is direct and yet encouraging and hopeful.

John Grisham has always been one of my favorite authors. Maybe you're a fan too. In his novel *Street Lawyer*, Grisham opens with a description of an elevator scene in which a partner of a prestigious law firm notices the rather foul stench of a vagrant from the streets who enters the elevator and stands behind him. They ride together in this confined space up to his office floor. Grisham stresses the lawyer's ill feelings toward this man from the streets who would otherwise be invisible in society except for the fact that he's stuck in the elevator with him.[1]

Who would you want to be in this scene? Many, in our Asian American circles, would probably choose to be the lawyer and not the homeless person. How would we feel if this person stood behind us in the elevator? Would we fear for our safety or clutch tighter to our belongings? Would we be repulsed by his odor? Would feelings of pride and superiority set in? How would we feel? What words would John Grisham use to describe your inner dialogue in this situation?

In Nehemiah 5, we begin to see the condition of the human heart. Money is necessary in all parts of life. We need it to live. But there are moments where a switch happens, and money consumes us even to the point of exploiting the helpless. How do we feel when we witness injustices around the world or even here in this city? Turn with me to Nehemiah 5. What injustices are happening in Nehemiah's cultural context? How does Nehemiah respond to them? And how does God call us to respond to injustice?

I. Money Affects Our Relationship with God and with Others (vv. 1–5).

[Historical, Grammatical, and Literary Context] Before becoming the governor of Jerusalem, Nehemiah served King Artaxerxes as his cupbearer or the equivalent of the president's chief of staff. In the ancient world the cupbearer's job was to sample the king's wine to make sure it wasn't poisoned. How would you like that job? Well, in the middle of this rebuilding project, Governor Nehemiah is faced with a dilemma.[2]

[Author's Cultural Context] In these opening scenes in the first five verses of chapter 5, we get a glimpse into a common societal trend that exists even today. The rich are getting richer, and the poor are getting poorer. A great famine seizes the city. Scholars tell us that famines were fairly common in the ancient Near East. There wasn't enough supply to meet the demand due to natural causes as well as the human sin of greed. In verse 2, even within one community some were not getting their share of the food supply. People were starving to their literal death.

[**Illustration**] I remember that when I was younger, my brothers and I would sometimes complain about the food we were eating. Our dad would tell us stories about the difficult living standards during the Korean War. There was no food to eat, so he would find anything edible such as rolling into a ball the skins of brown rice and barley. Only those who could afford it ate *real* rice. So I asked, "Why didn't you just go to the store and cook some ramen noodles?" He smirked, "What are you talking about? There was no ramen until sometime in the 1970s. That's why we needed to eat *anything* in order to survive. So be grateful to God and eat your food." The same dire situation confronted the Israelites in Nehemiah's context.

[**Author's Cultural Context**] Three times the people cried out for food. First, in verse 2, there was a shortage because of the sheer number of Jewish family members needing food. Second, in verse 3, landowners were greedy, making a profit by charging them extra for food, which forced them to mortgage their land, vineyards, and homes.

[**Rituals**] The question for us today is clear: how do we use our money, power, and influence? Some of us find satisfaction in helping others, while others of us unconsciously extort others in the ways we manage resources, whether in the office, at home, or even at church.

[**Interpret in Your Context**] It's like an extreme version of the board game Monopoly. If you want to stay in the game, you have to mortgage your property and sometimes all of it just to keep playing. Admit it: sometimes your Monopoly partners are ruthless, or maybe that's you.

[**Author's Cultural Context**] But the big difference here is that these were *real* people with *real* money problems. It was about complete survival. They needed food to live, or else they would die. The third time the people cried out for food, verse 4 says that others were complaining about the king's high taxes, which kept them from feeding their families. At this time, Persian kings collected 20 million darics, or approximately 100 million dollars in taxes, rendering the people unable to buy food. In verse 5, because of this famine and extortion, the people were even sending their children into slavery.

[**Illustration**] Many injustices are happening in our world today as well. In Gary Haugen's book *Good News about Injustice*, he describes such tragedies:

World Vision India, a Christian relief and development agency, recently introduced me to a ten-year-old girl in a little village in the state of Tamil Naidu. Her name is Kanmani. From 8:00 in the morning until 6:00 at night, six days a week, she sits in the same little place on the floor and manufactures cigarettes. Her job is to close the ends with a little knife. She is required to complete 2,000 cigarettes a day. If she doesn't work fast enough, her overseers strike her on the head. Her ten-hour workday is broken only by a single thirty-minute lunch period. At the end of a long week she gets her wages—about seventy-five cents. Worst of all, she has been working like this for more than five years.[3]

[Theological Presuppositions/View of God] How do we respond when others face hardships? Some different thoughts enter our brains: (1) It's easy to blame God for his lack of provision for his people. (2) They deserve it because they probably sinned against God. (3) God permitted their suffering on account of their sin. (4) Someone else will come along and provide for them. (5) It's easy to judge and look the other way and say that's not my problem. Well, how does Nehemiah respond? As we continue reading, the people's problems became Nehemiah's problem. He couldn't look the other way.

[Language] The Holy Spirit grips our hearts when we see injustices happening around us. We are agents of God's love. We are distributors of God's peace. We are instruments of God's grace to a world that yearns for Christians to take action. And that's what Nehemiah models for us.

II. Caring for the Oppressed Means Speaking Up on Their Behalf (vv. 6–13).

[Author's Cultural Context] In verses 6–7 we read, "When I heard their outcry and these charges, I was very angry. I pondered them in my mind and then accused the nobles and officials. I told them, 'You are charging your own people interest!'" He doesn't stop there. He decides to act on their behalf and calls a meeting. He calls out the officials for their corruption. He demands that the usury be stopped and that they immediately return the fields, vineyards, olive groves, homes, and usury to them in verse 11.

[Beliefs] How do we respond when we see injustice happen? Has it ever angered us, like Nehemiah, to see injustices happening near us? Proverbs 31:8–9 says, "Speak up for those who cannot speak for themselves, for the rights of all who are destitute. Speak up and judge fairly; defend the rights of the poor and needy." For many of us, we may have the right intentions without the right heart.

[Illustrations] Perhaps we respond like Bobby in the following story. "Six-year-old Bobby and his dad were headed to McDonald's when they passed a car accident. The family had a practice of saying a prayer for those who might be hurt whenever they saw an accident, so dad said to [his] son, 'We should pray.' From the back seat Bobby began to pray fervently: 'Please, God, don't let those cars block the entrance to McDonald's.'"[4] Rather, Isaiah 1:16b–17 says, "Stop doing wrong. Learn to do right; seek justice. Defend the oppressed. Take up the cause of the fatherless; plead the case of the widow."

[Dreams] As Christians, God calls us to respond to injustices with a new dream. Instead of dreaming about our future only, God dreams that one day his children will speak up for the poor, the marginalized, the oppressed, the widow, and the orphan. In Genesis 1, we are told clearly that every single human being on the face of this earth, whether they are homeless people as in Grisham's story or marginalized Jews as in Nehemiah's story, are persons made in the image of God. If that is the case, how then can we simply turn our backs on them when they need our help?

[The Big Idea] *Out of reverence for God, care for others, and God will remember you.*

[Experiences] How can we do that, you ask? Maybe some of us have been tainted by negative experiences with the oppressed. Perhaps we've been taken advantage of by those who said they were in need. Yet God calls us to care for others, especially those who have no voice.

[Applications] Let's take a practical example close to home. Many Asian Americans, especially Chinese Americans and Korean Americans, are self-employed. Perhaps our parents own restaurants or businesses where they hire immigrants. The perception is that some Asian business owners mistreat their employees. They exploit their workers and do not pay them fairly. Perhaps they mistreat them and abuse them verbally. As Christians, we must speak out against such abuse and reverse our legacy. This is one way we can care for all who are made in God's image out of reverence for him.

In Denver and other parts of the world, there is increased slavery in the sex industry where "massage parlors" employ young girls to provide sex acts. This is an illegal activity that usually goes unnoticed and unvoiced. As a church, we can help to stop this activity from occurring. Like Nehemiah, we can speak out against this horrendous sin in our city. We can start caring for what God clearly cares about, which is speaking up on behalf of the oppressed. Perhaps we can partner with groups like International Justice Mission in DC to speak out against such crimes in our city. What else does Nehemiah do?

III. Caring for the Oppressed Means Living a More Modest Lifestyle (vv. 14–16).

[Author's Cultural Context] Nehemiah, as a government official, was living well. In that time period, during the reign of King Artaxerxes, he was easily making what we would call "six figures." He had the potential to live luxuriously. Yet, in order to care for the oppressed, Nehemiah chose not to eat the food of the king. Why? Because the government officials took food and money from the people so that they could live more lavishly. And Nehemiah says something out of the ordinary. In verse 15, he responds: "But out of reverence for God I did not act like that."

[Idols] If we care more about what God thinks of us than what other people think of us, then we can live as Nehemiah did. We can live a more modest lifestyle. We don't always have to play with the latest and fastest gadgets, wear the best name brands, drive the sleekest cars, and live in the most extravagant homes. Dare I say it? We don't even have to send our kids to the most expensive or prestigious colleges. Consider how much we could do to care for the widows and orphans and others if we lived more modestly.

[Illustration] Proverbs 30:8–9 says, "Give me neither poverty nor riches, but give me only my daily bread. Otherwise, I may have too much and disown you and say, 'Who is the LORD?' Or I may become poor and steal, and so dishonor the name of my God." Did you know that one of the most common misconceptions we evangelical Christians have is that if I give God my tithe, or 10 percent of my income, I can spend the rest of the 90 percent however I want to? Nowhere in the Bible does it say that. This is completely untrue. In all parts of life, we are God's stewards of every material and spiritual blessing.

IV. Last, Caring for the Oppressed Means Giving Generously to Them (vv. 17–18).

[Author's Cultural Context] Nehemiah showed love by sharing with others without counting the cost. He provided lavishly for others. It says in verse 17 that "a hundred and fifty Jews and officials ate at my table, as well as those who came to us from the surrounding nations." Verse 18 describes the extravagance of the meals: "Each day one ox, six choice sheep and some poultry were prepared for me, and every ten days an abundant supply of wine of all kinds." In most, if not all, cultures past and present, meat and wine are expensive commodities. This amount of food would be enough to feed "six or eight hundred people."[5] As one commentator explains, Nehemiah provided meals for "150 poor Judeans and Nehemiah's own household," in addition to "some four or five hundred people."[6] This was not a line item in the governor's budget but rather a sacrificial gift from his personal bank account.[7] Nehemiah clearly cared for others.

[Illustration] I remember a few years ago reading a sermon by a well-known preacher in Chicago, Joe Stowell, the former president of Moody Bible

Institute, who now serves as president of Cornerstone University in Michigan. In his sermon on caring for the poor, he shares this story about an interaction with a person on the streets:

> It was a bitterly cold January morning and I had already stopped by Starbucks and paid more than a buck for a measly cup of coffee. . . . [I asked the homeless woman selling newspapers,] "How are you today?" She looked at me and said, "I'm cold. I'm so cold." I turned to go, and told her matter-of-factly, "I hope the sun comes out, it warms up, and you have a good day." . . . For weeks I prayed that the Lord would let me see her again. To this day I would do anything to give her a cup of hot coffee in Christ's name.[8]

[**Trust**] The truth is that I'm not perfect. In the depths of my heart, I've done the same type of things or even worse. I'm ashamed that I've avoided eye contact to avoid having to say, "I'm sorry." I'm not perfect. I've refused to give even when I've had money in my pockets. I've ignored the street panderers standing at the exit of Colorado Boulevard and so many others. I've been cold and heartless, at times. Why is it that God tells us so many times in the Bible to care for those in need, yet we are somehow conditioned not to follow those instructions?

[**Illustration**] Joe Stowell continues: "We might never say the words out loud, but we act as though our God is the God of clean people, the God of the wealthy, the God of the middle and upper classes. But one quick glance at the heart of God in the Old Testament and the actions of Christ in the New Testament, and we see that God has a special interest in the disadvantaged and the oppressed. In fact, it is biblically clear that when God sees the disadvantaged that His response is one of active compassion."[9]

Notice Nehemiah's last statement in verse 19: "Remember me with favor, my God, for all I have done for these people." Dear church, God will remember everything that we did and did not do for people in desperate situations. This is not a sermon to heap on guilt and shame.

[**Embrace**] Yes, God forgives our mistakes in this area of life. He loves us no matter what—even when we've failed to love the oppressed. This is not a message to scold us but to encourage us to respond to God's invitation to act on his behalf. Of course, we can't do anything apart from the power of God, the example of Christ, and the Holy Spirit working on our hearts.

[**Dream**] Nehemiah's life reminds us that we can make a positive difference in Denver and in the world. God calls us to have new dreams. A group of purposeful Christians, called the church, can make that difference. We can change the world one person at a time. We can bring new life to those without hope. If we claim to know God and have no compassion toward injustice, then we are no better than those who do not know him.

[**The Big Idea**] *Out of reverence for God, care for others, and God will remember you.* He will remember every time we care for those in need. He will remember every time we give lovingly and sacrificially. He will remember. *Out of reverence for God, care for others, and God will remember you.*

Notes

Introduction

1. R. Roosevelt Thomas Jr., *Building a House for Diversity: How a Fable about a Giraffe and an Elephant Offers New Strategies for Today's Workforce* (New York: AMACOM, 1999), 3–4.

2. Donald McGavran, *Understanding Church Growth*, 3rd ed. (Grand Rapids: Eerdmans, 1990), 156, 174–75.

3. Gerald A. Arbuckle, *Refounding the Church: Dissent for Leadership* (Maryknoll, NY: Orbis Books, 1993), 223.

4. Thomas, *Building a House for Diversity*, 5.

5. David A. Livermore popularized the concept of "cultural intelligence" in *Serving with Eyes Wide Open: Doing Short-Term Missions with Cultural Intelligence* (Grand Rapids: Baker Books, 2006) and in his subsequent books. The term "cultural intelligence" was introduced originally by business professors P. Christopher Earley and Soon Ang in *Cultural Intelligence: Individual Interactions across Cultures* (Stanford, CA: Stanford University Press, 2003), 12.

Chapter 1: Preaching and Cultural Intelligence

1. See Kernwood Avenue Bridge, *Bridge Hunter*, https://bridgehunter.com/ma/essex/B110 05307MHDNBI.

2. Ibid.

3. John Stott, *Between Two Worlds: The Challenge of Preaching Today* (Grand Rapids: Eerdmans, 1982), 9.

4. Ibid., 135–79.

5. Laura Ziessel, "Why Christians Are Not in a Culture War," *Relevant Magazine*, October 14, 2011, http://www.relevantmagazine.com/god/church/features/27044-are-we-in-a-culture-war.

6. See, e.g., Dennis E. Johnson, *Him We Proclaim: Preaching Christ from All the Scriptures* (Phillipsburg, NJ: P&R, 2007); and Timothy Keller, *Preaching: Communicating Faith in an Age of Skepticism* (New York: Viking, 2015).

7. See Scott M. Gibson, *Preaching with a Plan: Sermon Strategies for Maturing Believers* (Grand Rapids: Baker Books, 2012).

8. See note on Acts 8:27 in *NIV Zondervan Study Bible*, ed. D. A. Carson (Grand Rapids: Zondervan, 2015), 2234.

9. See Lesslie Newbigin, *Foolishness to the Greeks: The Gospel and Western Culture* (Grand Rapids: Eerdmans, 1986), 3; and Aubrey Malphurs, *Look Before You Lead: How to Discern and Shape Your Church Culture* (Grand Rapids: Baker Books, 2013), 20.

10. The business world is not the only field to encourage cultural intelligence. To educate the medical field on cultural differences, e.g., Geri-Ann Galanti has written a helpful book: *Caring for Patients from Different Cultures*, 3rd ed. (Philadelphia: University of Pennsylvania Press, 2004).

11. P. Christopher Earley and Soon Ang, *Cultural Intelligence: Individual Interactions across Cultures* (Stanford, CA: Stanford University Press, 2003), 12.

12. Jared E. Alcántara, *Crossover Preaching: Intercultural-Improvisational Homiletics in Conversation with Gardner C. Taylor* (Downers Grove, IL: IVP Academic, 2015), 198.

13. See, e.g., David Livermore's website, "Cultural Intelligence (CQ)," http://davidlivermore.com/blog/cq.

14. Alcántara, *Crossover Preaching*, 218.

15. David A. Livermore, *Leading with Cultural Intelligence: The New Secret to Success* (New York: AMACOM, 2009), 26.

16. Ibid.

17. Ibid.

18. Ibid.

19. David A. Livermore, *Cultural Intelligence: Improving Your CQ to Engage Our Multicultural World* (Grand Rapids: Baker Academic, 2009), 121.

20. Livermore, *Leading with Cultural Intelligence*, 27.

21. Ibid.

22. Ibid.

23. Ibid.

24. Ibid., 28, emphasis original.

25. Michael J. Quicke, *Preaching as Worship: An Integrative Approach to Formation in Your Church* (Grand Rapids: Baker Books, 2011), 53.

26. Leonora Tubbs Tisdale, *Preaching as Local Theology and Folk Art* (Minneapolis: Fortress, 1997), 18.

27. Raymond J. Bakke, "The Challenge of World Urbanization to Mission Thinking and Strategy: Perspectives on Demographic Realities," *Urban Mission* 4, no. 1 (September 1986): 15.

28. Michael V. Angrosino, *Talking about Cultural Diversity in Your Church: Gifts and Challenges* (Walnut Creek, CA: Altamira, 2001), 53.

29. See Jolyon P. Mitchell, *Visually Speaking: Radio and the Renaissance of Preaching* (Louisville: Westminster John Knox, 1999).

30. Patty Lane, *A Beginner's Guide to Crossing Cultures: Making Friends in a Multicultural World* (Downers Grove, IL: InterVarsity, 2002), 18–19.

31. Ibid., 18.

32. See Gibson, *Preaching with a Plan*.

33. Here I am borrowing from and adding to Lane's perspective (Lane, *Beginner's Guide to Crossing Cultures*).

34. In some cultures time is viewed as being limited. These cultures value punctuality and awareness of others' busy schedules. Other cultures view time as being limitless. These cultures are less concerned with punctuality but rather focus energy on building bridges by spending time with others.

35. Lane, *Beginner's Guide to Crossing Cultures*, 46.

36. Eugene H. Peterson, *The Contemplative Pastor: Returning to the Art of Spiritual Direction* (Grand Rapids: Eerdmans, 1993), 4.

37. Livermore, *Cultural Intelligence*, 34.

Chapter 2: The Homiletical Template

1. E.g., see Joseph R. Jeter Jr. and Ronald J. Allen, *One Gospel, Many Ears: Preaching for Different Listeners in the Congregation* (St. Louis: Chalice, 2002); James R. Nieman and Thomas G. Rogers, *Preaching to Every Pew: Cross-Cultural Strategies* (Minneapolis: Fortress, 2001); and Leonora Tubbs Tisdale, *Preaching as Local Theology and Folk Art* (Minneapolis: Fortress, 1997).

2. E. Randolph Richards and Brandon J. O'Brien, *Misreading Scripture with Western Eyes: Removing Cultural Blinders to Better Understand the Bible* (Downers Grove, IL: InterVarsity, 2012), 12–13.

3. Haddon W. Robinson, *Biblical Preaching: The Development and Delivery of Expository Messages*, 3rd ed. (Grand Rapids: Baker Academic, 2014), 5.

4. I am relying on Robinson's preaching philosophy (see preceding note) and recognize that various readers may ascribe to other homiletical methods yet can still adapt this book to suit their preaching approaches.

5. For "historical-cultural context," see Terry G. Carter, J. Scott Duvall, and J. Daniel Hays, *Preaching God's Word: A Hands-On Approach to Preparing, Developing, and Delivering the Sermon* (Grand Rapids: Zondervan, 2005), 50–54.

6. For help in understanding ancient biblical cultures in the Old Testament, see Bill T. Arnold and Brent A. Strawn, eds., *The World around the Old Testament: The People and Places of the Ancient Near East* (Grand Rapids: Baker Academic, 2016).

7. Gary M. Burge, *Encounters with Jesus: Uncover the Ancient Culture, Discover Hidden Meanings* (Grand Rapids: Zondervan, 2010), 9.

8. Ibid., 9–10.

9. For a complete description of the big idea philosophy, see Robinson, *Biblical Preaching*, 15–26.

10. John Koessler, *Folly, Grace, and Power: The Mysterious Act of Preaching* (Grand Rapids: Zondervan, 2011), 87.

11. John Goldingay, "How Far Do Readers Make Sense? Interpreting Biblical Narrative," *Themelios* 18, no. 2 (January 1993): 9; and E. D. Hirsch, *Validity in Interpretation* (New Haven: Yale University Press, 1967), 8, 140.

12. James W. Sire, *Naming the Elephant: Worldview as a Concept*, 2nd ed. (Downers Grove, IL: IVP Academic, 2015), 18.

13. "Values" are "principles or standards of behavior; one's judgment of what is important in life." https://en.oxforddictionaries.com/definition/us/value. D. A. Carson explains: "A 'worldview,' after all, is nothing other than a view of the 'world'—that is, of all reality." See D. A. Carson, *Christ and Culture Revisited*, rev. ed. (Grand Rapids: Eerdmans, 2012), 95.

14. See "Belief," http://www.oxforddictionaries.com/us/definition/american_english /belief?q=beliefs.

15. Steve Wilkens and Mark L. Sanford, *Hidden Worldviews: Eight Cultural Stories That Shape Our Lives* (Downers Grove, IL: IVP Academic, 2009), 22.

16. Ibid.

17. Albert M. Wolters, *Creation Regained: Biblical Basics for a Reformational Worldview*, 2nd ed. (Grand Rapids: Eerdmans, 2005), 2.

18. "Customs" or "traditions" may be more comfortable terms for the preacher. A "custom" is "a traditional and widely accepted way of behaving or doing something that is specific to a particular society, place, or time." https://en.oxforddictionaries.com/definition/us/custom. A "tradition" involves both beliefs and customs: "The transmission of customs or beliefs from generation to generation, or the fact of being passed on in this way." https://en.oxforddictionaries .com/definition/us/tradition.

19. See "Ritual," http://www.oxforddictionaries.com/us/definition/american_english/ritual ?q=rituals.

20. Thomas A. Robinson and Hillary P. Rodrigues, *World Religions: A Guide to the Essentials*, 2nd ed. (Grand Rapids: Baker Academic, 2014), 11.

21. "Identity" can be defined as "the characteristics determining who or what a person or thing is." https://en.oxforddictionaries.com/definition/us/identity.

22. Timothy Keller and Katherine Leary Alsdorf, *Every Good Endeavor: Connecting Your Work to God's Work* (New York: Dutton, 2012), 131–32.

23. Gregory K. Beale, *We Become What We Worship: A Biblical Theology of Idolatry* (Downers Grove, IL: IVP Academic, 2008), 16, emphasis original.

24. Eric Geiger, *Identity: Who You Are in Christ* (Nashville: B&H, 2008), 7.

25. Timothy Keller, "Gospel Preaching That Radically Changes Lives: How to Discern, Expose, and Challenge the Idols," *Preaching Today*, August 17, 2009, http://www.preachingtoday.com/skills/themes/preachingwithauthority/gospelpreachingthatradically.html.

26. Hazel Rose Markus and Paula Nurius, "Possible Selves," *American Psychologist* 41, no. 9 (1986): 954.

27. For information on spiritual possible selves, see Matthew D. Kim, *Preaching to Second Generation Korean Americans: Towards a Possible Selves Contextual Homiletic* (New York: Peter Lang, 2007), 129–60.

28. Dan Harris and Enjoli Francis, "A Look at the 4 Ways Americans View God," ABCNEWS, October 7, 2010, http://abcnews.go.com/WN/book-religion-examines-ways-americans-perceive-god/story?id=11825319.

29. Henri J. M. Nouwen, *The Wounded Healer* (New York: Doubleday, 1979), 80.

30. Kenneth Burke, *A Grammar of Motives and a Rhetoric of Motives* (Cleveland: World Pub. Co., 1962), 579.

31. David J. Hesselgrave, *Communicating Christ Cross-Culturally: An Introduction to Missionary Communication*, 2nd ed. (Grand Rapids: Zondervan, 1991), 46, emphasis original.

32. "Dialect," https://en.oxforddictionaries.com/definition/us/dialect.

33. Clive Upton, "English Dialect Study—an Overview," http://public.oed.com/aspects-of-english/english-in-use/english-dialect-study-an-overview.

34. Rick Aschmann, "North American English Dialects, Based on Pronunciation Patterns," http://aschmann.net/AmEng.

35. Maria Khodorkovsky, "10 Spanish Dialects: How Spanish Is Spoken around the World," *ALTA Language Services*, November 13, 2008, http://www.altalang.com/beyond-words/2008/11/13/10-spanish-dialects-how-spanish-is-spoken-around-the-world.

36. Calvin Miller, *Marketplace Preaching: How to Return the Sermon to Where It Belongs* (Grand Rapids: Baker, 1995), 55.

37. Wayne Harvey, "Illustrating with Integrity and Sensitivity: Seven Questions for Staying above Reproach," in *The Art and Craft of Biblical Preaching*, ed. Haddon W. Robinson and Craig Brian Larson (Grand Rapids: Zondervan, 2005), 523, emphasis original.

38. Ibid.

39. Matthew Soerens and Jenny Hwang, *Welcoming the Stranger: Justice, Compassion and Truth in the Immigration Debate* (Downers Grove, IL: InterVarsity, 2009), 91.

40. Abraham Kuruvilla, *A Vision for Preaching: Understanding the Heart of Pastoral Ministry* (Grand Rapids: Baker Academic, 2015), 6.

41. Haddon W. Robinson, "The Heresy of Application: It's When We're Applying Scripture That Error Most Likely Creeps In," in Robinson and Larson, *The Art and Craft of Biblical Preaching*, 306.

42. Koessler, *Folly, Grace, and Power*, 87.

43. Timothy Keller, Ockenga Lectures, Gordon-Conwell Theological Seminary, April 5, 2006; in his *Preaching: Communicating Faith in an Age of Skepticism* (New York: Viking, 2015), 186.

44. Robinson, "The Heresy of Application," 309.

45. Ibid.

46. Ibid.

47. Kathleen Tracy, *Islamic Culture in Perspective* (Hockessin, DE: Mitchell Lane, 2015), 26.

48. Richard H. Cox, *Rewiring Your Preaching: How the Brain Processes Sermons* (Downers Grove, IL: InterVarsity, 2012), 44, emphasis original.

49. See Woosung Calvin Choi, *Preaching to Multiethnic Congregation: Positive Marginality as a Homiletical Paradigm* (New York: Peter Lang, 2015), 3.

50. Mark Labberton, *The Dangerous Act of Loving Your Neighbor: Seeing Others through the Eyes of Jesus* (Downers Grove, IL: InterVarsity, 2010), 49, emphasis original.

51. Scott M. Gibson, *Preaching with a Plan: Sermon Strategies for Maturing Believers* (Grand Rapids: Baker Books, 2012), 28.

52. Jeffrey D. Arthurs, *Preaching with Variety: How to Re-create the Dynamics of Biblical Genres* (Grand Rapids: Kregel, 2007), 175.

Chapter 3: Hermeneutics and Cultural Intelligence

1. See E. Randolph Richards and Brandon J. O'Brien, *Misreading Scripture with Western Eyes: Removing Cultural Blinders to Better Understand the Bible* (Downers Grove, IL: InterVarsity, 2012), 34.

2. Anthony Thiselton, *Hermeneutics: An Introduction* (Grand Rapids: Eerdmans, 2009), 1.

3. John Goldingay, *Models for Interpretation of Scripture* (Grand Rapids: Eerdmans, 1994), 8; and James I. Packer, "Preaching as Biblical Interpretation," in *Inerrancy and Common Sense*, ed. Roger Nicole and J. Ramsey Michaels (Grand Rapids: Baker, 1980), 189.

4. J. Scott Duvall and J. Daniel Hays, *Grasping God's Word: A Hands-On Approach to Reading, Interpreting, and Applying the Bible*, 3rd ed. (Grand Rapids: Zondervan, 2012), 139–40, emphasis original.

5. Water C. Kaiser Jr. and Moises Silva, *Introduction to Biblical Hermeneutics: The Search for Meaning*, rev. ed. (Grand Rapids: Zondervan, 2007), 223.

6. See Abraham Kuruvilla, *Mark: A Theological Commentary for Preachers* (Eugene, OR: Cascade, 2012), xi. Kuruvilla articulates a vision for hermeneutics called pericopal theology, focusing less on what the text says and more on what the text does. See Abraham Kuruvilla, *Privilege the Text! A Theological Hermeneutic for Preaching* (Chicago: Moody, 2014), 111.

7. Duvall and Hays, *Grasping God's Word*, 176.

8. Kaiser and Silva, *Introduction to Biblical Hermeneutics*, 332.

9. Andreas J. Köstenberger and Richard D. Patterson, *Invitation to Biblical Interpretation: Exploring the Hermeneutical Triad of History, Literature, and Theology* (Grand Rapids: Kregel, 2011), 58.

10. John A. Broadus, *On the Preparation and Delivery of Sermons*, 4th ed. (San Francisco: Harper, 1979), 24.

11. Kaiser and Silva, *Introduction to Biblical Hermeneutics*, 266–67.

12. Milton S. Terry, *Biblical Hermeneutics: A Treatise on the Interpretation of the Old and New Testaments* (New York: Eaton & Mains, 1890), 70. See also Raymond F. Surburg, "The Presuppositions of the Historical-Grammatical Method as Employed by Historic Lutheranism," *The Springfielder* 38, no. 4 (1974): 280.

13. Haddon W. Robinson, *Biblical Preaching: The Development and Delivery of Expository Messages*, 3rd ed. (Grand Rapids: Baker Academic, 2014), 8.

14. Ibid., 21.

15. Bryan Chapell, *Christ-Centered Preaching: Redeeming the Expository Sermon* (Grand Rapids: Baker Books, 2001), 23.

16. Ramesh Richard, *Preparing Expository Sermons: A Seven-Step Method for Biblical Preaching* (Grand Rapids: Baker Books, 2007), 19.

17. Robinson, *Biblical Preaching*, 5.

18. For assistance on understanding the author's cultural context, see Craig S. Keener and John H. Walton, eds., *NIV Cultural Backgrounds Study Bible* (Grand Rapids: Zondervan, 2016).

19. Kaiser and Silva, *Introduction to Biblical Hermeneutics*, 238.

20. Mark L. Strauss, *How to Read the Bible in Changing Times: Understanding and Applying God's Word Today* (Grand Rapids: Baker Books, 2011), 212.

21. Leslie C. Allen, *Psalms 101–150*, Word Biblical Commentary (Waco: Word, 1983), 214.

22. John Goldingay, *Psalms 90–150*, Baker Commentary on the Old Testament Wisdom and Psalms (Grand Rapids: Baker Academic, 2008), 564.

23. Ibid., 565.

24. Allen, *Psalms 101–150*, 213–14.

25. John Calvin, *John Calvin's Commentaries*, "Psalm 133," http://biblehub.com/commentaries/calvin/psalms/133.htm.

26. Ibid.

27. Goldingay, *Psalms 90–150*, 568.

28. Allen, *Psalms 101–150*, 215.

29. Craig C. Broyles, *Psalms*, New International Biblical Commentary (Peabody, MA: Hendrickson, 1999), 474.

30. Goldingay, *Psalms 90–150*, 567.

31. Broyles, *Psalms*, 474.

32. Allen, *Psalms 101–150*, 214.

33. Hans-Joachim Kraus, *Psalms 60–150: A Commentary* (Minneapolis: Fortress, 1993), 485.

34. Gordon D. Fee and Douglas Stuart, *How to Read the Bible for All Its Worth: A Guide to Understanding the Bible*, 2nd ed. (Grand Rapids: Zondervan, 1993), 193.

35. Kevin Green, *Zondervan All-in-One Bible Reference Guide* (Grand Rapids: Zondervan, 2008), 513.

36. Charles August Briggs and Emilie Grace Briggs, *A Critical and Exegetical Commentary on the Book of Psalms*, International Critical Commentary (Edinburgh: T&T Clark, 1925), 475.

37. Green, *Zondervan All-in-One Bible Reference Guide*, 80.

38. Ibid., 237.

39. See note on Ps. 133:2 in *NIV Cultural Backgrounds Study Bible: Bringing to Life the Ancient World of Scripture*, ed. John H. Walton and Craig S. Keener (Grand Rapids: Zondervan, 2016), 1008.

40. See note on Ps. 133:3 in ibid.

Chapter 4: Exegeting the Preacher

1. E.g., see articles in part 2, "The Spiritual Life of the Preacher," in *The Art and Craft of Biblical Preaching*, ed. Haddon W. Robinson and Craig Brian Larson (Grand Rapids: Zondervan, 2005), 71–113.

2. Chuck DeGroat, *Toughest People to Love: How to Understand, Lead, and Love the Difficult People in Your Life—Including Yourself* (Grand Rapids: Eerdmans, 2014), 19.

3. Charles E. Hummel, *Tyranny of the Urgent*, rev. ed. (Downers Grove, IL: InterVarsity, 1994), 6.

4. Michael Duduit, "Preaching and the City: An Interview with Erwin Lutzer," *Preaching* 13, no. 5 (March–April 1998): 16, available at http://www.preaching.com/resources/articles/preaching-and-the-city-an-interiew-with-erwin-lutzer.

5. Jared E. Alcántara, *Crossover Preaching: Intercultural-Improvisational Homiletics in Conversation with Gardner C. Taylor* (Downers Grove, IL: IVP Academic, 2015), 223, emphasis original.

6. Michael V. Angrosino, *Talking about Cultural Diversity in Your Church: Gifts and Challenges* (Walnut Creek, CA: Altamira, 2001), 51–52.

7. James R. Nieman and Thomas G. Rogers, *Preaching to Every Pew: Cross-Cultural Strategies* (Minneapolis: Fortress, 2001), 140.

8. Ibid.

9. "Xenophobia," http://www.merriam-webster.com/dictionary/xenophobia.

10. David I. Smith, *Learning from the Stranger: Christian Faith and Cultural Diversity* (Grand Rapids: Eerdmans, 2009), 19.

11. "Empathy," http://www.oxforddictionaries.com/definition/english/empathy.

12. "Sympathy," https://en.oxforddictionaries.com/definition/us/sympathy.

13. Nieman and Rogers, *Preaching to Every Pew*, 142.

14. Jennifer M. Durham, "Bounded Set Trends and Conformity to Group Norms at a Non-Denominational Church" (DMin thesis, Ashland Theological Seminary, 2005), 3.

15. Ibid., 4.

16. See Patty Lane, *A Beginner's Guide to Crossing Cultures: Making Friends in a Multicultural World* (Downers Grove, IL: InterVarsity, 2002), 39.

17. Ibid., 41.

18. Here I will adapt Terry Walling's "time-line" approach to self-understanding, which will "help you recognize those critical incidents that God has used to shape your life and give you purpose." See Terry B. Walling, *Perspective Time Line* (Bloomington, MN: ChurchSmart Resources, 1996), 13.

19. Ibid., 14.

20. Ibid.

21. Ibid.

22. DeGroat, *Toughest People to Love*, 114.

23. Paula Harris and Doug Schaupp, *Being White: Finding Our Place in a Multiethnic World* (Downers Grove, IL: InterVarsity, 2009), 102.

24. DeGroat, *Toughest People to Love*, 122.

25. Soong-Chan Rah, *Prophetic Lament: A Call for Justice in Troubled Times* (Downers Grove, IL: InterVarsity, 2015), 23.

26. Ibid., 21.

27. DeGroat, *Toughest People to Love*, 109.

28. Parker Palmer, *A Hidden Wholeness: The Journey toward an Undivided Life* (San Francisco: Jossey-Bass, 2004), 20.

29. DeGroat, *Toughest People to Love*, 124.

30. Paul Tokunaga, introduction to *Following Jesus without Dishonoring Your Parents*, ed. Jeanette Yep, Peter Cha, Susan Cho Van Riesen, Greg Jao, and Paul Tokunaga (Downers Grove, IL: InterVarsity, 1998), 15.

31. Curt Thompson, *Anatomy of the Soul: Surprising Connections between Neuroscience and Spiritual Practices That Can Transform Your Life and Relationships* (Carol Stream, IL: Salt River, 2000), 3, 23.

Chapter 5: Preaching and Denominations

1. List of Christian denominations provided in a study conducted by Gordon-Conwell Theological Seminary.

2. Derek Penwell, *The Mainliner's Survival Guide to the Post-Denominational World* (St. Louis: Chalice, 2014), 4–5.

3. Due to limitations of space, we are unable to explore preaching in the Roman Catholic Church.

4. Timothy George, "Evangelicals and the Present Ecumenical Movement," in *Critical Issues in Ecclesiology: Essays in Honor of Carl E. Braaten*, ed. Alberto L. Garcia and Susan K. Wood (Grand Rapids: Eerdmans, 2011), 50.

5. Erwin Lutzer, *The Doctrines That Divide: A Fresh Look at the Historic Doctrines That Separate Christians* (Grand Rapids: Kregel, 1998), 13.

6. Billy Graham, introduction to *The Evangelicals: An Illustrated History*, by John D. Allan (Grand Rapids: Baker, 1989).

7. Steve Wilkens and Don Thorsen, *Everything You Know about Evangelicals Is Wrong (Well, Almost Everything): An Insider's Look at Myths and Realities* (Grand Rapids: Baker Books, 2010), 203.

8. David T. Olson, *The American Church in Crisis* (Grand Rapids: Zondervan, 2008), 175.

9. Craig Groeschel, foreword to *The American Church in Crisis*, by David T. Olson (Grand Rapids: Zondervan, 2008), 8.

10. D. A. Carson, ed., *NIV Zondervan Study Bible* (Grand Rapids: Zondervan, 2015), 2394.

11. Ibid.

12. Harold W. Hoehner, *Ephesians: An Exegetical Commentary* (Grand Rapids: Baker Academic, 2002), 79.

13. Clinton E. Arnold, *Ephesians*, Zondervan Exegetical Commentary Series on the New Testament (Grand Rapids: Zondervan, 2010), 30.

14. Ibid., 33.

15. Ibid., 228.

16. Hoehner, *Ephesians*, 61.

17. Jeffrey D. Arthurs, *Preaching with Variety: How to Re-create the Dynamics of Biblical Genres* (Grand Rapids: Kregel, 2007), 155.

18. Francis Foulkes, *The Letter of Paul to the Ephesians: An Introduction and Commentary*, rev. ed., Tyndale New Testament Commentaries (Grand Rapids: Eerdmans, 1989), 19–20.

19. Arthurs, *Preaching with Variety*, 153.

20. Foulkes, *The Letter of Paul to the Ephesians*, 119–20.

21. Arnold, *Ephesians*, 44.

22. Walter C. Kaiser Jr., ed., *NIV Archeological Study Bible* (Grand Rapids: Zondervan, 2005), 1917.

23. Ibid., 1921.

24. John F. MacArthur, *Ephesians*, MacArthur New Testament Commentary (Chicago: Moody, 1986), 118.

25. Jonathan Swift, *Thoughts on Various Subjects*, https://ebooks.adelaide.edu.au/s/swift/jonathan/s97th.

26. Jackson W. Carroll, *Mainline to the Future: Congregations for the 21st Century* (Louisville: Westminster John Knox, 2000), xii.

27. Daniel Treier, *Introducing Theological Interpretation of Scripture: Recovering a Christian Practice* (Grand Rapids: Baker Academic, 2008), 32.

28. George, "Evangelicals and the Present Ecumenical Movement," 46.

29. Ibid.

30. Robert Stephen Reid and Lucy Lind Hogan, *The Six Deadly Sins of Preaching: Becoming Responsible for the Faith We Proclaim* (Nashville: Abingdon, 2012), 7.

31. Martin E. Marty, *Lutheran Questions, Lutheran Answers: Exploring Christian Faith* (Minneapolis: Augsburg, 2007), 19.

32. Alix Spiegel, "Why Even Radiologists Can Miss a Gorilla Hiding in Plain Sight," *Shots: Health News from NPR*, February 11, 2013, http://www.npr.org/sections/health-shots/2013/02/11/171409656/why-even-radiologists-can-miss-a-gorilla-hiding-in-plain-sight.

33. Walter B. Shurden, "What Comes into Your Baptist Mind When You Think about God?," *Baptist History and Heritage* 40, no. 2 (2005): 6.

34. W. David Buschart, *Exploring Protestant Traditions: An Invitation to Theological Hospitality* (Downers Grove, IL: IVP Academic, 2006), 22.

35. C. Michael Patton, "Essentials and Non-Essentials in a Nutshell," *Credo House Blog*, June 8, 2011, http://www.reclaimingthemind.org/blog/2011/06/essentials-and-non-essentials-in-a-nutshell.

36. Kevin P. Emmert, "A New School Year Starts, and Many Seminarians Are Staying Put," *Christianity Today*, August 26, 2015, http://www.christianitytoday.com/ct/2015/august-web -only/new-school-year-starts-many-seminarians-staying-put.html.

37. Derek Tidball, *Ministry by the Book: New Testament Patterns for Pastoral Leadership* (Downers Grove, IL: IVP Academic, 2008), 131.

38. Ibid., 132.

39. James F. White, *Protestant Worship: Traditions in Transition* (Louisville: Westminster John Knox, 1989), 21.

40. Buschart, *Exploring Protestant Traditions*, 17.

41. Zack Eswine, *The Imperfect Pastor: Discovering Joy in Our Limitations through a Daily Apprenticeship with Jesus* (Wheaton: Crossway, 2015), 113.

42. See, e.g., David S. Dockery, ed., *Southern Baptist Identity: An Evangelical Denomination Faces the Future* (Wheaton: Crossway, 2009); Mark Granquist, *Lutherans in America: A New History* (Minneapolis: Fortress, 2015); Alan Jones, *Common Prayer on Common Ground: A Vision of Anglican Orthodoxy* (Harrisburg, PA: Morehouse, 2006); Scott J. Jones and Bruce R. Ough, eds., *The Future of the United Methodist Church: 7 Vision Pathways* (Nashville: Abingdon, 2010); and more.

43. Sharon A. Christopher Brown, introduction to Jones and Ough, *The Future of the United Methodist Church*, xxi.

44. David S. Dockery, introduction to *Southern Baptist Identity: An Evangelical Denomination Faces the Future*, ed. David S. Dockery (Wheaton: Crossway, 2009), 13–14.

45. Ibid., 14.

46. See Matthew D. Kim, *Preaching to Second Generation Korean Americans: Towards a Possible Selves Contextual Homiletic* (New York: Peter Lang, 2007), 171.

47. Abraham Kuruvilla, *A Vision for Preaching: Understanding the Heart of Pastoral Ministry* (Grand Rapids: Baker Academic, 2015), 91–109.

48. Tara Klena Barthel and David V. Edling, *Redeeming Church Conflicts: Turning Crisis into Compassion and Care* (Grand Rapids: Baker Books, 2012), 52.

49. Thabiti M. Anyabwile, *What Is a Healthy Church Member?* (Wheaton: Crossway, 2008), 27.

50. Chris Jackson, *Loving God When You Don't Love the Church: Opening the Door to Healing* (Grand Rapids: Chosen, 2007), 12.

51. Roger E. Olson, "Why I Like Denominations," *Patheos: Hosting the Conversation on Faith*, October 11, 2012, http://www.patheos.com/blogs/rogereolson/2012/10/why-i-like-denominations.

52. Thom S. Rainer, "The Future of Denominations," *Rainer on Leadership*, June 5, 2015, http://thomrainer.com/2015/06/the-future-of-denominations-rainer-on-leadership-130.

53. Olson, "Why I Like Denominations."

54. E.g., Kevin DeYoung writes in a blog post: "Since 2002, the year I was ordained, I estimate that I've preached almost 500 times. It took about 450 sermons to find my voice" ("Learning to Be Yourself as a Preacher," *9Marks: Preaching and Theology*, https://9marks.org/article /learning-to-be-yourself-as-a-preacher-from-one-still-trying-to-do-just-that).

55. Charles B. Bugg, "A Look at Baptist Preaching: Past, Present, and Future," *Baptist History and Heritage* 40, no. 2 (Spring 2005): 17.

56. David Dunn-Wilson, *A Mirror for the Church: Preaching in the First Five Centuries* (Grand Rapids: Eerdmans, 2005), xv.

57. Dave Stone, *Refining Your Style: Learning from Respected Communicators* (Loveland, CO: Group, 2004), 12–13. Read the entire book for an in-depth understanding of each of these thirteen categories.

58. Phillips Brooks, *Lectures on Preaching* (New York: Dutton, 1877), 5.

59. Wayne McDill, *12 Essential Skills for Great Preaching*, 2nd ed. (Nashville: B&H, 2006), 240.

60. Ibid., 143.

61. Penwell, *The Mainliner's Survival Guide*, 82, emphasis original.

62. For resources to improve our illustrating, see Bryan Chapell, *Using Illustrations to Preach with Power*, 2nd ed. (Wheaton: Crossway, 2001); and Mark Galli and Craig Brian Larson, *Preaching That Connects: Using the Techniques of Journalists to Add Impact to Your Sermons* (Grand Rapids: Zondervan, 1994).

63. David W. Bebbington, *Evangelicalism in Modern Britain: A History from the 1730s to the 1980s* (London: Unwin Hyman, 1989), 2–17.

64. National Association of Evangelicals, "What Is an Evangelical," http://nae.net/what-is-an-evangelical.

65. Michael Brothers, *Distance in Preaching: Room to Speak, Space to Listen* (Grand Rapids: Eerdmans, 2014), 2, emphasis original.

66. John G. Stackhouse Jr., *Evangelical Landscapes: Facing Critical Issues of the Day* (Grand Rapids: Baker Academic, 2002), 187.

67. Bugg, "A Look at Baptist Preaching," 12.

68. Bryan Chapell, *Christ-Centered Preaching: Redeeming the Expository Sermon* (Grand Rapids: Baker Academic, 2001), 40–44.

69. Anthony Robinson, "Theological Themes and Twenty-First Century Public Witness: Beyond the Feckless and the Bland," *International Congregational Journal* 8, no. 2 (Fall 2009): 80.

70. Scott M. Gibson, *Preaching with a Plan: Sermon Strategies for Maturing Believers* (Grand Rapids: Baker Books, 2012), 28.

71. Michael Horton, foreword to *Preaching the Whole Counsel of God: Design and Deliver Gospel-Centered Sermons*, by Julius J. Kim (Grand Rapids: Zondervan, 2015), 10.

72. For assistance with sermon planning and determining the spiritual maturity of one's congregation, see Gibson, *Preaching with a Plan*.

73. Mark Meynell, *A Wilderness of Mirrors: Trusting Again in a Cynical World* (Grand Rapids: Zondervan, 2015), 128, emphasis original.

74. J. Kim, *Preaching the Whole Counsel of God*, 180–81.

75. John Burke, *No Perfect People Allowed: Creating a Come-as-You-Are Culture in the Church* (Grand Rapids: Zondervan, 2005), 57.

76. Lutzer, *The Doctrines That Divide*, 19.

77. Russell Moore, "Baptist Born? Baptist Bred?," *Ethics and Religious Liberty Commission of the Southern Baptist Convention*, http://www.russellmoore.com/2006/09/07/baptist-born-baptist-bred.

Chapter 6: Preaching and Ethnicities

1. David A. Anderson, *Gracism: The Art of Inclusion* (Downers Grove, IL: InterVarsity, 2007), 18.

2. For five indicators of a racist heart, see Bryan Loritts, "The Multi-Ethnic Preacher," *The Journal of the Evangelical Homiletics Society* 13, no. 1 (March 2013): 8–9.

3. See Jared E. Alcántara, *Crossover Preaching: Intercultural-Improvisational Homiletics in Conversation with Gardner C. Taylor* (Downers Grove, IL: IVP Academic, 2015), 192.

4. Kenneth A. Mathews and M. Sydney Park, *The Post-Racial Church: A Biblical Framework for Multiethnic Reconciliation* (Grand Rapids: Kregel, 2011), 30.

5. Richard T. Schaefer, *Racial and Ethnic Groups*, 6th ed. (New York: HarperCollins, 1996), 9.

6. See Kwame Anthony Appiah, "Race," in *Critical Terms for Literary Study*, ed. Frank Lentricchia and Thomas McLaughlin (Chicago: University of Chicago Press, 1990), 276; Mark Lau Branson and Juan F. Martínez, *Churches, Cultures & Leadership: A Practical Theology of Congregations and Ethnicities* (Downers Grove, IL: IVP Academic, 2011), 86.

7. Lesli A. Maxwell, "U.S. School Enrollment Hits Majority-Minority Milestone," *Education Week*, August 19, 2014, http://www.edweek.org/ew/articles/2014/08/20/01demographics.h34.html.

8. Sandra L. Colby and Jennifer M. Ortman, "Projections of the Size and Composition of the U.S. Population: 2014 to 2060: Current Population Reports, P25-1143," US Census Bureau, 2014, http://www.census.gov/content/dam/Census/library/publications/2015/demo/p25-1143.pdf.

9. See Matthew D. Kim, "The Preacher as Culture Maker: Creating a Church Culture through Sermons," *Preaching* (September/October 2012): 8–10.

10. Soong-Chan Rah, *The Next Evangelicalism: Freeing the Church from Western Cultural Captivity* (Downers Grove, IL: InterVarsity, 2009), 138.

11. F. F. Bruce, *The Book of the Acts*, New International Commentary on the New Testament (Grand Rapids: Eerdmans, 1988), 282.

12. Rah, *Next Evangelicalism*, 138.

13. David J. Williams, *Acts*, New International Biblical Commentary (Peabody, MA: Hendrickson, 1990), 262.

14. Eckhard J. Schnabel, *Acts*, Exegetical Commentary on the New Testament (Grand Rapids: Zondervan, 2012), 626, emphasis original.

15. Ibid., 620.

16. Stephen Um and Justin Buzzard, *Why Cities Matter* (Wheaton: Crossway, 2012), 108–9.

17. Bruce, *Book of the Acts*, 284.

18. Schnabel, *Acts*, 628–29.

19. Williams, *Acts*, 261.

20. William H. Willimon, *Acts*, Interpretation: A Bible Commentary for Teaching and Preaching (Atlanta: John Knox, 1988), 130.

21. Richard T. Schaefer, *Racial and Ethnic Groups*, 6th ed. (New York: HarperCollins, 1996), 7.

22. Leonora Tubbs Tisdale, *Preaching as Local Theology and Folk Art* (Minneapolis: Fortress, 1997), 134.

23. Rah, *Next Evangelicalism*, 139.

24. Gary L. McIntosh and Alan McMahan, *Being the Church in a Multi-Ethnic Community: Why It Matters and How It Works* (Indianapolis: Wesleyan Publishing House, 2012), 189.

25. M. Daniel Carroll R., *Christians at the Borders: Immigration, the Church, and the Bible* (Grand Rapids: Baker Academic, 2008), 67.

26. Bruce Milne, *Dynamic Diversity: Bridging Class, Age, Race and Gender in the Church* (Downers Grove, IL: IVP Academic, 2007), 13.

27. Thanks to Jared E. Alcántara for this important insight during a conversation on September 29, 2015.

28. Adapted from "Cultural Values Profile," *Cultural Intelligence Center*, http://www.culturalq .com/tmpl/research/cvalues.php.

29. Michael O. Emerson and Christian Smith, *Divided by Faith: Evangelical Religion and the Problem of Race in America* (New York: Oxford University Press, 2001), 2.

30. See Gregg A. Ten Elshof, *Confucius for Christians: What an Ancient Chinese Worldview Can Teach Us about Life in Christ* (Grand Rapids: Eerdmans, 2015).

31. Jung Young Lee, *Korean Preaching: An Interpretation* (Nashville: Abingdon, 1997), 139.

32. Rodney L. Cooper, "African-American Preaching," in *The Art and Craft of Biblical Preaching: A Comprehensive Resource for Today's Communicators*, ed. Haddon W. Robinson and Craig Brian Larson (Grand Rapids: Zondervan, 2005), 198.

33. Noel Castellanos, Jesse Miranda, and Alfredo Ramos, "Hispanic-American Preaching," in Robinson and Larson, *Art and Craft of Biblical Preaching*, 195.

34. David A. Anderson, *Multicultural Ministry: Finding Your Church's Unique Rhythm* (Grand Rapids: Zondervan, 2004), 81.

35. Timothy Keller and Katherine Leary Alsdorf, *Every Good Endeavor: Connecting Your Work to God's Work* (New York: Dutton, 2012), 135.

36. See Rodger Woodworth, "Cultural Idolatry," *Cross-Cultural Convergence*, February 3, 2011, http://www.crossculture.ccojubilee.org/?p=162.

37. Ralph Ellison, *The Invisible Man*, 2nd ed. (New York: Vintage, 1995), 3.

38. Timothy P. Fong, *The Contemporary Asian American Experience: Beyond the Model Minority* (Upper Saddle River, NJ: Prentice-Hall, 1998), 108.

39. In sociology, terms like "racialization" or "racialized" have become normative to associate race and ethnicity with general aspects of life that were not originally tied to issues of race or ethnicity, such as the racialization of work or politics. See Michael Omi and Howard Winant, *Racial Formation in the United States: From the 1960s to the 1980s*, 3rd ed. (New York: Routledge, 2014), 142.

40. See Caleb Colley, "God Is No Respecter of Persons," *Apologetics Press*, http://www.apologeticspress.org/apcontent.aspx?category=12&article=1440.

41. See Mark Labberton's Facebook page, August 15, 2015, https://www.facebook.com/mark.labberton/posts/10153560095458669.

42. Milton M. Gordon, *Assimilation in American Life: The Role of Race, Religion, and National Origins* (New York: Oxford University Press, 1964), 71–85.

43. See Bryan Loritts, "Ethnicity and Culture in Preaching, Lecture Two: 1 Corinthians 9:19–23," *Journal of the Evangelical Homiletics Society* 13, no. 1 (2013): 14–15; and Bryan Loritts, *Right Color, Wrong Culture: A Leadership Fable* (Chicago: Moody, 2014), 122.

44. Herbert J. Gans, "Symbolic Ethnicity: The Future of Ethnic Groups and Cultures in America," *Ethnic and Racial Studies* 2 (1979): 1–20.

45. George A. Yancey, *Beyond Black and White: Reflections on Racial Reconciliation* (Grand Rapids: Baker, 1996), 121.

46. Noel Castellanos, *Where the Cross Meets the Street: What Happens to the Neighborhood When God Is at the Center* (Downers Grove, IL: InterVarsity, 2015), 20.

47. McIntosh and McMahan, *Being the Church in a Multi-Ethnic Community*, 192.

48. Gretchen Livingston, "Today's Multiracial Babies Reflect America's Changing Demographics," *Pew Research Center*, June 24, 2015, http://www.pewresearch.org/fact-tank/2015/06/24/todays-multiracial-babies-reflect-americas-changing-demographics.

49. Emerson and Smith, *Divided by Faith*, 55.

50. Jenell Williams Paris, "Race: Critical Thinking and Transformative Possibilities," in *This Side of Heaven: Race, Ethnicity, and Christian Faith*, ed. Robert J. Priest and Alvaro L. Nieves (New York: Oxford University Press, 2007), 19.

51. Ibid., 26.

52. See Kate Kinsella, "Creating an Enabling Learning Environment for Non-Native Speakers of English," in *Multicultural Course Transformation in Higher Education: A Broader Truth*, ed. Ann Intili Morey and Margie K. Kitano (Boston: Allyn & Bacon, 1997), 113–14.

53. Christena Cleveland, *Disunity in Christ: Uncovering the Hidden Forces That Keep Us Apart* (Downers Grove, IL: InterVarsity, 2013), 51–52.

54. Patty Lane, *A Beginner's Guide to Crossing Cultures: Making Friends in a Multicultural World* (Downers Grove, IL: InterVarsity, 2002), 25.

55. Paris, "Race," 22.

56. Elise Mae Cannon, Lisa Sharon Harper, Troy Jackson, and Soong-Chan Rah, *Forgive Us: Confessions of a Compromised Faith* (Grand Rapids: Zondervan, 2014), 156.

57. Paris, "Race," 26.

58. Emerson and Smith, *Divided by Faith*, 57–58.

59. Anthony Bradley, "Race and Grace," lecture at Gordon-Conwell Theological Seminary, March 11, 2015, https://www.youtube.com/watch?v=CKegxA2SiHA.

60. Ibid.

61. Anderson, *Gracism*, 21.

62. Ibid.

63. Ibid., 47–150.

64. Lane, *A Beginner's Guide to Crossing Cultures*, 125. In many non-Western or "Eastern-collectivistic" cultures, however, David Augsburger reveals philosophical differences to conflict resolution. See David W. Augsburger, *Conflict Mediation across Cultures* (Louisville: Westminster John Knox, 1992), 9.

65. See note on 15:2ff. from the *Life Application Study Bible: New International Version* (Carol Stream, IL: Tyndale, 2005), 1841.

66. See "Famous Idioms—Meaning: Commonly Used Idioms," *English Language: Smart Words*, http://www.smart-words.org/quotes-sayings/idioms-meaning.html.

67. Woosung Calvin Choi, *Preaching to Multiethnic Congregation: Positive Marginality as a Homiletical Paradigm* (New York: Peter Lang, 2015), 106.

68. James R. Nieman and Thomas G. Rogers, *Preaching to Every Pew: Cross-Cultural Strategies* (Minneapolis: Fortress, 2001), 45. See also Matthew D. Kim, "A Blind Spot in Homiletics: Preaching that Exegetes Ethnicity," *Journal of the Evangelical Homiletics Society* 11, no. 1 (March 2011): 74, 78; and Joseph R. Jeter Jr. and Ronald J. Allen, *One Gospel, Many Ears: Preaching for Different Listeners in the Congregation* (St. Louis: Chalice, 2002), 110.

69. Michael Pocock and Joseph Henriques, *Cultural Change and Your Church: Helping Your Church Thrive in a Diverse Society* (Grand Rapids: Baker Books, 2002), 119.

70. See Jeff Brumley, "Raleigh Church Finds 'Very Baptist' Way to Be Multicultural," *Baptist News Global*, February 24, 2014, https://baptistnews.com/ministry/congregations/item/28392-raleigh-church-finds-very-baptist-way-to-be-multicultural. See also "A Mosaic of Membership: Four Congregations Hold Bimonthly Joint Services Celebrating Their Different Cultures," *Outreach* (September–October 2014): 42.

71. See John S. McClure, *The Roundtable Pulpit: Where Leadership and Preaching Meet* (Nashville: Abingdon, 1995); and Lucy Atkinson Rose, *Sharing the Word: Preaching in the Roundtable Church* (Louisville: Westminster John Knox, 1997).

72. M. Kim, "A Blind Spot in Homiletics," 76–77.

73. Mathews and Park, *The Post-Racial Church*, 258.

74. Emmanuel Katongole and Chris Rice, *Reconciling All Things: A Christian Vision for Justice, Peace and Healing* (Downers Grove, IL: InterVarsity, 2008), 29.

75. Mathews and Park, *The Post-Racial Church*, 225.

76. Emerson and Smith, *Divided by Faith*, 55.

77. Cannon et al., *Forgive Us*, 31.

78. Ibid., 98.

79. Anthony B. Bradley, *Aliens in the Promised Land: Why Minority Leadership Is Overlooked in White Christian Churches and Institutions* (Phillipsburg, NJ: P&R, 2013), 16.

80. Paul Tokunaga, *Invitation to Lead: Guidance for Emerging Asian American Leaders* (Downers Grove, IL: InterVarsity, 2003), 137.

81. Eric Russ, "Discipling African Americans in An Urban Context," *GCD: Gospel-Centered Discipleship*, http://gcdiscipleship.com/2011/10/31/discipling-african-americans-in-an-urban-context/.

82. David A. Livermore, *The Cultural Intelligence Difference: Master the One Skill You Can't Do Without in Today's Global Economy* (New York: AMACOM, 2011), 9.

Chapter 7: Preaching and Genders

1. Alice P. Mathews, *Preaching That Speaks to Women* (Grand Rapids: Baker Academic, 2003), 17.

2. David Murrow, *Why Men Hate Going to Church* (Nashville: Thomas Nelson, 2005), 53.

3. Haddon W. Robinson, foreword in Mathews, *Preaching That Speaks to Women*, 7.

4. Mathews, *Preaching That Speaks to Women*, 26.

5. Ibid., 27.

6. Larry Crabb, *Men and Women* (Grand Rapids: Zondervan, 1991), 133.

7. Adapted from Virginia Sapiro, *Women in American Society* (Palo Alto, CA: Mayfield, 1986), 260.

8. Deborah Tannen, *You Just Don't Understand: Women and Men in Conversation* (New York: William Morrow, 1990), 16.

9. Samuel Shem and Janet Surrey, *We Have to Talk: Healing Dialogues between Women and Men* (New York: Basic, 1998), 9.

10. Susan Nolen-Hoeksema, "The Truth about Women and Self-Esteem: Women and Girls Do NOT Have Low Self-Esteem," *Psychology Today*, January 21, 2010, from her book *The Power of Women: Harness Your Unique Strengths at Home, at Work, and in Your Community* (New York: Times Books, 2010), 37–40, https://www.psychologytoday.com/blog/the-power-women/201001 /the-truth-about-women-and-self-esteem. Yet Leslie Leyland Fields writes, "Women and girls enjoy a generous allowance that recognizes the athlete, the supermodel, the CEO, and the mother as equally valid expressions of femaleness. . . . But cultural expectations of masculinity are far stingier. If a man is gentle, compassionate, artsy, empathetic, cultivates beauty in his life, talks with his hands, enjoys the friendship of women, his masculinity and sexuality is instantly questioned." See Leslie Leyland Fields, "How We Made Too Much of Gender: Reclaiming an Identity More Meaningful than Manhood or Womanhood," *Christianity Today*, July 7, 2015, http://www.christianitytoday.com/women/2015/july/how-we-made-too-much-of-gender.html.

11. Robert H. Mounce, *Matthew*, New International Biblical Commentary (Peabody, MA: Hendrickson, 1991), 4.

12. Michael J. Wilkins, *Matthew*, NIV Application Commentary (Grand Rapids: Zondervan, 2004), 20–21.

13. Kurt Aland, ed., *Synopsis of the Four Gospels*, 2nd ed. (New York: United Bible Societies, 1985), 96.

14. Mounce, *Matthew*, 98.

15. John Charles Wynn, "The Family of God," in *Pastoral Preaching*, ed. Charles F. Kemp (St. Louis: Bethany, 1963), 192.

16. Grant R. Osborne, *Matthew*, Exegetical Commentary on the New Testament (Grand Rapids: Zondervan, 2010), 405.

17. Craig S. Keener, *Matthew*, IVP New Testament Commentary Series (Downers Grove, IL: InterVarsity, 1997), 209.

18. Craig L. Blomberg, *Matthew*, New American Commentary (Nashville: Broadman & Holman, 1992), 181, emphasis original.

19. David L. Turner, *Matthew*, Baker Exegetical Commentary on the New Testament (Grand Rapids: Baker Academic, 2008), 281–82.

20. Mounce, *Matthew*, 99.

21. Keener, *Matthew*, 210, emphasis original.

22. Aland, *Synopsis of the Four Gospels*, 193.

23. Wilkins, *Matthew*, 32.

24. Osborne, *Matthew*, 400.

25. D. A. Carson, ed., *NIV Zondervan Study Bible* (Grand Rapids: Zondervan, 2015), 1951.

26. Wilkins, *Matthew*, 21.

27. See, e.g., Richard N. Longenecker, ed., *Patterns of Discipleship in the New Testament* (Grand Rapids: Eerdmans, 1996).

28. Keener, *Matthew*, 210.

29. Ibid.

30. Eric C. Redmond, *Where Are All the Brothers? Straight Answers to Men's Questions about the Church* (Wheaton: Crossway, 2008), 19.

31. *The Life Application Study Bible: New International Version* (Carol Stream, IL: Tyndale, 2005), 1554.

32. Adam S. McHugh, *The Listening Life: Embracing Attentiveness in a World of Distraction* (Downers Grove, IL: InterVarsity, 2015), 155.

33. Mathews, *Preaching That Speaks to Women*, 49.

34. See also Susan Adams, "How Women Breadwinners Can Save Their Relationships," *Forbes*, April 21, 2014, http://www.forbes.com/sites/susanadams/2014/04/21/how-women-bread winners-can-save-their-relationships/#33e3596839a7.

35. Brita L. Gill-Austern, "Love Understood as Self-Sacrifice and Self-Denial: What Does It Do to Women?," in *Through the Eyes of Women: Insights for Pastoral Care*, ed. Jeanne Stevenson Moessner (Minneapolis: Fortress, 1996), 305.

36. Maxine Glaz and Jeanne Stevenson Moessner, *Women in Travail and Transition: A New Pastoral Care* (Minneapolis: Fortress, 1991), 198.

37. Wynn, "The Family of God," 190.

38. Cynthia Long Westfall, "Family in the Gospels and Acts," in *Family in the Bible: Exploring Customs, Culture, and Context*, ed. Richard S. Hess and M. Daniel Carroll R. (Grand Rapids: Baker Academic, 2003), 125–29.

39. Timothy Keller, *Counterfeit Gods* (New York: Riverhead, 2009), xvi.

40. See Amy Chua, *Battle Hymn of the Tiger Mother* (London: Bloomsbury, 2011), 3–4.

41. Tom Nelson, *Work Matters: Connecting Sunday Worship to Monday Work* (Wheaton: Crossway, 2011), 169.

42. Mark Sayers, *The Vertical Self: How Biblical Faith Can Help Us Discover Who We Are in an Age of Self Obsession* (Nashville: Thomas Nelson, 2010), 21.

43. John Ortberg, foreword to *The Surprising Grace of Disappointment: Finding Hope When God Seems to Fail Us*, by John Koessler (Chicago: Moody, 2013), 9–10.

44. Carolyn Custis James, *Half the Church: Recapturing God's Global Vision for Women* (Grand Rapids: Zondervan, 2010), 19.

45. Denise George, "What Women Wish Their Pastors Knew," *Preaching*, May 1, 2007, http://www.preaching.com/sermons/11547304/?page=5.

46. Brennan Manning, *The Relentless Tenderness of Jesus*, 3rd ed. (Grand Rapids: Revell, 2004), 18.

47. George, "What Women Wish Their Pastors Knew."

48. Floyd McClung Jr., *The Father Heart of God* (Eugene, OR: Harvest House, 1985), 13–14, emphasis original.

49. Soong-Chan Rah, *Prophetic Lament: A Call for Justice in Troubled Times* (Downers Grove, IL: InterVarsity, 2015), 21.

50. Bev Hislop, *Shepherding Women in Pain: Real Women, Real Issues, and What You Need to Know to Truly Help* (Chicago: Moody, 2010), 15.

51. Ibid., 26–27.

52. Matthew D. Kim, "Match the Mood of the Text," in *Preaching Points: 55 Tips for Improving Your Pulpit Ministry*, ed. Scott M. Gibson (Wooster, OH: Weaver, 2016), 17–18.

53. Richard H. Cox, *Rewiring Your Preaching: How the Brain Processes Sermons* (Downers Grove, IL: InterVarsity, 2012), 29, emphasis original.

54. "Tone," http://www.merriam-webster.com/dictionary/tone.

55. Annette Simmons, *The Story Factor: Inspiration, Influence and Persuasion through the Art of Storytelling* (Cambridge, MA: Perseus, 2002), 86.

56. Patricia Morrison Batten, *Expository Story Sermons* (DMin thesis, Gordon-Conwell Theological Seminary, 2008), 108.

57. Mathews, *Preaching That Speaks to Women*, 20; and Tannen, *You Just Don't Understand*, 210.

58. Mignon R. Jacobs, *Gender, Power, and Persuasion: The Genesis Narratives and Contemporary Portraits* (Grand Rapids: Baker Academic, 2007), 210.

59. Daniel Overdorf, *One Year to Better Preaching: 52 Exercises to Hone Your Skills* (Grand Rapids: Kregel, 2013), 132.

60. "Illustration," http://www.dictionary.com/browse/illustration.

61. Erin Wheeler, "Preaching to Women: Things for a Pastor to Consider," *Preaching and Theology*, June 18, 2015, http://9marks.org/article/preaching-to-women-things-for-a-pastor-to-consider, emphasis original.

62. George, "What Women Wish Their Pastors Knew."

63. A similar puzzle is told by MECA Electronics Inc., http://www.rfcafe.com/miscellany/humor/lateral-thinking.htm.

64. James, *Half the Church*, 41.

65. Jay E. Adams, *Truth Applied: Application in Preaching* (Grand Rapids: Zondervan, 1990), 96.

66. Sam A. Andreades, *enGendered: God's Gift of Gender Difference in Relationship* (Wooster, OH: Weaver, 2015), 12–13.

67. Cox, *Rewiring Your Preaching*, 151.

68. See James O. Prochaska, "How Do People Change, and How Can We Change to Help Many More People?," in *Heart and Soul of Change*, ed. Mark A. Hubble, Barry L. Duncan, and Scott D. Miller (Washington, DC: American Psychological Association, 1999), 227–36.

69. Cox, *Rewiring Your Preaching*, 150.

70. Ibid., 151.

71. Ibid.

72. Mathews, *Preaching That Speaks to Women*, 38–39.

73. See Jacqueline A. Roese, "Training Women to Prepare and Deliver a Biblical Message" (DMin thesis, Gordon-Conwell Theological Seminary, 2010), 71.

74. Francis A. Schaeffer, *The God Who Is There: Speaking Historic Christianity into the Twentieth Century* (Downers Grove, IL: InterVarsity, 1968), 119.

75. See Jeffrey D. Arthurs, "Adapt to Genderlects," in Gibson, *Preaching Points*, 77–78.

76. Arthurs, "Adapt to Genderlects," 77–78.

77. Tannen, *You Just Don't Understand*, 77.

78. Ibid.

79. See Roese, "Training Women to Prepare and Deliver a Biblical Message," 72–73.

80. Arthurs, "Adapt to Genderlects," 78.

81. Roese, "Training Women to Prepare and Deliver a Biblical Message," 76.

82. Woodleigh Hope Volland, "Preaching That Engages and Instructs Male Listeners" (DMin thesis, Gordon-Conwell Theological Seminary, 2009), 116–17.

83. Dietrich Bonhoeffer, *Life Together* (New York: HarperOne, 2009), 97.

84. McHugh, *The Listening Life*, 168.

85. Ibid.

86. Ibid., 161.

87. Denise George, *What Women Wish Pastors Knew: Understanding the Hopes, Hurts, Needs, and Dreams of Women in the Church* (Grand Rapids: Zondervan, 2007), 189.

88. Cannon et al., *Forgive Us*, 114.

89. Jacobs, *Gender, Power, and Persuasion*, 18.

90. Rick Richardson, "Preaching across the Great Divide," *Leadership* 26, no. 2 (Spring 2005): 48.

91. Cox, *Rewiring Your Preaching*, 99.

92. Debra Rienstra and Ron Rienstra, *Worship Words: Discipling Language for Faithful Ministry* (Grand Rapids: Baker Academic, 2009), 129.

93. Justin Holcomb, "10 Things You Should Know about Sexual Assault," *Crossway*, April 4, 2016, https://www.crossway.org/blog/2016/04/10-things-you-should-know-about-sexual-assault.

Chapter 8: Preaching and Locations

1. Lawrence W. Farris, *Ten Commandments for Pastors New to a Congregation* (Grand Rapids: Eerdmans, 2003), 1.

2. These imaginary caricatures were written with the aid of information provided in surveys done with local church pastors serving in urban, suburban, and rural churches.

3. Thanks to Casey C. Barton, a pastor in rural California, for this observation.

4. The Bible is replete with examples from both urban and rural communities, pagan, Jewish, and Gentile. Nineveh, Corinth, Ephesus, Athens, and a plethora of other major cities were natural destinations for God's workers to proclaim his Word to more skeptical urban dwellers. Similarly, the inhabitants of rural areas were also given their own set of instructions for worship. For instance, Esther 9:19 reads: "That is why rural Jews—those living in villages—observe the fourteenth of the month of Adar as a day of joy and feasting, a day for giving presents to each other." Though technically a concept developed as early as 4,000 years ago in southern Mesopotamia in the land of Ur, our modern construct of suburban living has been more or less a development in the United States since the 1950s, after World War II veterans returned home from their military service. For more information on suburban contexts, see Albert Y. Hsu, *The Suburban Christian: Finding Spiritual Vitality in the Land of Plenty* (Downers Grove, IL: InterVarsity, 2006), 25.

5. Stephen Um and Justin Buzzard, *Why Cities Matter* (Wheaton: Crossway, 2012), 18.

6. Keith N. Schoville, *Biblical Archaeology in Focus*, 6th ed. (Grand Rapids: Baker, 1991), 188.

7. Douglas Rawlinson Jones, *Jeremiah*, New Century Bible Commentary (Grand Rapids: Eerdmans, 1992), 363.

8. Tremper Longman III, ed., *The Baker Illustrated Bible Dictionary* (Grand Rapids: Baker Books, 2013), 160.

9. Ibid.

10. LeMoine F. DeVries, *Cities of the Biblical World* (Eugene, OR: Wipf & Stock, 2006), 17–18.

11. Ibid., 14.

12. Ibid., 19.

13. Longman, *The Baker Illustrated Bible Dictionary*, 161.

14. Berel Wein, "Babylon and Beyond," *JewishHistory.org*, http://www.jewishhistory.org/babylon-and-beyond.

15. Alfred J. Hoerth, *Archaeology and the Old Testament*, 3rd ed. (Grand Rapids: Baker Books, 2001), 385–86.

16. Jones, *Jeremiah*, 363.

17. Timothy Keller, *Center Church: Doing Balanced, Gospel-Centered Ministry in Your City* (Grand Rapids: Zondervan, 2012), 171–72.

18. William D. Mounce, *Complete Expository Dictionary of Old and New Testament Words* (Grand Rapids: Zondervan, 2006), 502.

19. Gerald L. Keown, Pamela J. Scalise, and Thomas G. Smothers, *Jeremiah 26–52*, Word Biblical Commentary (Dallas: Word, 1995), 72.

20. David J. Zucker, *Israel's Prophets: An Introduction for Christians and Jews* (New York: Paulist Press, 1994), 1.

21. Terry G. Carter, J. Scott Duvall, and J. Daniel Hays, *Preaching God's Word: A Hands-On Approach to Preparing, Developing, and Delivering the Sermon* (Grand Rapids: Zondervan, 2005), 252.

22. Tremper Longman III, *Jeremiah, Lamentations*, New International Biblical Commentary (Peabody, MA: Hendrickson, 2008), 193.

23. Ibid., 194.

24. Zucker, *Israel's Prophets*, 76.

25. Hetty Lalleman, *Jeremiah and Lamentations*, Tyndale Old Testament Commentaries (Downers Grove, IL: IVP Academic, 2013), 217.

26. Harvie M. Conn, introduction to *Planting and Growing Urban Churches: From Dream to Reality*, ed. Harvie M. Conn, 4th printing (Grand Rapids: Baker Books, 2002), 33–34, emphasis original.

27. Steve Wilkens and Mark L. Sanford, *Hidden Worldviews: Eight Cultural Stories That Shape Our Lives* (Downers Grove, IL: IVP Academic, 2009), 46.

28. Mark R. Gornik, "Preaching in Communion: A View from the Inner City," *The Living Pulpit* (April–June 2002): 38, http://www.pulpit.org.

29. Matthew Henry, *Matthew Henry's Commentary*, https://www.biblegateway.com/resources/matthew-henry/Jer.29.1-Jer.29.7.

30. Thanks to Casey C. Barton for this insight.

31. Alvin C. Porteous, *Preaching to Suburban Captives* (Valley Forge, PA: Judson, 1979), 15.

32. Martin Giese, "Rurban Leadership," unpublished notes, Northern Idaho Leaders' Conference, Sagle, Idaho, February 1–2, 2013; cf. http://connection.ebscohost.com/c/articles/97196028/when-cultural-conflict-comes-church-understanding-rurban-collision.

33. Arthur H. DeKruyter and Quentin J. Schultze, *The Suburban Church: Practical Advice for Authentic Ministry* (Louisville: Westminster John Knox, 2008), 101.

34. Ibid., 100.

35. Shannon Jung, ed., *Rural Ministry: The Shape of the Renewal to Come* (Nashville: Abingdon, 1998), 14.

36. Giese, "Rurban Leadership."

37. Ibid.

38. Andrew Miles and Rae Jean Proeschold-Bell, "Exploring Rural/Non-Rural Differences among United Methodist Churches and Clergy in North Carolina," *Review of Religious Research* 53 (October 2011): 371.

39. Fred P. Edie, "A Liturgical Re-Imagining of Rural Church Youth Ministry," *Journal of Youth Ministry* 10, no. 2 (Spring 2012): 64.

40. Porteous, *Preaching to Suburban Captives*, 20.

41. Lee Eclov, "Preaching That Magnifies God," in *The Art and Craft of Biblical Preaching: A Comprehensive Resource for Today's Communicators*, ed. Haddon W. Robinson and Craig Brian Larson (Grand Rapids: Zondervan, 2005), 568.

42. Um and Buzzard, *Why Cities Matter*, 110.

43. Eric Russ, "Discipling African Americans," *Discipleship Defined*, http://discipleshipdefined.com/articles/discipling-african-americans.

44. Ray Bakke, *A Theology as Big as the City* (Downers Grove, IL: InterVarsity, 1997), 85–86, emphasis original.

45. Keith Willhite, "Connecting with Your Congregation," in *Preaching to a Shifting Culture: 12 Perspectives on Communicating That Connects*, ed. Scott M. Gibson (Grand Rapids: Baker Books, 2004), 102.

46. Thanks to Casey C. Barton for this helpful insight.

47. Leonora Tubbs Tisdale, *Preaching as Local Theology and Folk Art* (Minneapolis: Fortress, 1997), 9.

48. A survey conducted with a rural pastor in California, 2015.

49. Jennifer L. Lord, *Finding Language and Imagery* (Minneapolis: Fortress, 2010), 14.

50. A survey conducted with a rural pastor in California, 2015.

51. See Jeffrey Arthurs, "The Fundamentals of Sermon Application (Part 1)," in *Interpretation and Application*, ed. Craig Brian Larson (Peabody, MA: Hendrickson, 2012), 70.

52. Murray Capill, *The Heart Is the Target: Preaching Practical Application from Every Text* (Phillipsburg, NJ: P&R, 2014), 97–98.

53. Arthurs, "The Fundamentals of Sermon Application," 72.

54. Kenneth Lorne Bender, "The Differences in Pastoral Role Expectation between Rural Agrarian Churches and Urban Churches in the Baptist General Conference in Alberta" (DMin thesis, Canadian Theological Seminary [Regina, SK], 1997), 95.

55. Roger S. Greenway, "Role of the Urban Pulpit," *Urban Mission* 4, no. 1 (September 1986): 3.

56. Mark Gornik, "Preaching in Communion: A View from the Inner City," *The Living Pulpit* (April–June 2002): 39.

57. Michael Duduit, "Preaching and the City: An Interview with Erwin Lutzer," *Preaching* 13, no. 5 (March–April 1998): 14.

58. Ronald J. Allen, "What I Need from Urban Preaching: Reflections of an Urban Dweller," *Christian Ministry* 30, no. 6 (November–December 1999): 22.

59. Ed Rowell, "Before You Preach," in Robinson and Larson, *Art and Craft of Biblical Preaching*, 580.

60. Peter Rhea Jones Sr., "Learning to Preach in Varied Pastoral Settings," *Review and Expositor* 110 (Summer 2013): 366–67.

Chapter 9: Preaching and Religions

1. Winfried Corduan, *Neighboring Faiths: A Christian Introduction to World Religions* (Downers Grove, IL: InterVarsity, 1998), 21.

2. David M. Howard Jr., introduction to *Biblical Faith and Other Religions: An Evangelical Assessment*, ed. David W. Baker (Grand Rapids: Kregel, 2004), 11.

3. Thomas A. Robinson and Hillary P. Rodrigues, *World Religions: A Guide to the Essentials*, 2nd ed. (Grand Rapids: Baker Academic, 2014), 2–3.

4. Timothy C. Tennent, *Invitation to World Missions: A Trinitarian Missiology for the Twenty-first Century* (Grand Rapids: Kregel, 2010), 192.

5. See Gerald R. McDermott, *Can Evangelicals Learn from World Religions? Jesus, Revelation & Religious Traditions* (Downers Grove, IL: InterVarsity, 2000), 187.

6. Pew Center Research, *The Future of World Religions: Population Growth Projections, 2010–2050*, April 2, 2015, http://www.pewforum.org/2015/04/02/religious-projections-2010-2050.

7. Two helpful books to understand the religiously unaffiliated population in America referred to as "the nones" are by James Emery White, *The Rise of the Nones: Understanding and Reaching the Religiously Unaffiliated* (Grand Rapids: Baker Books, 2014); and George Barna and David Kinnaman, eds., *Churchless: Understanding Today's Unchurched and How to Connect with Them* (Carol Stream, IL: Tyndale, 2014).

8. Raymond B. Dillard and Tremper Longman III, *An Introduction to the Old Testament* (Grand Rapids: Zondervan, 1994), 152.

9. Lissa M. Wray Beal, *1 and 2 Kings*, Apollos Old Testament Commentary (Downers Grove, IL: IVP Academic, 2014), 244.

10. Ibid.

11. Ibid.

12. Thomas G. Long, *Preaching and the Literary Forms of the Bible* (Philadelphia: Fortress, 1989), 75.

13. Iain W. Provan, *1 and 2 Kings*, New International Biblical Commentary (Peabody, MA: Hendrickson, 1995), 10.

14. Ibid., 11.

15. Kenneth Barker, ed., *The NIV Study Bible* (Grand Rapids: Zondervan, 1995), 459.

16. Alfred J. Hoerth, *Archaeology and the Old Testament*, 3rd ed. (Grand Rapids: Baker Books, 2001), 220.

17. *Life Application Study Bible: New International Version* (Carol Stream, IL: Tyndale, 2005), 529.

18. Hoerth, *Archaeology and the Old Testament*, 310.

19. Ibid.

20. Ibid., 220.

21. Ibid., 310.

22. Ibid., 221.

23. Ibid., 220, 327.

24. Ibid., 220.

25. John R. Kohlenberger III, *The NIV Exhaustive Bible Concordance*, 3rd ed. (Grand Rapids: Zondervan, 2015), 88.

26. See Ellen White, "Asherah and the Asherim: Goddess or Cult Symbol? Exploring the Biblical and Archaeological Evidence," *Bible History Daily*, November 4, 2014, http://www.biblical archaeology.org/daily/ancient-cultures/ancient-israel/asherah-and-the-asherim-goddess-or-cult -symbol.

27. Lee Strobel, foreword, in *Paul Meets Muhammad: A Christian-Muslim Debate on the Resurrection*, by Michael R. Licona (Grand Rapids: Baker Books, 2006), 10.

28. Richard Wolff, *The Popular Encyclopedia of World Religions: A User-Friendly Guide to Their Beliefs, History, and Impact on Our World Today* (Eugene, OR: Harvest House, 2007), 28–29.

29. Derek Cooper, *Christianity and World Religions: An Introduction to the World's Major Faiths* (Phillipsburg, NJ: P&R, 2013), 138–41.

30. E.g., Kenneth J. Thomas explains this perspectival difference of beliefs about prophets: "A Muslim reading the biblical accounts for the first time is shocked at the realism of the portrayals of sins committed by 'prophets,' and a Christian reading the Qur'ân is amazed at the purity and ideal qualities imputed to these same 'prophets.'" See Kenneth J. Thomas, "The Qur'an and the Bible," in *Christian Approaches to Other Faiths: A Reader*, ed. Paul M. Hedges and Alan Race (London: SCM, 2009), 142.

31. Philip Yancey, *Disappointment with God: Three Questions No One Asks Aloud* (New York: Harper Paperbacks, 1991), 87.

32. Harold A. Netland, "Religious Pluralism and the Question of Truth," in *Biblical Faith and Other Religions: An Evangelical Assessment*, ed. David W. Baker (Grand Rapids: Kregel, 2004), 22–23.

33. See Cooper, *Christianity and World Religions*; Timothy C. Tennent, *Christianity at the Religious Roundtable: Evangelicalism in Conversation with Hinduism, Buddhism, and Islam* (Grand Rapids: Baker Academic, 2002); and Robinson and Rodrigues, *World Religions*.

34. David Platt, *Follow Me: A Call to Die, A Call to Live* (Carol Stream, IL: Tyndale, 2013), 53.

35. Robinson and Rodrigues, *World Religions*, 136.

36. Corduan, *Neighboring Faiths*, 35.

37. Cooper, *Christianity and World Religions*, 123.

38. Wolff, *The Popular Encyclopedia of World Religions*, 32.

39. Jane I. Smith, *Islam in America*, 2nd ed. (New York: Columbia University Press, 2010), 3.

40. Robinson and Rodrigues, *World Religions*, 93.

41. Corduan, *Neighboring Faiths*, 200, 115.

42. Ibid., 202.

43. Hans Küng, "Muhammad: A Prophet?," in Hedges and Race, *Christian Approaches to Other Faiths*, 135.

44. Andreas Maurer, *Ask Your Muslim Friend: An Introduction to Islam and a Christian's Guide for Interaction with Muslims* (Kempton Park, South Africa: AcadSA, 2008), 109.

45. David Burnett, *The Spirit of Hinduism: A Christian Perspective on Hindu Life and Thought* (Oxford: Monarch, 2007), 284.

46. Robert Wuthnow, *America and the Challenges of Religious Diversity* (Princeton: Princeton University Press, 2005), 37.

47. Keith Stump, "Sharing Your Faith . . . with a Muslim," *Grace Communion International*, accessed February 17, 2017, http://www.gci.org/gospel/sharing/muslim.

48. Michael Green, *"But Don't All Religions Lead to God?": Navigating the Multi-Faith Maze* (Grand Rapids: Baker Books, 2002), 48.

49. Robinson and Rodrigues, *World Religions*, 123.

50. Ibid.

51. Miroslav Volf, *Allah: A Christian Response* (New York: HarperOne, 2011), 129.

52. Ibid., 137.

53. Ibid., emphasis original.

54. Ibid., emphasis original.

55. Cooper, *Christianity and World Religions*, 17.

56. Corduan, *Neighboring Faiths*, 201.

57. Cooper, *Christianity and World Religions*, 17.

58. Ibid.

59. Ibid.

60. Ed Stetzer, "Proselytizing in a Multi-Faith World: Why Mutual Respect and Tolerance Require Us to Witness for Christ," *Christianity Today*, March 28, 2011, http://www.christianity today.com/ct/2011/april/proselytizingmultifaith.html.

61. Fred Craddock, *Preaching* (Nashville: Abingdon, 1985), 95–98.

62. Ibid., 97.

63. Ibid.

64. William Wagner, "Mistakes Christians Make When Trying to Reach a Muslim," *North American Mission Board*, accessed February 17, 2017, http://www.namb.net/apologetics /mistakes-christians-make-when-trying-to-reach-a-muslim?pageid=8589953031.

65. Gerald R. McDermott, *Can Evangelicals Learn from World Religions? Jesus, Revelation & Religious Traditions* (Downers Grove, IL: InterVarsity, 2000), 186.

66. Nantachai Mejudhon, "Meekness: A New Approach to Christian Witness to the Thai People," in *Sharing Jesus Effectively in the Buddhist World*, ed. David Lim, Steve Spaulding, and Paul De Neui (Pasadena, CA: William Carey Library, 2005), 150.

67. Mark Cahill, *One Thing You Can't Do in Heaven* (Rockwall, TX: Biblical Discipleship, 2007), 146–47, emphasis original.

68. Maurer, *Ask Your Muslim Friend*, 131, 134.

69. Earl Palmer, "Letting the Listeners Make the Discoveries: Scripture Can Speak for Itself," in *The Art and Craft of Biblical Preaching: A Comprehensive Resource for Today's Communicators*, ed. Haddon W. Robinson and Craig Brian Larson (Grand Rapids: Zondervan, 2005), 247.

70. Wagner, "Mistakes Christians Make When Trying to Reach a Muslim."

71. Don Little, *Effective Discipling in Muslim Communities: Scripture, History and Seasoned Practices* (Downers Grove, IL: IVP Academic, 2015), 26.

72. Eugene A. Nida and Charles R. Taber, *The Theory and Practice of Translation, with Special Reference to Bible Translating* (Leiden: Brill, 1969), 200, emphasis original.

73. James R. Nieman, *Knowing the Context: Frames, Tools, and Signs for Preaching* (Minneapolis: Fortress, 2008), 12.

74. E. Randolph Richards and Brandon J. O'Brien, *Misreading Scripture with Western Eyes: Removing Cultural Blinders to Better Understand the Bible* (Downers Grove, IL: InterVarsity, 2012), 70.

75. Timothy C. Tennent, *Christianity at the Religious Roundtable: Evangelicalism in Conversation with Hinduism, Buddhism, and Islam* (Grand Rapids: Baker Academic, 2002), 13.

76. Timothy George, "Evangelicals and the Present Ecumenical Movement," in *Critical Issues in Ecclesiology: Essays in Honor of Carl E. Braaten*, ed. Alberto L. Garcia and Susan K. Wood (Grand Rapids: Eerdmans, 2011), 59.

77. Thomas, "The Qur'an and the Bible," 138.

78. Stump, "Sharing Your Faith . . . with a Muslim."

79. Ibid.

80. M. S. Vasanthakumar, "Difficulties and Devices in Depicting the Deity of Christ to the Theravada Buddhist Mind," in Lim, Spaulding, and De Neui, *Sharing Jesus Effectively in the Buddhist World*, 65–66.

81. Vinoth Ramachandra, *Faiths in Conflict? Christian Integrity in a Multicultural World* (Downers Grove, IL: InterVarsity, 1999), 87–88.

82. Stump, "Sharing Your Faith . . . with a Muslim."

83. Derek J. Morris, "The 10/40 Window: Far Away and Next Door," *Ministry*, June 2012, https://www.ministrymagazine.org/archive/2012/06/the-10/40-window:-far-away-and-next-door.

84. Ian Pitt-Watson, *Preaching: A Kind of Folly* (Philadelphia: Westminster, 1978), 58.

85. Paul Louis Metzger, *Connecting Christ: How to Discuss Jesus in a World of Diverse Paths* (Nashville: Thomas Nelson, 2012), xvii.

86. Ibid., xviii.

87. Thabiti Anyabwile, *The Gospel for Muslims: An Encouragement to Share Christ with Confidence* (Chicago: Moody, 2010), 124.

88. Cahill, *One Thing You Can't Do in Heaven*, 11.

89. Ibid., 17.

Conclusion

1. See "The Challenge of Multicultural Preaching: An Interview with Gabriel Salguero," *Grace and Peace: A Dialogical Magazine for Nazarene Clergy*, October 5, 2010, http://www.graceandpeacemagazine.org/articles/12-issue-october-2010/61-the-challenge-of-multicultural-preaching-an-interview-with-gabriel-salguero.

2. Walter Brueggemann, *The Practice of Prophetic Imagination: Preaching an Emancipating Word* (Minneapolis: Fortress, 2012), 145.

Appendix 3: Sample Sermon

1. See also Joe Stowell, "Called to Christ, Called to Compassion: Putting Faith into Action," in *A Heart for the City: Effective Ministries to the Urban Community*, ed. John Fuder (Chicago: Moody, 1999), 41.

2. Walter C. Kaiser Jr., ed., *NIV Archaeological Study Bible* (Grand Rapids: Zondervan, 2005), 687.

3. Gary V. Haugen, *Good News about Injustice: A Witness of Courage in a Hurting World* (Downers Grove, IL: InterVarsity, 1999), 43.

4. "Illustration: Prayer, Priorities," *Preaching*, July 23, 2013, http://www.preaching.com/sermon-illustrations/11696064.

5. Loring W. Batten, *The Books of Ezra and Nehemiah*, International Critical Commentary (New York: Charles Scribner's Sons, 1913), 246.

6. Ibid., 247.

7. Mervin Breneman, *Ezra, Nehemiah, Esther*, New American Commentary (Nashville: Broadman & Holman, 1993), 208.

8. Stowell, "Called to Christ," 42.

9. Ibid.

Index

Note: Page references followed by an *f* or *t* indicate information contained in figures and tables, respectively.

achievement, 166–67
Adams, Jay E., 148
affluenza, 165
African Americans, hate crimes against, 175
Alcántara, Jared E., 46
Allen, Ronald J., 181
Alsdorf, Katherine Leary, 107
America and the Challenges of Religious Diversity (Wuthnow), 200
American Church in Crisis, The (Olson), 67
American citizenship, 48–49
America's Four Gods (Froese and Bader), 23
Anderson, David, 118
Andreades, Sam, 148
Ang, Soon, 5, 6, 46
Angrosino, Michael, 9, 46
Antioch, 35
Anyabwile, Thabiti, 212
application, addressing in sermons
   about, 26–27
   denominationalism and, 87
   ethnicity and, 118–19
   gender and, 148–50
   locations and, 177–79
   world religions and, 206–7
Arnold, Clinton, 84, 86
Arthurs, Jeffrey D., 30, 150–51, 178
Asherah, 190
Asian American cultural experience, 48–49, 107–8

Asian theologies, 106
Ask Your Muslim Friend (Maurer), 199
assimilation, cultural, 50–51, 97, 110–13, 123
atheism, 23
authority and power, 78–79
autobiography, 51

Baal, 190
Bader, Christopher, 39
Bakke, Raymond, 9, 173
Baptists, 83
Batten, Patricia, 161
Battle Hymn of the Tiger Mother (Chua), 140
Beal, Lissa M. Wray, 188
Beale, Gregory K., 21
Bebbington, David, 87
behaving, culture as way of, 11–12
being versus doing, 27, 105
Being White: Finding Our Place in a Multiethnic World (Harris and Schaupp), 55
beliefs, addressing in sermons
   about, 19–20
   denominationalism and, 75–77
   ethnicity and, 104–6
   gender and, 137–38
   locations and, 166–68
   world religions and, 194–96
Bender, Kenneth Lorne, 180
Berean Christians, 76
biblical author's cultural context, 16–17

biblical exegesis. *See* hermeneutics (HABIT)
Biblical Preaching (Robinson), 16, 35–36
black theologies, 106
Blomberg, Craig, 131
Bonhoeffer, Dietrich, 152
Bradley, Anthony, 117, 124
bridge-building. *See* homiletical connection to
    listeners (BRIDGE)
Briggs, Charles, 41
Broadus, John, 35
Brothers, Michael, 88
Brown, Sharon A. Christopher, 79
Bruce, F. F., 98
Brueggemann, Walter, 215
Buddhism, 186, 187, 196t
Bugg, Charles, 83, 90
Burge, Gary, 32
Burke, John, 92
Burke, Kenneth, 24
Buschart, David, 75, 77
Buzzard, Justin, 99

Cahill, Mark, 205, 212
Calvin, John, 39, 74, 80
Cannon, Elise Mae, 123
Capill, Murray, 178
Carleton College, 89
Carroll, Daniel, 104
Carroll, Jackson, 73
Carson, D. A., 132
Castellanos, Noel, 112
Chapell, Bryan, 36
Cho, John, 111
Choi, Woosung Calvin, 120
*Christianity and World Religions: An Introduc-
    tion to the World's Major Faiths* (Cooper),
    195
*Christianity at the Religious Roundtable: Evan-
    gelicalism in Conversation with Hinduism,
    Buddhism, and Islam* (Tennent), 195
Chua, Amy, 140
church-state separation, 203
circumcision, 100
class and ethnicity, 117–18
Cleveland, Christena, 115
collectivism, 7, 26, 82, 105, 118, 206–7
Colley, Caleb, 109
communication. *See* homiletics
Communion, 20, 76, 77, 87, 169
compassion, 28, 48, 211
confession, public, 123–24
confessional beliefs, 19
conflict resolution, 118–19

Confucianism, 108
Conn, Harvie, 164
*Connecting Christ: How to Discuss Jesus in a
    World of Diverse Paths* (Metzger), 212
consumerism, 59, 165, 205
contemplation, 149
content, of sermons
    about, 29
    denominationalism and, 90–91
    ethnicity and, 122–23
    gender and, 154
    locations and, 181–82
    world religions and, 209–11
conversion, 207
convictional beliefs, 19–20
Cooper, Derek, 192, 197, 201
Corduan, Winfried, 185, 199
corporate application, 26–27
Cox, Richard, 28, 145, 149
CQ. *See* cultural intelligence
Crabb, Larry, 128–29
Craddock, Fred, 202
Crossover Preaching (Alcántara), 46
cultural assimilation, 50–51, 97, 110–13, 123
cultural attitudes, journaling about, 57–58
cultural beliefs, 20
cultural empathy, 48–50, 113–14, 153
cultural exegesis, 9, 15, 18. *See also* cultural
    intelligence (CQ); homiletical connection to
    listeners (BRIDGE)
cultural intelligence (CQ)
    about, 5–6
    CQ action, 8
    CQ drive, 6–7, 46–51
    CQ knowledge, 7
    CQ strategy, 7–8
    defined, 5
    four stages of, 6–8
    model of, 10–12
Cultural Intelligence Center, 104–5
*Cultural Intelligence: Individual Interactions
    across Cultures* (Earley and Ang), 5
culture
    as behaving, living, and thinking, 10–12
    being- versus doing-oriented, 7, 27, 105
    defined, 5
    ethnicity and, 96–97
    and homiletics, 4–5
    majority-culture attitudes, 56
    objective and subjective, 10
    Scripture-culture relationship, 33–34, 35f

DeGroat, Chuck, 45, 58, 59
DeKruyter, Arthur, 167
demographics, U.S., 97
denominationalism and preaching
    about, 65–66
    beliefs, 75–77
    building BRIDGE to congregants, 75–83
    dreams, 79–80
    God and, 80–81
    Great Commission, 67–68
    hermeneutics and, 68–75
    homiletics and, 83–92
    idols and idolatry, 78–79
    life experiences and, 81–83
    Protestantism, 66–67
    rituals, 77–78
    sermon application, 87
    sermon content, 90–91
    sermon delivery, 83–85
    sermon embracement, 88–90
    sermon illustrations, 85–87
    sermon language, 88
    sermon trust, 91–92
disappointment in life, 141–42
discipleship, 132–33, 139, 207
distance, in preaching, 88
Dockery, David, 79–80
Doctrines That Divide, The (Lutzer), 66
Does Christianity Squash Women? (Jones), 128
doing versus being, 7, 27, 105
dreams, addressing in sermons
    about, 21–22
    denominationalism and, 79–80
    ethnicity and, 108–9
    gender and, 141–42
    locations and, 171–72
    world religions and, 200–201
Duncan, Ligon, 76
Dunn-Wilson, David, 84
Durham, Jennifer, 50
Duvall, J. Scott, 32
dynamic equivalence, 207–8

Earley, P. Christopher, 5, 6, 46
Eastern religions, 185, 193. *See also* religions
    (world) and preaching
ecclesiology, 73
Eclov, Lee, 170
Edie, Fred, 169
Effective Discipling in Muslim Communities
    (Little), 207
eisegesis, 34

Elijah, 193
Ellison, Ralph, 108
embracement, addressing in sermons
    about, 28–29
    denominationalism and, 88–90
    ethnicity and, 120–22
    gender and, 152–54
    locations and, 180–81
    world religions and, 208–9
emotional intelligence, 5
empathetic imagination, 202
empathy, cultural, 48–50, 113–14, 153
enGendered (Andreades), 148
Eswine, Zack, 78
ethnicity, journaling about, 55–57
ethnicity and preaching
    about, 95–96, 125
    assimilation, 110–11
    beliefs, 104–6
    building BRIDGE to congregants, 104–13
    and class, 117–18
    versus culture, 96–97
    dreams and, 108–9
    ethnocentrism, 97–98, 100, 118
    God and, 109–10
    gracism and, 118
    hermeneutics and, 98–104
    homiletics and, 113–24
    idols and idolatry, 107–8
    life experiences, 110–13
    liminality and shame, 111–13
    location, language, and, 179–80
    versus race, 96
    racism, 115–17, 124
    rituals, 106–7
    sermon application, 118–19
    sermon content, 122–23
    sermon delivery, 113–14
    sermon embracement, 120–22
    sermon illustrations, 115–18
    sermon language, 119–20
    sermon trust, 123–24
Eurocentric preaching, 95, 105, 108, 114
evangelicalism, 67, 106, 196, 212
exegeting congregations, 9
exilic circumstances, 160, 166
experiences, life. *See* life experiences, address-
    ing in sermons
Exploring Protestant Traditions (Buschart), 75
expository preaching, 16, 36
extroverts, 60

familial celebration, 169
family, idol of the, 139–40
family dysfunctions, 54–55
"Family of God, The" (Wynn), 139
Farris, Lawrence, 157
Father Heart of God, The (McClung), 143
focus groups, 153
food rituals, 196–97
forgiveness, asking for, 117, 123–24, 155–56
Forgive Us: Confessions of a Compromised Faith (Cannon et al.), 123
Foulkes, Francis, 70
Froese, Paul, 23

Gender, Power, and Persuasion (Jacobs), 145–46
gender and preaching
  about, 127–28, 156
  beliefs, 137–38
  building BRIDGE to congregants, 137–45
  dreams, 141–42
  gender spectrum, 128–29, 130f
  God and, 142–43
  hermeneutics and, 130–36
  homiletics and, 145–56
  idols and idolatry, 139–41
  life experiences, 143–45
  rituals, 138–39
  sermon application, 148–50
  sermon content, 154
  sermon delivery, 145–46
  sermon embracement, 152–54
  sermon illustrations, 146–48
  sermon language, 150–52
  sermon trust, 154–56
genderlects, 150–51
George, Denise, 142, 143, 147, 153
George, Timothy, 66, 73, 208–9
Gibson, Scott M., 29, 90
Giese, Martin, 168
Gill-Austern, Brita L., 138
Glaz, Maxine, 138–39
God, addressing perspectives on
  about, 23
  denominationalism and, 80–81
  ethnicity and, 104, 109–10
  gender and, 142–43
  locations and, 172
  world religions and, 201–2
God, impartiality of, 109–10
Goldingay, John, 32
Gornik, Mark, 165
Gospel for Muslims, The (Anyabwile), 212

gracism, 118
Graham, Billy, 51, 67
Green, Kevin, 57
Greenway, Roger, 181
Groeschel, Craig, 67

Half the Church (James), 141–42
Harris, Paula, 55
Harvey, Wayne, 25
hate crimes, 175
Hays, J. Daniel, 32
Henriques, Joseph, 121
Henry, Matthew, 166
hermeneutics (HABIT)
  about, 15
  authorial-cultural model, 16–17, 36–38, 41–42, 70–71, 100–101, 133, 163, 190
  authorial intention versus reader-response, 33, 37
  big idea of text, 17, 34–36, 42, 72, 101, 134, 163–64, 191
  examples of Scriptural, 39–44, 68–75, 98–104
  historical, grammatical, and literary context, 16, 35, 37–38, 39–41, 68–70, 98–100, 130–33, 160–63, 187–89
  for homiletics, 32
  interpretational context, 17–18, 42–43, 72–73, 101–3, 134–36, 164–65, 191–93
  preunderstanding, 32–33, 74
  Scripture-culture relationship, 33–34, 35f
  single meaning of text, 17, 34–36, 42, 72, 101, 134, 163–64, 191
  theological presuppositions, 18, 43–44, 74–75, 104, 136, 165–66, 193–94
Hesselgrave, David, 24
Hiding Place, The (ten Boom), 51
Hinduism, 186, 187, 193, 196t, 201–2
Hislop, Bev, 144
Hispanic Americans, 107, 108, 115
historical-grammatical hermeneutics, 16, 35, 36–37, 39–41, 68–70, 98–100, 130–33, 160–63, 187–89
Hitchens, Christopher, 23
Hoehner, Harold, 69
Hoerth, Alfred, 161
Hogan, Lucy Lind, 74
Holy Spirit, 4–5, 16, 33, 36, 44, 73, 149
homiletical connection to listeners (BRIDGE)
  about, 18–19
  applying, 60
  beliefs, 19–20, 75–77, 104–6, 137–38, 166–68, 194–96

dreams, 21–22, 79–80, 108–9, 141–42, 171–
  72, 200–201
experiences, 23–24, 81–83, 110–13, 143–45,
  172–73, 202–4
God, 23, 80–81, 109–10, 142–43, 172, 201–2
idols, 20–21, 78–79, 107–8, 139–41, 169–71,
  198–200
rituals, 20, 77–78, 106–7, 138–39, 169, 196–98
Homiletical Template
  about, 13–14
  building bridge to listeners, 18–24
  hermeneutics of sermon preparation, 15–18,
    31–44, 68–75
  homiletics, 24–30
homiletics (DIALECT)
  about, 24–25
  application, 26–27, 87, 118–19, 148–50,
    177–79, 206–7
  content, 29, 90–91, 122–23, 154, 181–82,
    209–11
  culture and, 4–5
  delivery, 25, 83–85, 113–14, 145–46, 173–75,
    204
  embracement, 28–29, 88–90, 120–22, 152–54,
    180–81, 208–9
  illustrations, 25, 85–87, 115–18, 146–48,
    175–77, 204–5
  language, 27–28, 88, 119–20, 150–52, 179–80,
    207–8
  trust, 29–30, 91–92, 123–24, 154–56, 182–83,
    211–12
honorific language, 119–20
hope, 175
Horton, Michael, 91
human trafficking, 166
Hwang, Jenny, 25

identity, 53, 57, 68, 72, 79–80, 93, 108, 112, 120,
  138–39
idioms, 119
idols and idolatry, addressing in sermons
  about, 20–21
  denominationalism and, 78–79
  ethnicity and, 107–8
  gender and, 139–41
  locations and, 169–71
  world religions and, 198–200
illustrations, using in sermons
  about, 25
  denominationalism and, 85–87
  ethnicity and, 115–18
  gender and, 146–48

  locations and, 175–77
  world religions and, 204–5
imago Dei, 104, 109
immigrants, 6–7, 49, 56, 57, 80, 110–13, 115,
  119–21
impartiality, God's, 109–10
Imperfect Pastor, The (Eswine), 78
indigenous theologies, 106
individualism, 7, 26, 31, 33, 105, 118, 149, 150,
  167
integrity, 29–30, 155
Invisible Man, The (Ellison), 108
Islam, 186, 187, 193, 196t, 197–98, 199, 200,
  201, 203, 207, 210, 212. See also religions
  (world) and preaching

Jackson, Chris, 81
Jacobs, Mignon, 145–46, 154–55
James, Carolyn Custis, 141–42, 148
Jehovah's Witnesses, 200
Jeong, Ken, 111
Jesus Christ, as the content of Christianity,
  209–11
Jones, Peter Rhea, Sr., 182
Jones, Rebecca, 128
Judaizers, 50
Just As I Am (Graham), 51

Kaiser, Walter C., Jr., 37
Katongole, Emmanuel, 122
Keener, Craig, 132
Keller, Timothy, 21, 26, 107
Kim, Julius, 91–92
Kim, Timothy David, 216
King, Martin Luther, Jr., 169
Koessler, John, 26
Korean American experience, 50, 53
Korean American Presbyterian Church, 80
Köstenberger, Andreas, 33
Küng, Hans, 199
Kuruvilla, Abraham, 26, 80–81

Labberton, Mark, 28
lament, 58, 143–44, 174–75
Lane, Patty, 10, 118–19
language, usage in sermons
  about, 27–28
  denominationalism and, 88
  ethnicity and, 119–20
  gender and, 150–52
  locations and, 179–80
  world religions and, 207–8

Lewis, C. S., 132
liberation theologies, 106
life experiences, addressing in sermons
    about, 23–24
    denominationalism and, 81–83
    ethnicity and, 110–13
    gender and, 143–45
    locations and, 172–73
    world religions and, 202–4
liminality, 111–13, 120
Little, Don, 207
Livermore, David, 5–6, 12
living, culture as way of, 10–11
locations and preaching
    about, 157–58
    beliefs and, 166–68
    building BRIDGE to congregants, 166–73
    dreams and, 171–72
    God and, 172
    hermeneutics and, 160–66
    homiletics and, 173–83
    idols and, 169–71
    life experiences and, 172–73
    rituals and, 169
    in rural situations, 159, 168, 169, 172, 176–77,
        180, 182
    sermon application and, 177–79
    sermon content and, 181–82
    sermon delivery and, 173–75
    sermon embracement, 180–81
    sermon illustrations and, 175–77
    sermon language and, 179–80
    sermon trust and, 182–83
    in suburban situations, 158–59, 167–68,
        169–70, 172, 182
    in urban situations, 158, 166–67, 168t, 172,
        181, 182
Long, Thomas, 189
Loritts, Bryan, 110
Loving God When You Don't Love the Church
    (Jackson), 81
Lutzer, Erwin, 66, 181

MacArthur, John, 72
majority-culture attitudes, 56
Manning, Brennan, 142
Markus, Hazel, 21
Marty, Martin, 74
Mathews, Alice, 128, 137–38, 150
Mathews, Kenneth, 96, 122
Maurer, Andreas, 199
McClung, Floyd, Jr., 143

McClure, John, 121–22
McDermott, Gerald, 203
McDill, Wayne, 86
McHugh, Adam, 152, 153
meekness, 204
Mejudhon, Nantachai, 204
metanoia, 117, 123–24, 155–56
Metzger, Paul Louis, 212
Meynell, Mark, 91
Miles, Andrew, 169
Miller, Calvin, 25
Milne, Bruce, 104
Ministry by the Book (Tidball), 77
minority cultural experience, 56–57, 102–3,
    108–9
Misreading Scripture with Western Eyes (Rich-
    ards and O'Brien), 15
Moessner, Jeanne Stevenson, 138–39
Morris, Derek, 211
Mounce, Robert, 132
Muhammad, 199
Murrow, David, 128
Muslims. See Islam
My Big Fat Greek Wedding (film), 56–57

Neighboring Faiths (Corduan), 185
Nelson, Tom, 140
Netland, Harold, 195
Nida, Eugene, 207
Nieman, James, 46, 120–21
Niles, Philip H., 89
Nolen-Hoeksema, Susan, 129
Nones, the, 187
No Perfect People Allowed (Burke), 92
Nouwen, Henri, 24
Nurius, Paula, 21

objective culture, 10
O'Brien, Brandon J., 15, 208
Olson, David, 67
Olson, Roger, 82
One Thing You Can't Do in Heaven (Cahill),
    205, 212
Ortberg, John, 141
Osborne, Grant, 131
Overdorf, Daniel, 146

pain, 143–44
pain, journaling about, 58–60
Palmer, Earl, 206
Palmer, Parker, 59
Paris, Jenell Williams, 113–14, 115

Park, M. Sydney, 96, 122
Park, Randall, 111
partiality and favoritism, God's, 109–10
pastoral concern, 149–50, 182–83, 211–12
pathos, 113–14
Patterson, Richard, 33
Paul, 4, 8, 68–75
Penwell, Derek, 86
Peterson, Eugene, 12
Philip, 4–5
Platt, David, 195
pluralism, 208–9
Pocock, Michael, 121
Porteous, Alvin, 169–70
possible selves theory, 21–22
power dynamics, 155
preachers and preaching. *See also* homiletics
    about, 45–46, 60–61
    bridge-building and, 3, 8–10, 47
    developing CQ drive, 46–51
    four types of, 84–85
    and Homiletical Template, 60
    journaling, 54–60
    Preacher's Timeline, 51–54
    unity and disharmony in churches, 65–66
Preaching as Local Theology and Folk Art (Tisdale), 175–76
Preaching That Speaks to Women (Mathews), 128
Preaching to Every Pew: Cross-Cultural Strategies (Nieman and Rogers), 46
Preaching to Suburban Captives (Porteous), 169–70
precontemplation, 149
prejudice, 47, 95–96
preparation, before application, 149
presence, 155
pride, 124
privacy, 167–68
Prochaska, James, 149
Proeschold-Bell, Rae Jean, 169
prosperity, 165
Protestantism, 66–68
Protestant Worship: Traditions in Transition (White), 77
Provan, Iain, 189
public confession and apology, 124
Pullman, Philip, 23

Quicke, Michael, 9

race and racism. *See* ethnicity and preaching
racism, 115–17, 124

Rah, Soong-Chan, 58, 103, 143
Rainer, Thom, 82
Ramachandra, Vinoth, 210
rapport talk, 151
reconciliation, 122–24
Redmond, Eric, 135
Refining Your Style: Learning from Respected Communicators (Stone), 84
refugees, 160, 166
Reid, Robert Stephen, 74
relational delivery, 25
relationships, pastoral, 149–50, 182–83, 211–12
religions (world) and preaching
    about, 185–86
    affiliation worldwide, 186–87
    beliefs and, 194–96
    building BRIDGE to congregants, 194–204
    dreams and, 200–201
    God and, 192, 201–2
    hermeneutics and, 187–94
    homiletics and, 204–12
    idols and, 198–200
    life experiences and, 202–4
    rituals and, 196–98
    sermon application, 206–7
    sermon content, 209–11
    sermon delivery, 204
    sermon embracement, 208–9
    sermon illustrations, 204–5
    sermon language, 207–8
    sermon trust, 211–12
Remember the Titans (film), 116
report talk, 151
respect, 209
Rewiring Your Preaching: How the Brain Processes Sermons (Cox), 28, 145
Rice, Chris, 122
Richard, Ramesh, 36
Richards, E. Randolph, 15, 208
Richardson, Rick, 155
Rienstra, Debra and Ron, 155
right, need to be, 78
rituals, addressing in sermons
    about, 20
    denominationalism and, 77–78
    ethnicity and, 106–7
    gender and, 138–39
    locations and, 169
    world religions and, 196–98
Robinson, Anthony, 90
Robinson, Haddon W., 16, 17, 26, 35–36, 128
Robinson, Thomas, 197

Rodrigues, Hillary, 197
Roese, Jacqueline, 150
Rogers, Thomas, 46, 120–21
Rose, Lucy Atkinson, 121–22
roundtable preaching, 121–22
Rowell, Ed, 182
Rudy (film), 171
Russ, Eric, 171

Salguero, Gabriel, 215
salvation, 200–201, 210
Sapiro, Virginia, 129
Sayers, Mark, 141
Schaefer, Richard, 102
Schaeffer, Francis, 150
Schaupp, Doug, 55
Schnabel, Eckhard, 99
Schultze, Quentin, 167
self, idol of the, 139–40
self-awareness. *See* preachers and preaching
self-identity, 53, 138–39
sermon. *See also* preachers and preaching;
    homiletics
  application, 26–27, 87, 118–19, 148–50,
    177–79, 206–7
  beliefs, addressing in, 19–20, 75–77, 104–6,
    137–38, 166–68, 194–96
  content, 29, 90–91, 122–23, 154, 181–82,
    209–11
  delivery, 25, 83–85, 113–14, 145–46, 173–75,
    204
  dreams, addressing in, 21–22, 79–80, 108–9,
    141–42, 171–72, 200–201
  embracement, addressing in, 28–29, 88–90,
    120–22, 152–54, 180–81, 208–9
  idols and idolatry, addressing in, 20–21,
    78–79, 107–8, 139–41, 169–71, 198–200
  illustrations, 25, 85–87, 115–18, 146–48,
    175–77, 204–5
  language, usage in, 27–28, 88, 119–20, 150–
    52, 179–80, 207–8
  life experiences, addressing in, 23–24, 81–83,
    110–13, 143–45, 172–73, 202–4
  preparation, hermeneutics of, 15–18, 31–44,
    68–75. *See also* Homiletical Template
  rituals, addressing in, 20, 77–78, 106–7,
    138–39, 169, 196–98
  tone, 145–46, 174–75, 204
  trust, nurturing in, 29–30, 91–92, 123–24,
    154–56, 182–83, 211–12
sexual abuse and violence, 155–56
shame, 111–13
Shem, Samuel, 129

Shepherding Women in Pain (Hislop), 144
Simmons, Annette, 145
slavery, 166
Smith, David, 48
Smith, Jane, 198
Soerens, Matthew, 25
Southern Baptist Convention, 79–80
spending time with Others, 124
stereotyping, 48–50, 115–17, 129, 147–48
Stone, Dave, 84
Story Factor, The (Simmons), 145
Stott, John, 3
Strobel, Lee, 191
Stump, Keith, 200
subjective culture, 10
suffering, 143–44
Surrey, Janet, 129
Swift, Jonathan, 72
syncretism, 208–9

Tannen, Deborah, 129, 150–51
ten Boom, Corrie, 51
*Ten Commandments for Pastors New to a Con-
    gregation* (Farris), 157
Tennent, Timothy, 186, 208
Terry, Milton, 35
thinking, culture as way of, 11
Thiselton, Anthony, 32
Thomas, Kenneth, 209
Thompson, Curt, 61
Thorsen, Don, 67
Tidball, Derek, 77
Tisdale, Leonora Tubbs, 9, 175–76
tone, of sermons, 145–46, 174–75, 204
Torabi, Farnoosh, 138
Toughest People to Love (DeGroat), 45
transdenominationalism, 67
translation, 207–8
Treier, Daniel, 73
Trinity, 201
trust, nurturing in sermons
  about, 29–30
  denominationalism and, 91–92
  ethnicity and, 123–24
  gender and, 154–56
  locations and, 182–83
  world religions and, 211–12
12 Essential Skills for Great Preaching (Mc-
    Dill), 86

Um, Stephen, 99
uncertainty, 168

United Methodist Church, 79, 91
United States demographics, 97
Upton, Clive, 24

Vasanthakumar, M. S., 210
Vertical Self, The (Sayers), 141
Vision for Preaching, A (Kuruvilla), 81
voice, preaching. *See* sermon delivery
Volf, Miroslav, 201
Volland, Woodleigh Hope, 152

Wagner, William, 207
Walling, Terry, 51
Washington, Denzel, 110
wealth, idol of, 170–71
We Have to Talk: Healing Dialogues between Men and Women (Shem and Surrey), 129
Welcoming the Stranger (Soerens and Hwang), 25
Western religions, 185. *See also* religions (world) and preaching
Wheeler, Erin, 147
When She Makes More: 10 Rules for Breadwinning Women (Torabi), 138
Where Are All the Brothers? (Redmond), 135–36
White, James, 77
Why Cities Matter (Um and Buzzard), 170
Why Men Hate Going to Church (Murrow), 128

Wilderness of Mirrors: Trusting Again in a Cynical World (Meynell), 91
Wilkens, Steve, 67
Wilkins, Michael, 130
Willhite, Keith, 174
Williams, David, 98–99
Willimon, William, 100
Wilson, Lawrence W., 84, 85f
women, gender issues and. *See* gender and preaching
Women in Travail and Transition (Glaz and Moessner), 138–39
Woodworth, Rodger, 108
work, idol of, 140–41, 170–71
Work Matters (Nelson), 140
world religions. *See* religions (world) and preaching
World Religions: A Guide to the Essentials (Robinson and Rodrigues), 195
Worship Words (Rienstra and Rienstra), 155
Wuthnow, Robert, 200
Wynn, John Charles, 139

xenophobia, 47–48

Yancey, George, 111
Yancey, Philip, 194
Young, William Paul, 23